For
LOVE and the SEA

For LOVE and the SEA

A MEMOIR OF EXTRAORDINARY
TRAVEL IN THE 1960s

Jutta Townes

ASHWOOD
PUBLISHING

Copyright © Jutta Townes 2024

All rights reserved. Apart from as permitted under Australian copyright law, no part of this book may be reproduced without the written permission of the author. Contact the publisher for information.

ISBN (paperback): 978-0-6459137-7-4
ISBN (ePub): 978-0-6459137-8-1

Published by Ashwood Publishing, Cradoc, Tasmania.
https://ashwoodpublishing.com.au
info@ashwoodpublishing.com.au

Set in Adriane Text 11/16.
Cover & maps: Susan Young.
Cover images: Author's own image; Depositphotos/maryloo; Shutterstock/DrAndY, Triff.

The CJ Dennis quotations are from 'Washing Day' in *Doreen*, Angus & Robertson, 1917, and 'The Mooch o' Life' in *The Songs of a Sentimental Bloke*, Angus & Robertson, 1916.

As far as the author could discover, the lyrics quoted from Thursday Island are from a long-established folk song of unknown authorship. They are recorded here with appreciation and respect.

'Yes, We Have No Bananas' original lyrics by Frank Silver, 1923, public domain; author's own translation.

 A catalogue record for this work is available from the National Library of Australia

Contents

Part One 1
- The most beautiful boat in the world 3
- Two drops of water 8
- Don't fence me in 14
- A breath of freedom 24
- Changes of heart 34
- Weighing dreams and reality 40
- With this boat I thee wed 52
- A home on the harbour 63
- Mother 77
- Life examined 89

Part Two 99
- Finding my sea legs 101
- The sea and her disciples 110
- Aboriginal country 127
- Thirty days at sea 142
- Indian Ocean islands 152
- The Seychelles 175
- Africa – a whole new continent 185
- Durban 215
- The cape of storms 235
- The ocean of the seven feasts 245
- Rio de Janeiro 266
- South American coast 281
- Calypso country 297
- A homecoming 307

Part Three 315
- Home ... and away again 317
- Two rivers 329
- Travelling through communist countries 338
- The Black Sea 360
- Istanbul 369
- The Aegean 380
- Rhodes 394
- The journey ends 409

Part One

The most beautiful boat in the world

Sydney, December 1963: one of those hot blue summer days, a stiff nor'easterly sea breeze cooling things down a little. The planks of the L-shaped Mosman Bay Marina feel rough and splintery under my feet, and I scold myself for having left my sandals in the car. My boyfriend is a couple of steps ahead checking the names of boats looking for the yacht we've come to see.

Hope had been advertised as 'suitable for cruising'. We had read that line many times before and been disappointed, but when we saw her, the second-to-last boat on the marina, all the miserable boats we had seen were forgotten. This was it; this boat was definitely the one.

Hope was tied stern to, and looking down into her deep cockpit I saw red cushions bright against varnished teak – a tiny lounge room. A gleaming brass-capped tiller connected to the outside rudder. Laid decks, scrubbed to a velvety grey, curved broadly around a timber mast towards a long bowsprit. Teak bulwarks and cabin structure gleamed in burgundy hues and green canvas covers were laced neatly over booms and sails. She had an aura of gentle authority, a commanding presence; was at home in her element like a mother duck. It would have been impossible to walk past and not notice her. We admired her for a minute and then Graeme gave a 'Hoi *Hope*... anybody aboard?' A tanned face with deep laugh lines and a head of greying curls appeared in the hatch. Seconds later Johnnie Johnson was in the cockpit, pulling in the lines for us to step aboard. Invited below we met Irene, Johnnie's wife.

The Johnsons had sailed the Barrier Reef for the past eighteen months but felt it was time to switch to a motor sailer. 'We're getting on a bit' – Johnnie grinned boyishly – 'semi-retired now.' He worked as a merchant seaman, only doing the occasional coastal trip now. A little more small talk followed but soon Johnnie got down to business. Carefully unfolding a set of original shipyard blueprints, we learned that *Hope* was a little under 9 metres, designed by a man named Hobbs, that she was built in England in 1932, had a beam of 2.70 metres, and drew... Graeme was keenly interested but I had stopped listening, didn't need to know the details. From the moment I saw *Hope* I knew we would buy her, and in my heart she was mine already.

Johnnie and Graeme went up on deck to talk sails and rigging, and Irene showed me around below. *Hope*'s cabin space was tiny. A skylight raised above deck level gave standing room in the centre. Bunks on either side, furnished with red cushions like the cockpit, doubled as daytime settees. The port bunk had a chart table built above it, and whoever slept there would have to tuck their legs underneath it. The padded backrest of the starboard settee hinged forward to reveal wardrobe space behind it, and lockers under the seat held the bedding. A polished kerosene lamp sat in gimbals, and leadlight windows fitted into the bulkheads allowed light into the forward section. We snaked our way forward, and Irene showed me the closed-in toilet cubicle to port, storage space to starboard and two bunks angling into the bows. A canvas windsock hoisted above deck pushed a cool stream of air through the opened forward hatch. *Hope* smelled woody and sweet.

Heading aft again, Irene proudly showed me the galley directly beneath the main hatch. Brackets, brass catches and custom-built racks held china plates and bowls securely in place. *We'll have china*, I rejoiced silently. I hated plastic plates. But looking at the single-burner kerosene stove had me worried. Irene noticed and explained how to prepare a meal on one burner. 'Put your vegies on first and when they're nearly done you put them aside... they'll keep cooking just sitting in the boiling water while you do the chops,' and then she added a smiling 'Men are easy to feed, just make sure you fry plenty of onions.' Advice from a long-time married woman to one who was about to marry: Irene had seen my engagement ring.

The men came below again; we had mugs of tea and a couple of hours passed chatting about the joys of sailing, the beauty of *Hope*, what a wonderful boat she was, how well she handled at sea and what a great life cruising was. I didn't doubt any of it, but what impressed me most was that two young Australians had sailed *Hope* out from England three years earlier. She was a seagoing vessel. She had proved herself and that sealed it for me: we had found our boat; we would get married and sail the world forever…

After we left the Johnsons, Graeme and I behaved like kids in a fun park, laughing, hugging and jumping around: *we made it, we found our boat*. Trying to be sensible we forced ourselves to slow down, look beyond the plusses and search out possible minuses. One concern was her rig. *Hope* was gaff rigged, old-fashioned even in the 1960s, but that didn't stop our enthusiasm. *So she is gaff rigged, so what?* It already seemed rude to criticise 'our' boat. She was a Lady, and one didn't criticise a Lady. A bigger concern was her cost. She was expensive, her asking price twice as much as we had imagined we might need, but we argued our way out of that too. Since her voyage from England *Hope* had been completely overhauled, new sails, new running rigging and every inch repainted; *we won't need to spend a penny and living aboard is going to be cheap*. The last tiny sticking point was her name. She was built and commissioned as *Hope*, her name and 'Luke Brothers Shipyard, Hamble' cast into the bronze sleeve fastened over the rudderpost. Like expectant parents we had dreamed up our own name, but we graciously accepted that changing *Hope* was unthinkable and would anger every god above and below the sea.

John and Irene took us for a sail on the following Sunday, a mere formality. Spending the day on the harbour became a meeting of friends and an introduction to *Hope*'s little quirks. Our concerns over her rig vanished as the day unfolded. The gaff was high peaked and although her performance to windward wasn't brilliant, we forgave her when she romped along on a broad reach – her best point of sailing, exhilarating, pure joy. Sailing to windward was of lesser importance to us anyway; we were planning to sail the world westwards, the trade winds pushing us from behind.

Finding *Hope* was pivotal to our venture, the shift from imagination to reality, from talk to commitment. She became my encouragement and my mentor, the bond I had with her beyond reason. I tried to tell myself that a boat was merely an object, a 'thing' that needed our skill to take it places but *Hope* was never that. For me she was alive, a personality, 'someone' I could trust like a friend from a half-forgotten past.

Two drops of water

It catches my breath to think how easily Sydney could have become two-dimensional, a set of beautiful colour slides in my collection and not my homeport. I had arrived a migrant and the two years I had signed up for were nearly over. I had no intention of staying. My passage home was booked, I had money in my pocket and after a duty visit home I had plans to work in Canada or the Middle East perhaps. I had merrily overlooked that everything I had dreamed of as a child was right here: sunshine, palm trees, boats and ocean. More importantly I hadn't banked on falling in love and whoever – or whatever – is in charge of such things was cutting it fine.

Alluvial Mining, the company Graeme worked for, was behind schedule on their Port Kembla job. An extra draftsman was needed and my agency, which rarely mentioned that they were sending a woman, gave me the contract. 1960s Australia had few draftswomen, and walking into Alluvial's Jamison Street city office wearing a tight skirt and heels (trousers for women were not yet tolerated) I picked up the by-now-familiar hum of incredulous voices: *is she going to work here?*

Mining was an especially male environment, the drawing office rough and functional. Around forty drawing boards lined the walls of two large rooms with rows of trestle tables in front of them. There wasn't a woman in sight, and watching from the corner of my eye I saw the fuss I was causing. Playboy pin-ups were taken down, men put their shoes back on, the door to the toilet was shut and eventually I was assigned a drawing board in the farthest corner of the office, next to Graeme. He had failed most of his previous year's university subjects, and Bill, the chief draftsman, deemed him too busy to even look at girls.

Bill was wrong. I had barely unpacked my pens when Graeme began chatting, and almost the first thing he told me was that he and his mate Max were going to sail a yacht around the world. Wow, I had never heard of anybody doing such a thing. 'What gave you that idea?' I asked. 'I'll give you a book to read,' he said.

Two days later we had our first date: had I seen the views from the newly opened AMP building at Circular Quay yet? The AMP was Sydney's first modest skyscraper, twenty-six floors tall with an observation deck on top. I lied, not telling him that a German lift mechanic had smuggled me up months earlier when the building was still an unfinished shell. I saw no point in knocking back a date with the first Australian who'd ever asked me out.

I liked Graeme, his awkward grin and his crazy plan to sail around the world. He was different from the smooth-skinned Europeans I had dated – wiry-looking, sinewy, with wide shoulders and strong legs. There was something rough about him, his body a sculpture not quite finished, sharp edges, the planes not filled in. Only his hands were perfect, gentle, capable, working away at his slide rule, his calculations fast and decisive. I began to imagine how good it would be to be touched by those hands and soon I no longer had to imagine it.

A crazy time began. Graeme would call at my Paddington flat on his way home from university and we'd make love half the night. Hours later we'd meet again to work side by side, pretending collegial friendship. Lunchtime had us leaning against the wrought-iron fences at Circular Quay with the sun on our backs, talking sailing and going places, and like two drops of water our lives and our dreams joined up. I was leaving for Europe soon and our falling-in-love madness had the added urgency to strengthen the relationship; neither wanted to let go of the other.

Sealed into an exclusive aura of careless summer, we became inseparable. A colour slide from that time brings back the ease and lightness we felt. The tiny square of film shows wheels of crimson poinsettia against an azure expanse of ocean, the shimmering heat almost palpable. I'd caught a glimpse of it, driving down the winding road towards Whale Beach, and had insisted on going back to photograph it. The poinsettia tree was tall; it was difficult to capture flowers and the sea in one shot and I ended up standing on top of Graeme's car, a white Austin with a cute BUB number plate.

Evenings would find us at the movies or having dinner out in one of the newly opened restaurants. I recall a special treat night at Beppi's down from Hyde Park; minestrone with fresh spinach leaves, osso bucco, and gelato for dessert. Later still we'd drift towards Kings Cross where motley crowds sat over bad coffee in smoky lounges, listening to emerging artists singing and playing for free. Graeme played the guitar and sometimes joined in, singing about Wild Colonial Boys and some crazy 'Shearer by name Bluey Brink'. Alex Hood, keen and dedicated advocate of Australian folk music, became a friend. His long frame arranged around his banjo, he told fascinating stories about travelling outback to record Australian folk songs, afraid that they would be lost. Times were a-changing. American culture had begun to push in. People were dancing the Twist. It became fashionable to talk about 'life', encounter groups were springing up and the promise of liberation through sex and baring one's soul permeated the air like the smell of fresh bread.

An important date: a drive to West Head, the northern tip of the Ku-ring-gai Chase National Park, a little way north of Sydney and one of the most majestic places I know. Leaving designated pathways and parties of Sunday picnickers behind, we trekked through the bush over fallen tree branches and leaf-filled gullies to finally settle on a huge boulder a good 200 metres above the sea. Holding hands and dangling our legs over the edge, we played King of the Castle, holding court over sheets of silvery water and golden sunshine. Palm Beach lay far below us, a thin line of white sand curving towards a solid wooded mound topped with a lighthouse. A short jump had us claim Lion Island, a green beast crouched in glittering water. Another jump and we felt our way along the northern coastline, dark headlands repeating themselves in lighter shades of grey all the way to Queensland.

Sails in all sizes dotted the ocean, and gazing at the sharp line of distant horizon I insisted that I could see the curve of our planet. We grew silent. I can't remember who spoke first but the decision to marry and sail a yacht around the world was unanimous. Neither of us had ever sailed before but I had read the book Graeme had lent me. I knew it could be done and we would do it. I would visit my parents as promised, Graeme would finish his engineering degree, and when that was done we would make proper plans. Love, boats and the sea rolled effortlessly into one tight bundle of shimmering excitement.

Graeme introduced me to his family as the girl he worked with, 'going back to Germany soon'. Our engagement was a secret, our plans too tentative for exposure and certain condemnation. His mother was not fond of me. She objected to my morals; to her son hardly being home and creeping into the house at ungodly hours. Taking off for a camping weekend one Friday after work, Graeme felt it was better for me to wait in the local park while he raced home to get his gear. His mother had made it clear that 'If that girl comes in the front door I'll go out the back door.'

Underneath her censure Jean (as I came to call Graeme's mother) was a softy. She told me later how worried she'd been about us that Friday night. Woken up by a fierce storm and exceptionally heavy rain sweeping up the coast, she couldn't go back to sleep, thinking about *that poor girl and her Graeme* camping out in that weather, hoping we'd be safe.

She needn't have worried. The storm did blow our tent down, we did get drenched, but for all that we were lucky. The rain soon stopped, the sky cleared, and abandoning our flattened tent until morning we found shelter inside the shell of a large corrugated iron water tank dumped in the dunes. Rusty and without a roof, it had split at the joint, leaving a gap just wide enough for us to squeeze inside it. Tucked into a single sleeping bag we slept like swagmen, safe from the wind, and the stars above us framed into a perfect circle.

More magic came with the crisp clear dawn. Racing Graeme along the beach for a warm-up I was about to jump onto a rounded, half-submerged rock near the water's edge when a sudden impulse stopped me. With a beating heart I realised I had almost jumped on top of a sea lion. Smooth and dark, the huge creature lay unmoving, stranded. One of his flippers was hurt, bleeding a little, and like Tarzan and Jane we sat with him, feeling helpless and worrying about his injury. The poor thing hardly moved, but as the sun climbed higher the creature slowly lifted his head, whiskers all bent and sandy, gave a growl and slowly lumbered into the water. Graeme swam with him, out past the surf to make sure he didn't get stuck on the sandbank.

⁓

November 1962: the ship taking me home is leaving from Sydney's overseas terminal. My brother and fellow immigrant will join the ship in Melbourne and five weeks later two dutiful children will be back with their parents in Germany.

Leaving is surreal. Graeme and I have dawdled carelessly, almost playing dare. *So what if I miss the boat?* We've left my flat too late, can't find a parking spot and end up having to rush like crazy. There is barely enough time for me to get aboard and push in among the passengers crowding the ship's rail. Frantically searching among the sea of people I find Graeme's bearded face and the woman next to me thrusts a whole packet of paper streamers into my hand. I furiously throw one after the other and he catches two of them, and minutes later the ship pulls away.

His first letter arrived en route, folded around a colour slide showing the M/V *Neptunia* leaving the harbour, a white ship in an afternoon indigo sea, North Head massive in the background. He had followed the ship's progress down the harbour, driving recklessly along South Head Road, trying to catch glimpses along the way, *crying and wishing he could sprout wings to follow me.*

Don't fence me in ...

I'd grown up in post-war Germany in a tight-knit family – too tight. We were Prussians, refugees in our own country and not especially welcomed in the Ruhr Valley. Rumour had it that the government was giving us money and *why should they get anything when everyone is doing it tough?*

Father worked at the coal mine because he had no other choice. The mining authorities assigned us two upstairs rooms in a narrow slice of house, part of a row of terraces left standing among bombed-out rubble like train carriages off the rails. The coal range in the kitchen took up a quarter of the room and left just enough space for a table, chairs and a sideboard for crockery. Mutti's treadle sewing machine was pushed hard into the corner next to the window, and near the door stood two covered buckets, one for clean and one for dirty water. The nearest tap was in the basement, down three flights of wooden stairs. Across the landing from the kitchen was our bedroom, double bunks for my brother and me and a double bed for my parents. We lived there until I was 11 years old.

Pappi, as we respectfully called him, had a classical university education and spoke precise High German. He was hacking coal from the ground on hands and knees, we were sitting on chairs pulled from the ruins but his children, he said, would behave. He insisted on perfect manners and correct speech. I was praised if I deserved it and transgressions were punished with a lecture, followed by a cooling-off period in which he simply ignored me. Mutti's way, giving me a quick slap around the ears, was easier to bear.

Unlike other miners I never saw Pappi with grimy hands or dark-rimmed eyes. When he was on morning shift my brother and I would sometimes pick him up, waiting for him outside the steel gates. Always the last one out, we could see him walking across the yard, tall and thin, his shoulders pushed back and always alone. He must have spent more time than anyone washing off every trace of coal dust. On Fridays it was customary for the miners to carry a bundle of dirty pit clothes home for their wives to wash. Father never did, *wouldn't do that to Mutti*. He wore the same filthy rags until he was eventually given an above-ground job manning the First Aid station.

My brother Frank, two years older than me, was taught to protect me and I had to obey. Amazingly, it is one hierarchy I never challenged. He was my big brother, my anchor and guardian angel. I loved and adored him and would happily have slept in his bed but for Mutti's permission to smack my hands if I tried to climb up into his bunk. I honestly believe that without him I would not have survived my childhood. He was my companion when our crowded rooms felt like a pressure cooker about to blow apart, and when Mutti and Pappi had their dreadful fights we would sit quietly, hold hands and wait for it to be over.

The thought of the four of us stranded in two small rooms for so many years brings up contradictory feelings. I sense the frustration of being trapped and under constant surveillance, but also the warmth of our tiny kitchen, the safety of all of us sleeping in the same room and the all-embracing intimacy of a family that had survived terrible trauma. I loved it when my parents talked about the life we'd had back in Prussia, how beautiful the Baltic had been *and right on our doorstep*. Mutti had saved our photographs and I look at myself, amazed that I had so many dresses, a different one in every picture. There is Frank holding my hand, and one of Mutti on a yacht. She looks beautiful in a dark sailor suit, perched high up on the boom, one arm hooked loosely around the mast. The pants of her suit are ridiculously wide at the bottom, the jacket tight, with a double row of shiny buttons. Mutti shows me how she had to swing her legs outwards to walk in those pants, covering the length of our kitchen in three quick strides. My heart burns with jealousy; I want to be a sailor too and swing my legs just like her.

Another picture, a beach scene, intrigued me. I am about 2 years old, perched naked on Pappi's knee feeding him a bit of apple. Mutti said he called me his Eve, like the paradisiacal Eve tempting Adam. I can't imagine that I ever sat on Pappi's knee. As I grew up we would shake hands at bedtime and wish each other good night, and sometimes he would touch the top of my head.

I have almost total recall of the seven years in our two small rooms, the good and the bad. I lived my life inside a Pappi/Mutti/Frank/me bubble, a vibrant and intense universe that rendered everything outside of it hazy and of no consequence. I had no need for friends. Crouched in the corner of our tiny kitchen, half-hidden under my mother's treadle sewing machine, I would disappear inside my brother's

African adventure books, shape clouds into carpets, into birds or ships; I'd make landfall in Zanzibar, talk to pirates and princes, wear fabulous clothes and feast on bananas and coconuts, fruits I'd never seen. I knew early that I would leave Germany. Unlike the girls at school, I had no wish to become a salesgirl in a shoe shop (the favourite occupation of the day) and then get married. Some girls had already worked out how many children they would have and picked out their names.

Left: Mutti in her sailor suit. *Right*: Mutti, my brother Frank and I in Elbing, my birthplace in East Prussia, in 1944. It is now Elblag, Poland.

The family bubble began to disperse when I was 11 and we moved to a bigger house. We now had a basement, a kitchen and a lounge room above it, and two bedrooms above that. Frank and I shared one of the bedrooms. A little more self-conscious now, we dragged a wardrobe into the middle of the room and closed off the gap left between it and the wall with a curtain. It gave us a 'room' each and best of all, we could continue to talk at bedtime the way we always had, our grievances, plans and ideas floating over the top of the wardrobe.

Frank longed for a BMW motorbike. I, more than ever, wanted to get away, feeding my imagination by gazing at a colour illustration cut from a magazine and tacked to the wall at the end of my bed. It showed a young man carrying a small suitcase, standing by the side of a rain-streaked city street. Neon advertisements and brightly lit buildings were mirrored on wet asphalt and the caption read '... *alone in a big town.*' It was supposed to be a sad picture illustrating the plight of lost and lonely youth. To me it looked like a gate to freedom. I wanted to be 'alone in a big town' and often imagined the gleaming rain-soaked street to be in Hamburg with large ships and a vast sea just around the corner.

Frank got his BMW motorbike soon after he began his apprenticeship as a fitter and turner. The fulfilment of my desires took a little longer, but my relentless wishing and wanting must have helped to arrange universal forces to make it possible, one slow step at a time. The most important step was to attain a career that freed me financially, and I got that thanks to Pappi augmenting my education and to Mutti's charm and tenacity. I had finished primary school, was not yet 14, when she took me to one of the large steel companies in the city. Telling lies, she brazened her way past the security gate and did not stop until the two of us sat in the CEO's office, where she presented me as the smartest girl in town, deserving of a drafting apprenticeship. Dr Witte gave us both the benefit of the doubt. Mutti was asked to leave, and I was put through a 4-hour aptitude test right there and then. Three months later I started my drafting apprenticeship, the youngest of the 1954 batch of thirty apprentices.

Working in town meant catching trains and buses and opened up my world. I made friends, went to the movies and played with the idea of enrolling in a language school, *French would be lovely and English would be useful* ... Pappi was pleased, didn't want me to get stuck in suburbia. Born into a well-off Prussian family, he'd moved in elite circles for most of his life; he wanted me to make contact with people away from coalmines – *enter a different milieu* as he put it. He suggested I join the one and only tennis club in town, forgetting that exclusive clubs were no longer within his social or financial reach.

I joined a dancing school instead and learned to waltz, foxtrot and cha-cha. Pappi gave me lots of freedom and on special occasions, such as balls or carnival celebrations, I was allowed to stay late and catch the last train home. It left the city at 0055 and took twenty-five minutes to reach our suburb. A twenty-minute walk from the train station took me along a tarred road with grazing pasture on both sides and got me home at twenty minutes to two. To keep me safe Pappi had bought me a knuckleduster and shown me how to use it. 'A man will always be stronger than you,' he said. 'If you get attacked hit him in the face as hard as you can, twice, you must hit twice ... then bring up your knee, scream and run.' It felt marvellous to walk through the night singing the latest hit, one hand holding a bunch of keys and the other encased in my cool smooth knuckleduster. No one could hurt me. I was invincible.

Pappi had given me the knuckleduster primarily to save me from being raped. German soldiers reported as dead or missing were returning from Russian prisoner-of-war camps as late as 1954. Ill and disoriented, they hid in fields and forests searching for wives (who may have remarried) and children that had grown up. As a rule they weren't violent but it was as well to be careful. I'd had my share of men hiding in corners, exposing themselves or beckoning for me to come with them. Pappi must have weighed the obvious danger against his (and my) wish for me to have a social life, and come up with the knuckleduster. Carefully worded comments had made it clear that it was up to me to protect my honour, at the very least until I met the man I wanted to marry.

Father's moralities were not based on religion, but on his own values and principles. Born in 1900, he was very much the stern and upright Prussian often referred to as being of the 'Old Guard'. In his world men looked after women and in return, women 'saved themselves' for that privilege. Father's rule clearly posed a dilemma for me, especially since my mind was firmly made up that I would not marry for a long, long time, if ever. A flurry of flirtations and the occasional boyfriend still had me follow his rules, but then I fell in love. He was gorgeous, heaven incarnate, and I had no trouble rearranging the morals I'd been taught. My heart and mind now required nothing more than mutual love and respect, and still intent on freedom and 'getting away', I simply dropped the prerequisite for a permanent bond. When Father found out that I had a lover he was deeply disappointed. In his mind I had abused the freedom he had given me, and my stubborn insistence that I had no intention to marry the man in question made things worse.

Pappi and I stood facing each other in our kitchen, he in front of the window, his silver hair lit from behind, and I, shaking and obstinate, in front of him: two combatants poised in an unwinnable contest. In an icy voice he pronounced my morals flawed and my behaviour disappointing and unforgivable. He could understand my transgression if it had happened spontaneously, in a dream at the end of a dance, but I had planned it. Of course I had planned it; it was winter, did he want me to do it on a park bench or in the muddy fields? He demanded to meet the young man and with that my humiliation turned to cold fury. For the first time in my life I found the strength to match my father's. Taking a deep breath, I stood tall and told him that I was responsible, not the young man, that it was my body and that it had been my decision to make. Still composed, I managed to walk past him, stopping just long enough to accuse him of ill manners for his failure to ask me if I was happy or not. Putting on my boots and coat in the hallway I took off into the fields, walking for hours and bawling my eyes out.

Standing up to Father shifted the balance between us. In an uneasy truce we became extremely polite with each other, careful to keep talk and discussions on neutral ground. He never mentioned my wrongdoing again and I saw no reason to talk about it either.

Luckily Mutti backed me up; a hug and 'it's okay, Kindchen' came from her. I hadn't told her that I'd met Lutz, that I was madly in love, but she must have guessed something. She must have remembered the day we'd sat in our favourite *Konditorei* after a shopping excursion, her smoking a cigarette and me tucking into *Schwarzwälder Kirschtorte.* Looking over my coffee cup I had asked her in a casual aside, 'Tell me, Mutti, how do I know who the right man is?' I was certain she knew what I meant because smiling impishly she'd replied, 'Oh, you'll know.' I'd known all right, but even Mutti was shocked by my adamant refusal to take the affair further. Lutz was a medical student and Mutti, still of a generation of women dependent on men, would not have let go of a chance to marry a doctor.

Frank was working in another town at the time, roaring in on his lovely motorbike at weekends. He missed the drama and I didn't tell him, both of us now grown up enough not to discuss such intimacies. It is unlikely that he noticed the frigid atmosphere between Pappi and me and if he did, he wouldn't have thought of it as odd. For Pappi to be so aloof I must have done something, whatever. We were used to his punishment of ignoring us until we knew how to behave ourselves again. Unfortunately losing my virginity was a transgression that could not be made good; there was no way I could 'behave myself' ever again.

The disagreement with Pappi brought me closer to leaving, and soon after our fight I sent off my application for immigration to Australia. To my dismay I received a letter explaining that although my professional qualifications fitted the immigration criteria, I needed to be 18 years old and have parental consent. I had to wait another year, nearly two actually...

1960 arrived, the year Pappi turned 60 and I turned 18. A new age dawned and changing winds engulfed me like an expected gift. Bill Haley unleashed rock-and-roll in concerts and movie houses. Elvis Presley, confident and laughing, served his army time in Germany surrounded by adoring girls in flared skirts and voluminous petticoats. Young people openly began to assert their right to live life their way, determined to create a new world of love and peace, of fun and sex. My exoneration from Pappi's harsh judgements arrived while watching *Breathless* with Jean-Paul Belmondo and Jean Seberg. It suddenly occurred to me that if gorgeous Seberg (playing Belmondo's girlfriend Patricia) could spend half the movie in bed with a sexy criminal, there was no reason to worry about my own failings.

Two glorious hours at the movies expanded my vision of

freedom beyond a simple escape from oppressive surroundings. It now included self-determination, independence and the right and the liberty to break outdated conventions. To make a statement, and to everyone's horror, I had my hair cut shorter than Jean Seberg's in *Breathless*.

On my eighteenth birthday I sent off my immigration papers a second time, enclosing my brother's application in the same envelope. It had been easy to talk Frank into coming with me, tempting him with enthusiastic visions of travel and sunshine. Frank's joining me helped and Pappi signed his consent with the terse remark that he had nothing more to teach me. Acceptance by Australian Immigration and the necessary travel documents dropped into our letterbox soon after, and Frank's and my bedtime talks over the top of the wardrobe took on a new intensity.

Four months later, on 2 September 1960 late in the afternoon, the *Castel Felice* pulled away from the German port of Cuxhaven. Frank took a photo of me leaning against the ship's timber rail wearing a light-coloured, three-quarter-length coat with the collar turned up. The North Sea stretches grey into the distance, my short, dark hair blows in the wind and I look relaxed and comfortable, ready to have a wonderful time. I am away ... at last.

A breath of freedom

In 1960 few Germans had the need to migrate for economic reasons. My own prospects were good, but the lure of adventure and desperately wanting to leave home proved stronger by far. Rebels like me had few options. Most sons and daughters lived at home until they married, in houses owned by the coal mine authorities. Flatting together was unknown and even if I had had the money, I was too young to sign a lease. We sometimes heard of young men joining the French Foreign Legion but the more accepted way, especially if one had qualifications, was to migrate to Canada or Australia.

Australia offered sunshine, my profession was in demand and having my fare paid made it an easy option. Women were welcomed, if not fast-tracked because years of immigration had skewed the male/female ratio. When I told people I was migrating to Australia it was often assumed that I was after a husband. Had I told them that marriage was the last thing on my mind, no one would have believed me.

On Pappi's insistence we'd agreed to write home every week. Frank and I took turns and Pappi saved our letters, neatly collated into a folder. Frank writes that '70 per cent of passengers cried when the ship pulled away', he describes the logistics of money transfer and the confusion of hundreds of people running around looking for their cabins. He records that the *Castel Felice* registered 17,000 tons (a medium modern cruise ship has 130,000 tons) and carried 1,464 migrants and a crew of 257.

I want my parents to know that I share a B Deck cabin with three other single girls, that my bunk has a soft mattress, two blankets, one pillow and a reading light. I write of seeing my first palm tree, of unbelievable heat, and give a detailed description of the food we were served, which to me seemed excessive: '*We are given a huge breakfast, a large meal at lunchtime and another large meal in the evening. And there are free carafes of wine on the table!*' One vignette describes how the two Italian stewards serving the ten people at our table fuss over me, one pulls out my chair at arrival while the other fills up my water glass, one hands me the menu and the other flaps a serviette onto my lap with a flourish. How my male German fellow diners jokingly roll their eyes skyward and grumble, '*when Italians see a woman they wake up.*'

I describe hilarious English lessons concluding with sing-alongs, a chorus of rough voices belting out 'How much is that doggy in the window?' ending in a drawn-out howl of *arf arf* and *ruff, ruuf*. They learn that I buy slippers with upturned toes in Port Said and a white bikini with its red and blue polka in Aden, delighted by the fact that '*without trying it on my bikini fits perfectly.*' I write of parties and captain's dinners and how I flout the dress code, turning up to dances in Brigid Bardot fashion wearing pale blue jeans and a man's shirt knotted at the waist.

Another vignette, probably a cheeky tease for Pappi, describes how a girl from my cabin spent hours sunbathing, carefully adjusting a bracelet on her wrist, a golden band engraved with the name of her boyfriend awaiting her in Australia. The white circle of skin on her suntanned arm would prove to him that she had been faithful. I imagined that Pappi would have liked a daughter like that, demure and chaste.

But reading the letters also brings back things I didn't tell: how overcrowded the ship was, how men and women drowned their anxiety over an uncertain future in duty-free drinks. I didn't write of the fights and tears, the anger and frustrations, or of the night when an insanely jealous husband raced through the corridors tearing open every door and screaming, 'Who's got my wife in bed?... I'll kill you!'

It wasn't for Pappi to know that I joined in on late night eggnog parties. The men in my group of shipboard friends insisted that the food we were given at table was mixed with chemicals to reduce libido... 'Bromide,' they said. 'We know, they used to mix the stuff into our food in the army.' I wasn't interested in the boys' libido, didn't want to risk pregnancy, but outraged at any wrong, I happily joined the adventures to procure uncontaminated food. We girls would flirt outrageously with the smartly dressed Italian officer on watch, creating the distraction needed for the boys to raid the storerooms and come back with tins of nuts, cakes and whole trays of eggs. Later, with the ship steadily steaming into the night, we'd picnic on the dark foredeck, the stolen goodies washed down with drinks made from egg yolks separated out over the side of the ship and shaken up with red wine and sugar taken from the tables.

I no longer had to evaluate my actions through the eyes of my father, was no longer accountable to him or anyone. I could shape my life any way I wished. The world was mine now, and fired up by an exuberant mix of joy and optimism I spent hours leaning on the stern rail high above the water, charmed by the trail of an ever-changing stern wake. I had no idea what Australia would be like and didn't care; to be surrounded by endless horizon and blue sky was enough for me. To be any happier I would have needed wings to let me soar and swoop around crazily in my newfound freedom.

Approaching the Australian coastline near Fremantle was a comedown, almost disappointing. The low, flat strip of land didn't fit my idea that Australia was BIG. The houses were too low, the port looked empty and there wasn't a shop in sight. A group of us, keeping together for mutual support, began walking towards town along a flat, dusty and practically deserted road. Making out a plume of dust in the shimmering heat had us joking that Fremantle might not have paved streets, but the dust turned out to be a group of workers digging up the side of the road with jackhammers. The noise was horrific but Udo, the comedian in the group, managed to stop the workman. In the sudden silence he then (in what must have been very garbled English) tried to talk the men into letting him have a go with the jackhammer. The men, clearly unable to understand, looked puzzled, which only made Udo more determined still. He switched to sign language and finally one of the men got it. Grinning broadly, he handed over the hammer and next thing Udo, no stranger to the tool, jack-hammered away whooping and yelling at us to 'take a photo, quick'. Continuing our dusty walk into Fremantle he fantasised how he would trick his parents, sending them the picture and telling them that he got a job within hours of arrival in Australia.

We did eventually find life (and shops) in Fremantle city and had a great time buying drinks and strange white sandwiches cut into triangles. Unfamiliar with the confusing currency of pounds, shillings and pence, we carefully counted out the asking price and the change we were given. We were cautious with our spending, did not yet have a 'feel' for the money and, if nothing else, Udo's antics had reminded us that we were unemployed. Our money was finite, and it was better not to spend too much.

A few days later, just past dawn, the *Castel Felice* docked in Melbourne. The formalities of channelling over a thousand mostly German-speaking migrants through Customs and Immigration took all day. Hans and his wife, former work colleagues of mine, had signed as guarantors and we escaped transfer to Bonegilla, a migrant camp at the New South Wales/Victorian border, miles from anywhere and reputed to be as hot as hell. Hans picked us up after he finished work and took us to a boarding house in Windsor where he had rented a room for us. It was dark by the time we got there. I was battling a migraine (my curse since early childhood) and finding a big bed in one corner and going to sleep took only minutes.

Morning light captures my waking moment. I hear Frank's snoring. Sunbeams angle beneath ill-fitting curtains onto suitcases on the floor, their lids open and clothes strewn everywhere. I sense a table, chairs and a bulky wardrobe leaning into the room. Slowly turning onto my back I make out a stained ceiling, pitted with shallow craters, striped with wooden slats. In the centre a light bulb dangles from an unblemished ceiling rose, white and beautiful like a sugary upside-down wedding cake. Running steps outside the room shake the floor; one man shouts and another is laughing as if he can't stop.

⁓

The laughing man turned out to be Addi from Hamburg, in his early thirties and the most established tenant. He introduced us to the other tenants (mostly young German men) and did the introductory tour of our new residence, a house unlike any I'd ever seen before.

Threadbare wall-to-wall carpet stretched over broken floorboards in the hallway. Not all the rooms had power points, and a tangle of extension cords ran underneath doors and along corridors. To the right was a bathroom shared by at least ten people. It was fitted with a shower rose rising tall like a sunflower above a rusty bath, and a huge yellow basin set on a cracked china pedestal. A spotted mirror completed the décor. Hot water came via a temperamental gas heater. Addi demonstrated the quirks of the beast, using half a box of matches to light it, assuring us that the mighty *whoomph* when it sprang into action was what it was meant to do.

The toilet was outside in a vine-covered wooden outhouse. The kitchen, also accessible from the backyard, was little more than a lean-to shed. Once a laundry, it still had the concrete tubs attached to the wall. A high-legged cast iron gas stove stood on cracked concrete flooring and next to an icebox; blocks of ice could be fetched from the nearby ice works.

The place was as run-down as it was casual. Dr Reich, a dentist in St Kilda, had bought it as an investment and transformed it into a boarding house by simply fitting locks to the doors and putting in extra beds. Everything else was left as he bought it. He owned the house next door too, another boarding house, and it was rumoured that he planned to buy up the entire street. He called each Saturday morning to collect the rent, five pounds per person paid in cash, no lease and no questions asked. Frank and I, brought up to be polite visitors, had no criticism to make and loved almost all of it.

Addi shared the large front room with shy, round-faced Kalle, a gentle soul with soft St Bernard eyes. Kalle was Frank's age and they soon became friends. Addi, fourteen years older than me, made no secret of the fact that he wanted me to be more than a friend, but I let him know early that I wasn't the marrying kind. He seemed okay with that. Having made my point, I was happy to join in with the group, an accidental family hanging out together, bound by a common language, sharing food and drink and having lots of parties.

Kalle was often the butt of jokes, the unwilling comedian of the group. If somebody fell off a horse on a riding excursion it was Kalle, if someone lost his swimming trunks in the surf it would be him. Kalle had the annoying habit of reading the sizeable Saturday *Melbourne Age* in the one and only toilet, deaf to all demands to please get off. The toilet, one of Australia's famed dunnies, was out the back and one Saturday morning, Frank and Addi decided to cure Kalle of his habit. Secretly rigging up the backyard hose through a chink in the dunny roof, they waited until Kalle was nicely settled, jammed the door shut with a plank and turned the tap on full blast. Kalle's shrieks could be heard for miles.

My first drafting job was in South Melbourne, with an engineering consultancy at fifteen pounds per week. The drawing office was a simple steel structure put on top of an old brick building; the floorboards bare and the corrugated iron roof visible through steel beams. The summer heat was fierce. Keeping the back door leading onto the fire stairs open let in a breeze, and when that wasn't enough we worked with damp towels around our necks. The boss was Austrian and employed Germans, Hungarians and Russians, all of us happy to have a job. I worked hard, anxious about making the switch from metric to imperial (still the measure in the sixties) until Hungarian Frieda, a draftswoman working on a board next to me whispered at me to 'slow down, for heaven's sake... people in this country don't work that hard. You'll ruin it for everybody.' Frieda spoke a little German, and with her help I soon found my bearings.

Olive, the secretary of the firm, became my casual language tutor. Olive was Australian, impeccably made up and dressed in stockings and high heels no matter how hot it got. She sat in a separate, more presentable office at the front of the building, where clients were received. She coached me in my lunch hour, and I advanced from the shipboard 'doggie in the window' to studying the *Women's Weekly*. Olive would flip the pages, extend a polished fingernail and name what she was pointing at: blouse, tissues, scarf, girdle, steak and kidney pie.

Olive helped me understand Australian dress sizes and told me to ask for Modess at the chemist, not sanitary towels as my dictionary suggested; shops were not self-serve and one had to ask for things. One day she wanted to know about my fiancé. 'But I do not have a man,' I said. 'What do you mean?' Mutti had given me one of her rings as a keepsake before I left, a small sapphire with a tiny diamond on either side. Unaware that it signified being engaged to be married, I had been wearing it on my left hand.

Olive was engaged to be married and proudly showed me her ring, a huge diamond. Her fiancé was clearly generous; he had something to do with cars, whether selling or repairing them I couldn't understand. The wedding was to be in six months' time, and my lunchtime lessons switched from women's magazines to wedding catalogues. Admiring one of the pictured couples I innocently said, 'I like flies on men.'

Olive looked at me in silent horror and it took a while to explain that in German a bowtie is called a fly. Now Olive wanted to know the German word for fly. Checking my dictionary, I translated to *Hosenschlitz* – meaning 'trouser slit'. She didn't like that and so I tried *Hosenstall*, a German popular expression for fly, literally meaning trouser stable (as in horse's stable). She must have thought the Germans a weird mob.

∽

Melbourne held me for a year, almost entirely in the company of fellow Germans. It became difficult to move outside our established social circle. Frank made more German friends through work, and combined with our boarding house crowd we had ongoing rounds of parties, sightseeing tours and camping trips. The day I was invited to join a German folk-dancing group became my day of reckoning. This was not what I wanted. I had not left Germany to put on a dirndl and swirl around boys in lederhosen. To make things worse, Addi and I had added sex to our friendship and he was hurt and increasingly angry at my steadfast refusal to marry him. Addi wasn't the only one; I'd been dodging a few advances. German migrant men wanted to marry their own kind and any newly arrived German girl would have had similar chances.

I wondered if Australian men were as keen to marry as the migrants. As far as I could tell they didn't seem to be interested in women, full stop, let alone in migrant girls. Coming home from work I'd see throngs of them drinking beer at the hotel opposite Flinders Street Station, outside, standing on the footpath with rows of drinks lined up on the windowsill. There wasn't a woman among them and a peek into the Ladies Lounge showed only old ladies wearing too much make-up.

The hotels shut at six and the streets were deserted soon after. In Germany I could sit in a tavern late into the night if I wanted to, have a beer or two with a girlfriend and flirt with the boys. *Where do the young folk hang out?* I wondered. *Where do they party?* Sydney was rumoured to be more cosmopolitan, more beautiful, and I decided to check it out. Frank was happy in Melbourne and, loyal to his friends, he stayed on. We finally parted ways.

Changes of heart

Having lived in Sydney for many years since makes it difficult to recall my first impressions. Sharp iridescent colours rise up, and words like 'bright' and 'light' want to push in. And while Sydney was all of that it held a deeper, less tangible essence for me; feelings of easiness, a devil-may-care attitude I could align with. Perching on a cliff top, the sea spread out below me, brought back familiar echoes of longing and rekindled dreams of freedom. I felt as if I had just arrived, as if Melbourne had never existed.

For all my secret joy the first couple of months were difficult. My plan to leave Addi behind hadn't worked, and he insisted on coming with me. Not particularly worried, I thought he'd catch on in time, but it turned out not to be so. His mother in Germany died and he was desperate to settle, to have a place to call home and start his own family. My continued refusal upset him, and he began to threaten suicide, even murder. I believed he was capable of it. A terrible time followed trying to comfort him, talk, explain and encourage. He was a friend, I didn't want to hurt him, and for a long time I couldn't see a way out.

My problem wasn't solved until the company Christmas party, a glamorous dress-up affair at the Kings Cross Hilton. Late into the night, with only a few stragglers left,

I found myself sitting at a table next to Lajos, a Hungarian work colleague. Dizzy with champagne and exhausted from dancing, my composure left me, and weeping miserably I told him about Addi and his threats, how scared I was, how Addi followed me around and was sure to be waiting for me when I got home... what was I to do?

Lajos turned out to be the right confessor. About the same age as Addi, he told me how he too had tried to kill himself over a woman, 'Not that long ago actually. Three times I tried,' he said. 'Honestly, seriously... believe me I tried but couldn't do it.' He was adamant that if Addi did kill himself he didn't belong in this world. 'When you try to give life away it proves too precious,' he said. Lajos would know the value of life; he had escaped the bloody 1956 revolution along with hundreds of thousands of other Hungarians. And being dark and handsome, life-affirming and a little drunk, Lajos naturally had another solution for my dilemma. Leaning closer, his eyes dark and deep, he whispered, 'Forget this Addi man, come to bed with me.'

My talk with Lajos gave me the courage to carefully organise a secret escape. I switched boarding houses, suburbs and my job and bundled my belongings into a taxi, making sure I left no trace behind. Discreet enquiries at a later date assured me that Addi was okay, dating an English girl. I was happy for him and for me. And Lajos was happy too because after a time he also got his wish, and we became friends and lovers, no strings attached and perfect rapport. I had found a companion for whom living and loving was enough.

Lajos' favourite word was 'sophistication'. He was a man of the world and the first person to tell me that a pill had been invented to stop women from falling pregnant 'and hey wouldn't that be great?' Cheeky rather than sophisticated, he told me that he watched his neighbours make love through a window set high above his double bed. 'But only if they're not being boring,' he reassured me, and by then I'd grown up enough not to be shocked. We liked shopping for clothes, dressed up to go out for dinner, and Lajos made sure we saw the latest Art House movies. I remember sitting in his car after watching Ingmar Berman's *Seventh Seal*, depressed and crying, more so after Lajos' admission that he knew I wouldn't like the movie but that he had wanted to see it. Simple kindness did not tally with his idea of sophistication.

I sometimes wondered about the woman he had tried to kill himself for and realised that quoting 'preciousness of life' as his reason for not doing it may have been a little glib. No doubt it had some truth to it, but his resilience and robust ego would have provided far more purpose. Besides, he had plenty of reasons to live. Unlike Addi he had family back home, a mother and father who loved him, neighbours who'd ask after him and his town still standing. Lajos left for Hungary a few months later when a brand-new Australian passport made it safe for him to visit his folks.

My own time in Australia was running out. Frank and I had promised to be back by Christmas, and in May I flew to Melbourne to sort out the logistics. It was my twentieth birthday and my first ride on a plane. I tried to be jet-setting cool about it, but as we landed in wet and grey Melbourne I couldn't stop telling Frank how only a few minutes ago I'd flown in brightest sunshine over clouds looking like snowfields.

Frank still lived in the Windsor boarding house, still had the same job and was surrounded by the same group of German friends. By contrast, I'd had half a dozen moves and as many jobs but for all that, 'cosmopolitan' Sydney had not widened my circle of friends to include Australians. The only difference was that I now spent time with migrants from other nationalities: Hungarians, Russians and Italians. There seemed to be 'new Australians' and 'old Australians' – the former busily working away, forming construction companies, opening fruit shops and restaurants, while the latter, both hosts and spectators to the activities, quietly kept their distance.

In a small way I managed to bridge the gap when I left boarding houses behind. Confident in my work and with my English much improved, I made good money and could afford to rent a small flat, the downstairs of Mr and Mrs Cook's private residence in Paddington, the first Australians I got to know well. Mrs Cook liked me and adopted me as a substitute for her recently married daughter. Board was added to my rent and I ate my meals with the Cooks, upstairs around their dinner table. I had my first taste of haddock with parsley sauce, crumbed lamb chops, roast leg of lamb and good mashed potatoes and gravy. I witnessed the making of pavlova and got hooked on rockmelon and ice cream.

Mr Cook was a builder and came home from work at exactly the same time every day. He'd stop at the local pub for a couple of beers to 'wet the whistle' and arrive soon after, carrying two bottles of Toohey's for us to share over dinner. And if I happened to be home on a Saturday night, the Cooks would take me with them to the Paddington Returned Servicemen's Club (RSL) down the road. Big crowds, all dressed up 'for the club', enjoyed dancing, floorshows, bingo, cheap meals and 'chook raffles'. New Australians ridiculed the clubs as unrefined, unsophisticated entertainment (Lajos had been scathing) but for me it beat German folk dancing any day.

It wasn't the young crowd I'd been looking for – RSL patrons were mostly older Australians – but months of sunbaking at Bondi beach in my smart new black bikini had made me less keen to meet Australians. Lifesavers seemed a proud lot and I wasn't impressed by knots of suntanned boys roughhousing their girls, chucking sand at them and bodily picking them up to throw them into the water. Strange behaviour, but the girls seemed to like it.

In August, four months before my ship left for Germany, I met Graeme – my first Australian boyfriend, future husband and travelling companion. Full of nationalistic fervour, Graeme joked later that it took an Australian to make me change my mind about marriage, and he was right. Graeme was different from the migrant men I had dated. He had freshness, and an innocence about him; his childhood was one of treks through the bush and spearfishing with his mates, of normal schooling followed by university. He didn't have a history of dislocation and loss, didn't struggle with trauma barely concealed, didn't have to carry the burden of nationalism turned to evil, my burden and that of my fellow Germans forever.

War for him was an abstraction; his nationalistic fervour uncomplicated, straightforward; his stories about the Anzacs and Rats of Tobruk about mateship and glory. Sydney was his home, he *felt* at home and suddenly I wanted to become Australian, be part of his world. I still had reservations about getting married, but as I reassured myself over and over, we weren't getting married as in settling down and having a family. We would sail the world together, and although I was happy to flout the morals of my time, I still thought it right and proper to marry the man with whom I intended to share my life.

Weighing dreams and reality

I had caused so much trouble with my stubborn stance for independence and my fight for sexual freedom that the irony of coming home engaged to be married wasn't lost on me. Travelling home on the *Neptunia* I worked out what I would tell my parents, determined not to breathe a word about our sailing plans. Two years away hadn't changed my view of Pappi as my critic, and I wouldn't risk another rebuke. I would tell him what he wanted to hear and hold plans and rebellious thoughts in sweet revenge.

Frank joined the ship in Melbourne, and five weeks of travel gave us time to get used to the idea of coming home, each week losing a little more sunshine: Perth, Ceylon, India and the Suez Canal still hot, sleet in Sicily, pouring rain in Naples and howling winds in Genoa. A heated train to take us over steep mountains and through Alpine tunnels into the snow and ice of Germany and finally, a taxi to our doorstep.

Two of Graeme's letters were already waiting for me and all I needed to do was confirm what my parents had already guessed. Yes, this Graeme was my sweetheart and yes, I would be going back to Australia. As intended, I only told the conventional: how much we loved each other (for Mutti) and that he was well educated (for Pappi). Hundreds of colour slides projected large onto our lounge room wall contrasted two different worlds. Here I was, sitting with my family in a room made cosy by a coal fire, and on the wall glittered an ocean in every shade of blue, white beaches and long sweeps of green bushland. Pictures of Graeme in different settings helped to introduce him: barefoot, in shorts, in a suit, and one of him taken in Luna Park, bearded and posing behind iron bars like a convict. A picture of Graeme holding a slice of watermelon in one hand and the big knife he'd cut it with in the other, caused much laughter. I explained what kind of fruit it was, and that Graeme probably looked serious because he was trying to separate out the pips in his mouth, but Pappi (with the straightest look on his face) said 'You are tricking me, I know he's eating a slice of leg.'

We were still a close family, but life had moved on without us; the ties had loosened. The only thing familiar was my bedtime talks with Frank over the top of the wardrobe. We both missed Australia, our friends and the sunshine, and often the question of whether we could leave our parents again stood large in the room. Mutti had grown independent and had been promoted in her job. She was fine, got by without us, but what about Pappi? We could see how old he'd grown, how tired and unwell he looked. Frank accepted that of course I must go back, but could he?

Duty and highly structured Germany began to enclose us. I missed the easy living and Australia's casual work scene. I'd got used to contracting, working as much or as little as I wanted to and the simple hiring procedures of 'Okay, you can start tomorrow.' Now I had to write job applications and tell lies at interviews, assuring prospective employers that I had no intention of returning to Australia. Drafting was not casual employment; I would be part of a select team, and admitting that I only needed six months of work to sort out my finances would not have gone down well.

I wanted to return to Graeme and Australia, but as the weeks rolled by I realised how much I had heaped onto my plate. Graeme and I barely knew each other, our sailing venture was little more than a dream, and living in a coalmining town miles from the sea made such plans seem more elusive still, even crazy. Who'd ever heard of anyone sailing around the world? Who would believe me when I'd never even set foot on a yacht, let alone sailed one? How could I explain that I needed to do this? I couldn't even tell Frank and he knew me better than anyone.

Apart from going to work I stayed home and read, took walks around the countryside and did the round of Sunday visits to aunts and uncles. My self-imposed solitude formed protective armouring around me, my plans safely contained within. Mutti tried to draw me out, eager to know more about Graeme's and my prospective life in Australia, but I couldn't find the words to satisfy her. I didn't know myself and felt more confused as the months went by. My only hold was the letters Graeme and I wrote to each other, eight months of promises and thousands of words spun into a tenuous thread.

⁓

I've searched out the box containing our letters, his and mine tied together with ribbon. They've been sitting on my desk as I write, teasing me to come clean and tell the reader that the romantic love story, so central to my book, has no happy ending, that Graeme and I went our separate ways not long after we returned from our travels. I question myself whether it is necessary to tell. And the answer is yes it is, not only in the name of honesty but because I want to. My story may have its fairy tale moments, but above all that it is a real-life story, a big chunk of my life retold, lived experiences whose legacy reverberates with me to this day. What came before and after my years of roaming puts them into context, is important and needs to be told.

Yet telling or no telling still left me with the dilemma of whether to read the letters. Is it wise to re-read love letters after the relationship has ended and love has cooled? Is it fair? Is it ethical? Will it upset me? I had longed for those letters to arrive, racing up the stairs into my cubbyhole bedroom behind the wardrobe to read them. Now I'm afraid of what they might reveal. Isn't it said that one should let sleeping dogs lie?

Eventually I did untie the bundle, and almost immediately the flow of words carried me away into timeless realms, where I found myself face to face with a younger Graeme and a younger me, easily recognisable, our individual quirks and ideals evident to this day. Smiling, almost laughing, I decided that reading our letters wasn't going to be a problem, it wouldn't hurt anyone. It felt comfortable to go back and revisit the feelings of long ago. Reading one letter at a time became seductive, a languid search for the forgotten, a leisurely basking in the excitement of when it all began. Touched by the innocence of our letters I felt again the bond we had, the belief in each other and the determination to make each other happy.

But disappointment and confusion also surfaced again, my sadness at finding so much casual matter-of-factness in his letters, so many words, but hardly any of his thoughts or feelings, no romantic flights of fancy, and only a few intimacies reserved for the closing paragraphs. I felt for the young woman I was, 20 years old, craving more intimacy and ardour, wondering if she had imagined it all. How was I going to know? What should I do?

In the end love played the winning hand. After knowing Graeme (the real live person) for only three months and the letter-writing Graeme for eight months I returned to Sydney. Marriage and travelling the world together would become our reality.

Enough time has passed for me to no longer feel the sting of what we lost, but to see gain in it. Meeting when we did was timely; we were perfect for each other. Our joint enthusiasm and abilities made it possible for us to grab a huge slice of life and live it bigger and fuller than we might have had we not met. We weren't to know that our horizons would change, that our time together would end, later, in another decade, when we came to live at opposite ends of the Australian continent unable to reconcile our differences. My wanting to become part of Graeme's heedless and untroubled world hadn't been enough; too much Slavic gravity, my inward-looking nature and a need for closer bonds got in the way of it.

Warmth and compassion for both of us remains; that, and a ready acceptance that despite physical and emotional separation our journey binds us still, not in sadness or anger, but as a shared experience encapsulated in a time that no longer exists. It is impossible to separate us from our adventure.

Graeme's letters were long and full of information, with sketches of boats and newspaper clippings attached. Optimism jumped out of the pages; busy and exuberant, he packed all he could into the time 'before we get hitched', as he put it.

University was finished for the year; six passes, six credits, with special dispensation for one subject because 'he was in trouble with his fiancé'. Taking time off work, he was off on the Sydney to Hobart Yacht Race, jubilant over having cadged a crewing job on *Goodewind*. It was his very first ocean sail, his beaming face shown on the front page of the *Sydney Morning Herald*.

I can't wait for you to get back was usually followed by something he had done or wanted to do. Like the time he'd looked over a yacht for sale, moored off Middle Harbour Yacht Club. He deemed the boat suitable for our venture, attached a sail plan and wondered if he should put a deposit on it – but then conceded that it would be unfair to buy 'our boat' without me seeing it. *'Perhaps it will still be there when you get back ... and would it be possible for you to pick up a sextant duty free?'*

An impossible request. Even in Sydney I would not have known where to find such a thing, let alone in Dortmund.

Still intent on cramming all he could into his life before I returned, he spent a week trekking Cradle Mountain in Tasmania (a map of the route was attached). He wrote of the amazing experience and included beautiful colour slides of the trip. I didn't mind him having a good time, far from it, but the Tasmania hiking trip irked me. We had talked about Cradle Mountain and made plans that – one distant day – we would do the trek together. Why couldn't he wait? My only consolation was that he went with Max, the mate he had been going to sail the world with. I felt I owed Max.

Then the scene changed and letters began arriving from

Bella Vista, where he absolved his university practicum working at the site office of the Snowy Mountains Hydro-Electric Scheme, a huge project being built in southern New South Wales in the Australian Alps. Being away from yachts and stuck in the wilderness made him reflective, and at last his letters contained snippets of what I had longed for: descriptions of his small room, the peace and beauty of the mountains, his enjoyment of sitting alone at night writing and thinking of me, his wish that I could have been with him that morning, sharing the magic of a red sun rising over cold hard snow. He loved the 'Snowies' and imagined them to be like Germany.

My letters were pensive and subdued, my life defined by being with my parents, aunts, uncles and cousins whom Graeme did not know. I wrote of my work scene so different from his, of leaving for work in the dark and coming home in the dark and of saving money for my return fare. I could add nothing to the sailing front and seemed intent on building more of an emotional connection. In my early letters I still talked of love, of missing him and feeling sad, but Graeme scolded me for it: he loved me and there was no need for sadness, I should know that.

Graeme didn't open his heart easily. Even when his dad died, he wrote only the barest facts. I'd met his father, a quiet Scot who had come to Australia in the 1930s Depression, and had taken him my modest collection of books before I left Sydney. Already a shadowy figure marked by his illness, he rested on a daybed on the veranda and I stood tongue-tied, returning his gentle smile and sensing a suffering deeper than his illness. I knew Graeme would be upset, would be shaken by his father's death. I wanted to know how he felt, offer closeness and comfort perhaps, but Graeme wouldn't be drawn into it.

~

Although Graeme's letters were offhand and almost casual, I never doubted the genuineness of his feeling for me, but as the months went by, reservations about our compatibility began to creep in and I toyed with the idea of ending the relationship. One job application for Canada would be all it needed. Canada was said to be a beautiful country; I could ski, mountain climb – perhaps even sail.

I thought about ringing Lutz, my first lover, living a train ride away from my parents' place. Walking the same streets we had walked two years earlier had brought him back with unexpected force; the first time we slept together, how next morning we'd walked through near freezing temperatures to throw the talisman fish I wore around my neck into the Dortmund-Ems Canal. 'Fish are meant to swim, men and women are meant for love,' he'd teased me. Lutz was comfortable with feelings, his and mine.

Graeme was more likely to joke feelings away, put his foot on the brakes while I had mine on the accelerator. I remembered how offhand he could be. My parents would have been aghast had I told them that he teasingly called me 'squarehead', 'kraut' or 'reffo'. Or of the time when we sat over a romantic meal and he suddenly reached out to touch my face, telling me seconds later that my skin was softer than Sandra's and she was using pots of cream, forever putting stuff on.

Was charm and sensitivity a European trait?

In one letter (numbered by him as 'No. 35 – *received*

18 August 1963'), I question him about an evening coming back from Manly on the ferry when he'd pointed into the dark mass of Clifton Gardens, winked at me and said, 'Remember the night we went there?' My memory is good. I knew one hundred per cent that we'd never been to Clifton Gardens, and I didn't like the idea of being interchangeable. It must have bothered me a lot to write to him about it, but he did not reply to it.

Graeme steered clear of disagreements and 'Clifton Gardens' was not the only time I was left with the discomfort of an unanswered question.

~

But I like his lightheartedness, his freewheeling ways, I argued with myself, thinking of a time we climbed over rough terrain at Willi's Castle, near his home in Willoughby. Steep slopes dropped down to Middle Harbour and hopping over rocks wasn't without danger. I led the way, jumping crevices and scaling boulders until distant water views opened up. Resting side by side on a ledge, a sweep of green bush and glimpses of water far below us, Graeme suddenly said, 'You're different... the girls I've been going out with need a hand to step over every pebble. I don't have to worry about you... you're okay.'

I liked that; didn't want to be worried about. He'd be fair, wouldn't hem me in. A champion of fairness, I smiled as another snippet of conversation bounced into my head. Out on another hike he'd told me how, as a kid at bedtime, he'd take off his socks in the same order in which he had put them on in the morning. If he put his left sock on first it should also be the one to come off first, in fairness to his feet.

And then, suddenly, all arguments in my head stopped. A

parcel arrived by sea mail, badly squashed and barely held together with yellow customs repair tape. Without having to open it I pulled from it a yacht made of balsa wood, her hull flawlessly painted in pale blue, her sails made from thin white paper. Graeme had carved it for me, and the fragile little gem had survived thousands of miles of rugged travel, safe, unharmed and not a mark on her. I am an easy target for omens; I look for them, and this was a good omen.

Resting in its little varnished cradle my sloop 'sailed' on the shelf beside my bed. Gazing at the curve of her papery sails had me conjure up blue oceans and distant horizons. I thought of Graeme at home alone in his room carving her for me and of the magical day when we'd sat high above Pittwater playing King of the Castle. We'd been close then and would be again and restlessness overtook me like a turning tide. Letters were too difficult, I needed to go back, be with him, sense, touch and make love again. And if we were still okay with each other the sailing part would simply fall into place.

The sailing the world part was the least of my worries. I knew I wanted to do it and never doubted that I could.

~

When I listen to reports of adventurers returning from tough and sometimes heart-breaking journeys I'm intrigued not so much by how they did it, but by why they did it. What drives a person to traverse burning deserts or drag a sled over miles of ice to reach the South Pole? Sometimes the adventurers say 'I've always wanted to do it' and launch into the logistics of how they made it happen, but more often it's the elated statement that 'It's the fulfilment of a dream.'

I can't claim to have always wanted to do it – plans to

sail the oceans didn't enter my head until I was 19 – but the notion of fulfilling a dream reverberates strongly. I am willing to believe that dreams set up subtle echoes, bypass consciousness and direct us in ways we may find hard to fathom. Who's to say that the worlds I visited as a child travelling on ships and carpets were pure fantasy? The longing for those places was real to me, as real and as unexplainable as my grown-up love for the sea and my affinity for boats. I simply know that at some time, somewhere, a flame ignited that has refused to dim ever since.

I have never looked for verification for my strange inner knowing, but inadvertently, and purely by chance, my imaginings suddenly gained a solid footing. Turning the pages of a book on seafaring in the Baltic, I came across an illustration of the shipping seal of the port of Elbing (now called Elblag), my birthplace in Prussia. Elbing, as a member of the Hanseatic League, traded with countries as far away as England, France and Holland and shipping documents bearing the town's seal have been found as far back as the 13th century. Studying the intricate details of the seal left me stunned. Roughly the size of the palm of a hand, it shows a single-masted Baltic cog steered by an oversized man holding a tiller; another figure in the bows is on lookout pointing ahead. Elbing's insignia – two crosses, one above the other – is fixed to the stern.

The same insignia had hung in our lounge room for as long as I can remember, not as a flag but as a coat of arms painted onto a small shield. I had been told that centuries of history lay behind that shield but had never connected it with sailing. Here were two people in a sailing boat; the helmsman could actually be my great-great-grandfather from generations ago. How could I have been so blind?

My affinity for sea and boats was not imagined but had

carried through blood and genes, unchangeable like my blue eyes and the shape of my nose. Pride for my forebears and sweet feelings of belonging swept over me and took hold. I felt received and accepted as if membership to an exclusive club had been handed to me. I was a sailor; restlessness had been put in my cradle; it was okay to want to keep moving and have a home in many places.

In the strangest of ironies that realisation didn't come until after I had sailed many thousands of miles;[1] proof after the event, a cheeky 'told you so' wink from a great-great-grandfather. It's a pity he didn't wink earlier; the good man could have sunk a raft of insecurities.

---

1 Distances over water are measured in nautical miles, which are slightly longer than land miles. Sailing speed is measured in knots; one knot equals one nautical mile per hour.

With this boat I thee wed ...

My bank balance was healthy and, humouring my childish glee to complete one loop around the world, I decided to fly back to Sydney westwards, stopping over in Paris, San Francisco and Tahiti. Pappi insisted on a photo of the two of us standing in the doorway as I left. He wears a shirt and tie (as always) and holds my arm, smiling. I look down, disconnected and separate, already gone.

Frank took me to the airport and my cousin Werner brought the champagne. The plane left in darkness and resting my dizzy, drunken head against the oval aeroplane window, I earnestly and conscientiously said *Auf Wiedersehen* to every runway light as the plane taxied towards take-off... *goodbye, goodbye* ... right, left, left again ... *goodbye, goodbye* ... hundreds of lights and a thousand goodbyes.

I did the prescribed tourist thing and stood under the Eiffel Tower, marvelled at Notre Dame, but was equally amazed at the bidet in my hotel room; I'd never seen one of those before. And in Tahiti I nearly missed the once-a-week plane. Ignorant of the effects of jet lag, I stretched out on the hotel bed 'just for a minute' and was instantly asleep, woken up hours later by a maid coming in to clean the room. Her swiftness in packing my suitcase and the breakneck speed of a taxi got me to the airport in time. I was lucky. Departure was delayed, not because of me but because of the difficulty in rounding up the Tahiti soccer team. The boys, covered to their ears in flower leis, were flying to Nadi (Nandi) for their first inter-island competition. Rousing team songs, good-luck kisses and laughter slowed things down for well over an hour.

I didn't see my luggage again until Sydney, and my careful plan to look a million dollars walking across the tarmac towards Graeme was ruined. I was going to wear a fitted mustard-coloured gabardine suit, concealed buttons, small collar, tight skirt and all the matching accessories. Instead, I wore a cotton pyjama top printed with red poppies, cool and perfect for sightseeing in Tahiti. I had managed to dress in my yellow skirt, but my bare legs must have been blue as I emerged into a cold September dawn. I asked Graeme later whether my unusual outfit had shocked him, but he had only noticed my lack of stockings. Stockings and gloves were still the thing for girls in the early 1960s.

Mr and Mrs Cook, my friends in Paddington, had my flat ready for me and it took no time for me to settle in. Graeme had told his mother of my return only days before I arrived, and slow as she had been to catch on until then, she'd raced to the phone to tell her sister that *that girl was coming back*. Flossie's reply was instant: *Oh, I hear wedding bells; they can have the reception at my place*. I was invited to Graeme's house for Sunday roast: leg of lamb, baked pumpkin, onion, potatoes and mint sauce, rice pudding and custard. I was accepted and not long after Graeme insisted on tradition and sealed it with a diamond ring.

My first sail ever was on *Goodewind*, the yacht Graeme had crewed on in the Sydney to Hobart race. Mark, her new owner, offered Sunday sailing in exchange for working on the boat on Saturdays, and I was his greenest recruit. Leaving Rushcutters Bay, we sailed up the harbour towards Sydney Heads laughing and joking, the harbour calm and lovely. The wind was fresh and sailing out into open water felt marvellous, *wow, this is the life*. I couldn't have been more surprised to suddenly find myself irritated and tired, barely able keep my eyes open. Bitter fluid collected in the back of my mouth and minutes later I was gut-wrenchingly seasick. The placid motion of ocean liners had not prepared me for the fierce rolling and pitching of a small yacht.

My only consolation was that another girl aboard was sicker than I. Busy with my own troubles, I didn't see her but was told later that her face had turned green and concern for her safety had prompted our return. I never turned green, but seasickness stuck with me – a big nuisance, which I decided to put up with, like the migraines I'd had since childhood or a hangover after a party. I always got better, didn't I?

With this boat I thee wed ...

My brother was the first of my family to meet Graeme. Australia had proved too much of a magnet for him and he arrived in Sydney by ship, three months after I did. Stepping off the gangplank he shook hands with Graeme, the two men sizing each other up, very cool. I was a cauldron of emotions. What if they didn't like each other? Frank had been my closest friend and companion for so long, it felt strange to add a husband.

Later, in my flat in Paddington, Frank told me his news. He too was in love. In a strange reversal of my situation he'd met Helga, his future wife, shortly before his ship left and too late to cancel the passage. 'Copycat,' I teased him, 'now it's your turn to write love letters.' Beaming me his best boyish grin, he stacked his gear in my flat (Frank didn't travel light) and took off working as a pump specialist on the Snowy Mountain Scheme. He planned to stay for a year and make lots of money.

~

A month after Frank's arrival we found *Hope*, and six weeks later she was ours, a British-registered vessel listing Graeme as captain and myself as first mate. Raising the money to pay for her had been a nightmare. Graeme, a few semesters short of his engineering degree, was in regular employment, and I had returned to freelancing. Both of us earned big money, but the banks wouldn't touch us without a guarantor, *money for a house yes, any amount you want, but a boat?* Not one person in Graeme's extended family would guarantee us; *you can buy a house for that amount of money* was the usual refrain. *Yes, thank you, we know, but we don't want a house.*

We were about to sign for a high-interest private investment loan through a group of solicitors when Johnnie and

Irene, *Hope*'s owners, stepped in. Johnnie got furiously angry over 'those bastards wanting to make a quid out of you kids', fumed against 'shark money' and offered to finance us himself, at bank rates. Johnnie and Irene believed in dreams and trusted us, no check-ups, no fuss. Our self-chosen repayment plan was ambitious; we aimed to pay off *Hope* within two years and have enough money in the bank to start cruising.

Having a home now, we set a wedding date three months hence. And with that, suddenly, like the tide turning, all omens turned bad. First Mrs Cook, my beloved landlady, wanted my flat for a friend and asked me to leave. Racing upstairs after work one day to show her something I had bought, I crept back in tears feeling hurt and betrayed. I had lived with the Cooks like a daughter; I thought they liked me. I had imagined leaving for the wedding from her home; she was my friend. My antenna is usually pretty good, what had I missed? Why would she throw me out so close to the wedding? Did I mean so little to her that she would ditch me for a tenant who would stay longer? My silent questions were never answered, and I left within two weeks.

˜

The easiest solution was for Graeme to move aboard *Hope* and for me to move into his home, his boyhood room. His mother suggested it and I accepted her offer, not realising how difficult the coming months would be for me. Jean (she had suggested I call her by her first name) and I had got to know each other a little. We got on well, but moving into her home spelled the end of my freedom and bohemian existence. I was now a resident of Sydney's North Shore, heartland of uprightness and respectability. I was gently reminded that toilets were bathrooms, humans never busted

(Graeme's slang) and that dogs didn't piddle (Graeme's slang again). And while sex might exist, it was never mentioned. Graeme became the visiting fiancé whom I would see off outside the front door with a quick kiss. 'Not long now kiddo,' he would whisper, and then sprint along the side of the house, jump into his car and speed back to *Hope*.

The please-and-thank-you politeness seemed reminiscent of my own home, but I soon realised that refined manners were a brittle façade. Jean fought with the neighbours on both sides. The woman on the left earned her wrath for trimming the hydrangeas arching into their property, and Jean retaliated by hurling the dead rats she caught in a trap over into their backyard. Old man Marchant, living alone in the other half of her semi, was more of a worry. I don't know what started the fight but whenever Old Marchant got drunk he'd shout tirades of abuse into his fireplace, the words arriving hollow and garbled via the common flue shared by the two dwellings.

It didn't help that Graeme's sister Helen, three years younger than me, was into full-on teenage rebellion, screaming at her mum through slammed doors and using words I had only heard from the boys when things went wrong out sailing. If Mutti and I had shouted at each other like that just once, we would have died of shame. Jean simply ran around the house banging the casement windows shut so that the 'stickybeak neighbours' wouldn't hear. Deeply unsettled by the fights, I tried to sense Graeme's place in this strange family. Did he shout at his mum? Did he respect women?

The next upset came when Frank arrived unexpectedly in Sydney, having driven all night from some place he'd worked at. Mutti had written to him; Pappi wasn't well and she wanted Frank to come home straight after the wedding. The letter sounded urgent and we both felt it would be best if he left immediately. Things could be serious, and if something were to happen to Father, Mutti mustn't be alone. Frank was to give me away at the wedding, but I assured him that it was no big deal ... 'Don't worry, someone else can give me away. I'll ask my boss.'

'No big deal' bravado vanished in the night before the wedding. Afraid and close to panic I lay awake in Graeme's blue boyhood room, in his single bed, my mind frantically trying to balance the commitment I was about to make against my need to be free. Was I crazy to marry? What if I'd got it all wrong ... what if this wasn't love? Couldn't we just sail around the world and not marry ... if I climbed out the window now and ran away nobody would know where to find me ... I'd need my passport, bankbook, travel bag, shoes ...

Mach dich doch nicht verückt suddenly popped into my head, words my mother would speak if she saw me now. *You're right Mutti I am driving myself crazy* – and forcing myself to lie perfectly still, I calmed down. Dear Mutti. Extending an arm, I tried to touch the wedding dress she had made for me, a ghostly shape hanging in readiness outside the wardrobe door. I had begged her to make the dress, simply requesting something slim and elegant. Mutti knew my taste, she had made clothes for me all my life and the dress of heavy ribbon-embroidered French satin fitted perfectly, right down to the hem. Gazing at it in that long awful night brought Mutti as close to me as I could possibly have her. I missed her terribly and, crying and exhausted, I finally went to sleep.

The next day my head ached, my stomach churned and I looked ghastly. The hairdresser poured strong cups of tea into me, I swallowed tonics and powders, but nothing helped.

The day dragged on in an uncomfortable blur until the very moment I entered the church. In an almost miraculous recovery the fog in my head suddenly lifted and I felt incredibly, exuberantly well. Flowers and candles stood out, sharp and precise. I saw golden sunbeams slant at an angle touching the altar and felt the warm ambience of brick and timber. A large Union Jack on one wall and the Australian flag on the other gave an air of solemnity and as I slowly walked past the many smiling faces, my eyes found Graeme, dark-suited, his beard shaved off for the occasion. *Too late, all done* sang a cheery little voice within me, and stifling a sudden impulse to run to him, I forced myself to take small seemly steps.

The photo of Graeme and me leaving the church shows us smiling and radiant. Graeme is looking smart with a flower in his lapel and a pair of grey gloves held casually in his clasped hands. My arm is linked into his and I am wearing the loveliest dress ever.

And yet, on all counts it was an unusual wedding: the bride alone, not a single member of her family present, and yet not alone. Graeme's family had done everything they could to welcome me – his mum fussing over me, making my bouquet and filling the church with masses of flowers, his sister happily taking on the role of caring and attentive bridesmaid, while the wedding guests broke with custom and sat on both sides of the aisle. Willoughby was Graeme's home turf, and leaving the church we were greeted by dozens of neighbours smiling, cheering and wishing us well. But perhaps the most unusual detail – as weddings go – was Graeme's words as we drove off in the wedding car.

'It's a strong southerly,' he whispered. 'We may not get away tonight.'

We had plans to leave on our honeymoon on *Hope* that very evening.

The reception too had touches of quirkiness. Graeme's cousin Brian, an ardent Jerry Mulligan fan, played the saxophone and had organised a band to back him. I don't remember if the music was good or bad, nor even what was being played; only that it was loud and that we danced to Beatles music when the band took breaks.

Brian's mother, Aunt Flossie, had kept her promise to let us have the reception at her home overlooking Lane Cove River; plenty of room to accommodate the fifty guests; Graeme's family was big. I imagined them all having a lovely time after we left, sitting down on chintzy lounges for a quiet 'cuppa' and airing their opinions about this German girl who had married their Graeme. ... *and did you know they're going to live on a boat ... ridiculous ... what a silly idea, mark my words, that won't last.*

In spite of our protests we were given vases, serving trays, double bed sheets and mountains of huge bath towels as presents. Auntie Joyce insisted on giving us a fancy Royal Doulton sugar bowl and fluted silver spoon. 'Never mind the boat,' she told me. 'You'll need something pretty.' Auntie Joyce's bathroom was pink, right down to the toilet seat cover.

After the party Max and Helen, best man and bridesmaid, drove us down to *Hope*, tied up at Mosman marina, where Graeme became adamant that he would carry me 'over the threshold' of our new home. For this Max needed to pull the boat up close so Graeme could jump aboard with me hanging around his neck monkey style. The tide was out, the boat was way down, and discussion on how exactly we were going to do this ensued with the earnestness of people several notches past tipsy. Then Helen got a case of the giggles, badly, which quickly evolved into all of us laughing uproariously. I was carried aboard safely but would have laughed had I ended up in the water. My silken canary-yellow going-away dress billowing around me in the black water would have made a lovely sight.

Peter Kenny, living with his family aboard *Innisfail* on the opposite side of the marina, got out his Claxton foghorn to farewell us. His shouts of 'good luck' and sustained blasts of the foghorn followed us as we motored down the dark bay towards Sirius Cove, the first anchorage of our honeymoon. Next day we sailed to Pittwater, roughly 25 miles north of Sydney, a good day's sail through open water. It would be two years before we could leave on our big cruise, but not counting the days we explored bays and beaches, bathed under the waterfall in Refuge Bay, cooked leisurely meals and pretended that we'd left already.

A month later we sailed back through the Heads with me in tears, sad over having to return so soon and moved by the beauty of the setting sun casting peach and vermilion swirls onto darkening water. My tears flow easily. I weep at sadness and beauty, at goodbyes and homecomings and not infrequently at beautiful sunsets. On that day it may have been premonition of what awaited me.

I hadn't heard from my family since before the wedding. First a postal strike held up the mail and then we'd been away sailing. Sorting my stack of accumulated letters by date, I sat in the cockpit to read wedding cards, congratulations from Mutti, Pappi and Frank, from aunts and uncles and then, in the last letter, the news that my father had died a week before the wedding. Something was wrong here; I had only just read that Pappi was getting better. Frank's return had lifted his spirits; he was fine, how could he have died a week before the wedding?

I tried making sense of it and slowly the truth sank in. Mutti and Frank had lied to me, had written pretend-happy letters to shield me and not spoil my wedding. Pappi lay buried already when we had toasted his health. Confused and upset, I blurted all this out to Graeme. He came to sit with me, tried to hold me but I'd gone rigid and refused to be comforted, stuck in a nightmare, a layer of ice slowly freezing around me. 'I'm okay,' I said getting up stiffly, 'I'll start making dinner,' but peeling potatoes in our tiny galley everything suddenly stopped. I saw my hand holding the knife, the half-peeled potato and the pot of water sharply contained like a vision in spyglass, and then I couldn't stand up anymore.

A home on the harbour

We stayed at the marina for a time but soon the longing for privacy made us move onto a mooring far out in the bay. It was good to get away from Mosman Rowing Club, the party venue of the day, as fashionable as it was noisy. We no longer had to put up with curious sightseers crouched on hands and knees trying to peek inside the boat. On misty winter mornings the stillness was almost eerie. Standing on the cockpit seat with my arms draped over the boom, I could watch the Manly ferry move silently across the mouth of the bay, her familiar shape suspended in layers of grey. We took turns leaning on the boom, absorbing the morning. Graeme called his time the morning stare, sacred space in which to adjust to a busy day ashore.

At first, living aboard peppered me with an assortment of bruises from bumping into things, but before long the boat began to fit around me. My body acquired a radar system in the manner of bats, automatically twisting and turning to avoid solid corners. Even out sailing I could race forward through a wildly gyrating boat to fetch something and not bang into things. Occasionally the movement of the boat would follow me ashore, and working away at my drawing board the upright surface suddenly became fluid, gently swaying to and fro in front of me.

The one drawback of living out in the bay was when storms hit, especially at night. Mosman Bay is open to the south and when it stormed from that direction the misery was intense. Our nerves on edge, we'd lie awake and listen to *Hope* furiously bucking and yanking like a wild horse tethered against her will. Gusts rising and falling tightened and slackened the mooring chain, sending steely bangs and shuddering reverberations throughout the boat, the thought that the mooring might not hold ever on our minds. One night two neighbouring boats tore lose and skimmed past us at tremendous speed straight for the rocks behind us. Afraid that *Hope* would follow, we managed to drop the mooring, motor into the lee of the land and shelter behind *Radar*, a solid wooden charter boat moored against a private wharf. Tucking us against her broad topside, *Radar* was like a kind and generous patron saint, shielding us from the worst. In times to come we sought her shelter more than once, preferably before it got nasty – there was no point in toughing it out.

Mosman Bay had a community of live-aboarders, an odd collection of families, couples, drifters and old salts. Some, like us, were getting ready to go places; some were in transit and others simply loved living on the water. In the back of the bay lived a postman, evident by his uniform and postman's cap. On weekday mornings and always at the same time he rowed ashore in a slow and measured way. In the evening he made his way back again, threading his dinghy among the moored boats in the straightest possible line. Once aboard, he crawled underneath a canvas cover thrown over the boom and laced tightly to the scuppers like a steep tent. He never talked to anyone, but sometimes late at night I could hear him play music, clear piano notes drifting across the water. *He can't have a piano aboard, surely?* I thought him a silly man, he never talked to anyone, never sailed the boat, never painted her bottom and one day surely it would sink under him.

Another lone man lived aboard *Blue Waters*, a gaff-rigged ketch reputed to be older than *Hope*. I have forgotten his name, but unlike the postman he sailed his boat, and handled her beautifully. I would have liked to step aboard and look over the boat, but one of the other yachties warned me off. Bunny (he must have had another name but was Bunny to everyone) told us that *Blue Waters* was seething with cockroaches. Apparently the galley was equipped with two pots only: one for porridge, in constant use and never washed, and another for stew, ditto. Bunny had hung around for a drink, strongly alcoholic and served in an empty coffee jar.

Overall, we were a social lot. We knew everyone's dinghies and if more than one was tied up behind a yacht it amounted to an invitation to join the party. Boats were the favoured topic, but discussion could as easily do the rounds of John F. Kennedy's assassination (still raw), politics in general and idiotic council people in particular, *did you know they're trying to stop honest yachties living aboard?* Talk revolved around the ballot called by the government in an effort to boost troop numbers in Vietnam. A man carrying a 'Ban the Bomb' placard nailed to a stick ceaselessly walked the streets of Sydney. Friends and colleagues were called up but, lucky for us, Graeme's part-time university studies gave him an exemption. I was especially relieved, found the thought of war too horrible to contemplate. We were safe; it was okay to talk sailing for hours.

Two couples were ready to head north to sail the Barrier

Reef; a New Zealand couple had crossed the Tasman already. With all of us broke, trading, swapping and lending became our currency and charts, books, and tools made the rounds. Bargains were shared. I worked for the Colonial Sugar Refinery and could buy cases of high potency rum cheaply, unlabelled and in a choice of white or tan. Peter Kenny worked as a mechanic at the IXL canning factory, getting dented tins of food for little cost. Dented tins couldn't be put through the labelling machine and (if Peter can be believed) when collective demand outstripped supply he'd walk along the assembly line banging tins with a spanner. We soon learned to memorise the letters and numbers stamped onto the lids to determine the contents; SH stood for spaghetti and meatballs, our least favourite.

A homosexual couple, 'out' and impervious to poofter labels (the term 'gay' had not yet been adopted), lived aboard another yacht. Trevor, the 'better half' as he liked to introduce himself, was a Qantas steward and brought in whatever duty-free stuff might be called for. He was popular with us girls – sailing can be rough on skin and it was great to get French cosmetics duty-free.

But the best bargain to come our way ever was a Vespa motor scooter. Graeme had sold his car to save money and we had eyed the little machine for a while, leaning against the boatshed fence, barely visible under a lantana bush gone wild. A round of enquiries uncovered that a chap named Bill owned the Vespa, apparently *a nice bloke, kept a boat on the marina but away a lot, doing his second stint in Antarctica.* One day Graeme spotted him stepping onto his boat and after polite preliminaries he made him a joking offer for the Vespa: 'Five quid if she starts first go.' 'Okay,' said Bill, 'that's fair.' He fetched the key and the three of us trooped off to the back of the shed to drag the little grey thing from its leafy nest. Bill turned the ignition key and against all odds the machine started first go. Five quid changed hands and Bill and Graeme went for a quick spin around the car park, nearly crashing into the fence on the way back. The brake lever had become unworkable and stiff with rust. An oil bath and a bit of fiddling soon fixed the problem.

The Vespa became our darling, a patient mule bringing home our shopping and transporting us everywhere. On Friday evenings especially we must have been a strange sight. Graeme drove with a case of beer between his legs, topped by his briefcase. I hung onto him with the week's groceries and a bag of washing squashed tightly between us. Last stop before heading for home was the coin-in-the-slot machine at the North Sydney ice factory, a resourceful bit of engineering. A couple of coins set off a distant rumble and shortly afterwards a solid 2-cubic-foot ice block whooshed down a chute, landing with a mighty thump in the metal tray below. From there we lugged it into the yellow Esky strapped to the back of the Vespa and our weekend refrigeration was assured.

The next bit of excitement to come our way was Jinky, the cat. The Neutral Bay boatshed cat had had a litter and one warm little body with black fur, white boots, white bib and extra-long whiskers looked at me with such appeal that I could not help hugging him and taking him home. 'Jinky' seemed to suit him for a name and his pet name (so to speak) became 'Jinks'. His mother was known, and written up in the local paper, as the cat that could fish. Apparently, she would crouch along the planks of the marina at high tide, swipe her paw into the water and come up with a fish. I can't verify this, but knowing Jinky I believe it. Out on the mooring one morning we watched him, no more than eight weeks old, slide along the deck, his belly low and every fibre of his body focussed on a seagull swimming alongside *Hope*. 'Come on Jinks, don't be silly,' I warned, but Jinky wasn't listening. His crouch uncurled, his paws extended, and he threw himself full length on top of the bird almost twice his size. The gull took off with a screech and a flap and Jinky trod water until we fished him out. He wasn't at all pleased for me to be taking a photo of him, the look in his eyes fierce and his front paws defiantly planted onto the deck.

It's a pity I didn't get a picture of Graeme when he took an involuntary swim not long after Jinky's little faux pas. His engineering mind should have told him that walking on water would not work, not on plastic blow-up shoes anyway, but he got carried away by the glossy picture on the box showing a man doing just that. Graeme thought it would be great for getting the milk in morning. He couldn't wait to try the 'shoes' but waited until sunset and the privacy of dusk, thinking he'd do a trial walk across to *Ataruka*, tied to a mooring about 30 metres away. Skipper Rolli was sitting in the cockpit, and Graeme could barely contain his amusement imagining the stir it would cause when he walked up to him and asked if he could join him for evening drinks.

He put on his trunks and blew up his 'shoes'. Fully inflated they looked like narrowed-down kiddy pools, streamlined little boats about a metre long, with wooden planks a little wider than a human foot fitted into the bottom. Tightly blown up, the plastic 'uppers' closed around the ankles, and 'ski stocks' for pushing oneself along in the water completed the outfit.

Looking at my lean, half-naked husband standing on deck in very large Micky Mouse 'shoes' had me in fits of laughter. Watching him high-step over the handrail, ease himself into the water and cautiously 'walk' around the boat, one hand holding onto the cap rail and his bearded face bobbing up and down like a sailor in a puppet show, had me in helpless roars.

First Rolli, then his wife and soon all our neighbours got up on deck to see what was going on. Graeme had an audience now, and after his practice walk around *Hope* he grabbed the 'ski stocks' and pushed off. Rolli, quickly assessing the situation, jumped up with beer in hand and launched into a dry commentary, 'And here ladies and gentlemen we see the amazing feat of a man defying the elements', but then excitement got the better of him too and he began shouting, 'Come on JC, come on mate ... not far now.' Graeme had covered almost half the distance when the Mosman ferry rounded the point. The first ripples in the water reached him and next thing he was an upside-down man, his feet buoyed by two fat pale-blue plastic sausages. He wouldn't have seen the startled faces of the ferry passengers or heard the echoing laughter of the yachting crowd.

Taunts, jokes, parties and childish silliness found easy ground in our crowd of barefoot existentialists, but sailing was a different ballgame. Sailing was serious business and required good teamwork, and in that department Graeme and I still had major hiccups. When friends came along things tended to run smoothly, but when it was just the two of us we had some glorious fights. Here's one: I'm at the tiller headed for Mosman late one Sunday, Graeme comfortably on deck, leaning his back against the raised skylight smoking his favourite pipe. The wind is strong on the port quarter and

Hope's mighty mainsail is sheeted way out, almost at ninety degrees, and close behind us is the Manly ferry.

'Graeme, the Manly ferry is getting close, I'd like to jibe.'

He casts a casual glance astern and says, 'No, you're right, keep going.'

Sailing dead before the wind in a gaff-rigged boat can be tricky. On *Hope* the gaff boom extended beyond the stern, which meant there was no backstay to secure the mast. Instead, she had running backstays: two wires, coming off the mast just below the crosstrees, that fed into port and starboard levers screwed to the deck next to the cockpit. Bringing the boat about, but most importantly for a jibe, it was essential for one lever to be released and the other to be tightened at the precise moment when the boom swung across the boat. A jibe is when the sail shifts from one side to the other when the boat is running before the wind and can be very violent: failing to secure the running backstay (as would be the case in an uncontrolled accidental jibe) had the potential to bring the mast down.

I didn't like jibing *Hope* at the best of times, and the Manly ferry getting ever closer made me jittery. The slightest shift of the wind could bring the boom smacking across, I'd have to scramble like mad to pull the sheets in, secure the backstay and next thing we'd be bang in the path of the ferry. We should get out of the way, jibe safely, in time... pretty well right now.

'Graeme, I want to jibe. Now. I don't like this.'

He takes another look. 'No, keep going, he can see you.'

I am sure the captain has eyes, but Manly ferries have recently been given right of way over sail and *this bloke is pushing it.*

'Graeme!!! Can we please jibe – now!'

Graeme takes no notice of me, and with that my anxiety

and frustration boil over. Furious over his perverse stubbornness I drop the helm, scream at him to steer his own fucking course, and jump below.

I knew about the f-word, had heard it before, but it was the very first time it came out of my mouth. The effect was brilliant. Graeme jumped to the task, jibed the boat (single-handedly I might add) and half a minute later the ferry thundered past, rocking us in her wash. No doubt the ferry captain had seen us and a slight course alteration on his part would have cleared us, but that wasn't the point. As things stood, I'd been right to want to jibe but wrong to disobey the captain, and Graeme never let me forget it. I was the irresponsible one and he had absolutely nothing to do with it.

Our ideas on safety differed. I could, for example, see no reason to sail up close to North Head when there were miles of water to roll around in.

'Do we have to be this close?'

'It's deep enough, go and look at the chart.'

'I don't give a damn about the chart. I don't like to be this close... makes me nervous.'

'You worry too much.'

He was right. I did. For him it was okay for things to be 'safe enough'. I wanted things to be 'very safe', as safe as we could make it. It took fights and the occasional f-word to get my point across and for us to forge the necessary compromise.

I liked to talk things through, hypothesise what might go wrong and how it was to be fixed. I thought of my questions as sensible fact-finding missions; Graeme dismissed them as idiotic and silly: 'It's not going to happen.' I wanted at least a theoretical understanding of what needed to be done should we run aground on a reef, lose our mast in a storm or hit a log floating in the sea. I wasn't dreaming up problems, crazy things happen. One sailor crossing the Pacific reported that a whale had deliberately rammed his boat as punishment for sailing between her and her calf. The boat was so badly damaged that the crew barely made land.

In the matter of whales or floating logs knocking holes into the hull I figured out that I'd jump overboard with a canvas cover kept in the cockpit locker and drape it around the boat from underneath. The canvas would stop the water gushing in, which would give us time to figure out what to do next. I learned later that this wasn't such a silly idea; Captain James Cook employed a similar method to save the *Endeavour* from sinking when she hit a coral reef back in 1770. Draping canvas under water wouldn't be an easy job but it would have to beat drowning.

It began to dawn on me how much of a driving force I was in our venture. I became the schedule police, the one to insist that planned work be done, while Graeme was happy to party, sit in the cockpit, smoke his pipe and enjoy a glass of red wine. He'd not been out of Australia, and I began to wonder, did he really want to do this? His mate Max, with whom he had planned to sail the world, now had a wife and was nicely settled in the suburbs. No sign of him going anywhere, let alone sailing there. What if Graeme bailed out? I couldn't do it alone, wouldn't want to. I wanted to sail with him.

I didn't know any women sailing single-handedly. Women on yachts were an embellishment, a decoration, and if they could sail too that was merely a lucky coincidence. The sailors I met were less respectful of women than the men in the engineering offices I worked in. Speech wasn't monitored, jokes were uncensored and swearing compulsory; there was an air of *if you don't like it, tough, this is our domain, we're not about to rewrite centuries of seafaring.*

I tried not to mind Graeme's rough jokes: Effi, a girl sailing on *Goodewind*, was 'so strong she could bend a penny between her tits', others were 'silly twits' and at the slightest whiff of female upmanship he'd turn patronising. Party jokes ran along the lines of 'why buy a cow if you only want a glass of milk?' Or this one on fidelity: 'it doesn't matter where you get your appetite, as long as you eat at home.' Being charming with girls was un-Australian, left to Italian immigrants, ponces and other alien creatures. Tough mateship was it, although I developed doubts about that sacred myth too. Was this bond, this legendary fairness as honourable as it was made out to be? Did it include women (me for example) or was it simply men sharing drinks and covering up for each other?

This is the story of Angus and Zac (their names are invented). Angus and his wife lived on one boat. Zac and his wife lived on another. Angus, ruggedly handsome, had an affair with Zac's wife, not easy because Zac was his mate. For the illicit lovers to get together was difficult. If Zac had just rowed ashore and next thing Angus's dinghy was tied up behind Zac's boat, that would certainly have looked suspicious.

Zac, a trusting soul, was busy getting their boat ready to sail north, and one day he asked his mate Angus to pull him up the mast on the bosun's chair so he could check through the rigging. Angus of course did this. He securely tied up Zac 40 feet above the deck and then went below and hopped into the bunk with his mate's wife.

Usually a discreet chap, Angus couldn't resist telling the punch line, was choking on it. It went something like this: 'And there we were ... couldn't tell who was rocking the boat – Zac on top of the mast, or me and X on the bunk below.' A ménage à trois with a difference, and fluent in

Aussie slang by then all I could think was *you bastard, how's that for mateship ... and did you have to tell?*

Obviously Zac's wife wasn't blameless, but Angus was double the bastard: once for exposing Zac's wife by telling the story, and twice for doing the dirty on his mate right within earshot.

Graeme nearly killed himself laughing, and that bothered me too. I didn't know at the time that he also was having an affair with a woman married to one of *his* mates. Would I have walked out had I known? Probably not. It would have hurt and I would have screamed, but the free and easy sixties had begun to cast their spell. 'Make love not war' was gaining credence and by then we had too much to lose.

∼

Graeme's lovable side came out in other ways. Fiercely nationalistic, he loved all things Australian, wanted me to know and love his country. I got to understand the fine differences between cobbers, larrikins and wankers (apparently the latter were plentiful). He pointed out birds, caught cicadas to show me pissers and bakers. One time, rowing a hire boat on Lane Cove River we actually saw a platypus in the wild. I knew how rare such a sighting was by how breathless and exited Graeme became, pleased and happy to be able to show me.

He talked about Australia's involvement in both world wars, proud of the bravery and mateship of Australian diggers and making light of the fact that his country and mine had stood on opposite sides of the fence. He told me how at Christmas time, Germans and Allied Forces had emerged from the trenches in France to shake hands in a Christmas ceasefire. Nobody had ever told me this before and I loved the story.

On quiet evenings, with *Hope* gently swaying at her mooring, he taught me songs about shearers, drovers and swagmen. He read Henry Lawson's stories to me and introduced me to the poetry of Dorothea Mackellar and CJ Dennis. *The Sentimental Bloke* by CJ Dennis was his favourite. Written in slang, it was impossible for me to understand, and Graeme read it aloud with all the right inflections and the occasional aside. Listening to him and seeing his face soften showed me the flipside of his often rude and show-off Aussie bravado, it brought out his gentleness and vulnerability and I loved him for it. It's a pity I didn't like the actual poetry, the sentiments expressed by the Bloke.

Doreen, the Bloke's sweetheart (and later his wife) was Graeme's favourite woman. He loved the way she jammed up the clothes prop after she hung out the washing, all the while making coaxing noises to get her husband to do his job.

> *An' I like the dinkum woman 'oo ... (She jerks the clothes-*
>   *prop, so,*
> *An' sez, so sweet an' dangerous, 'The stove-wood's gittin'*
>   *low.')*

I couldn't relate to CJ Dennis' work and regarded it as the most low-key love poetry ever written. To me Sweet Doreen was an innocent darling with her eyes shut, but not wanting to hurt Graeme's feelings I kept that opinion to myself.

Here is another stanza from 'Washing Day', lines I found particularly vexing, a cop-out for not bothering to understand women. It's too hard; CJ Dennis says so:

> *Now, a woman, she's a woman. I 'ave fixed that fer a cert.*
> *They're jist as like as rows uv peas from 'at to 'em uv skirt.*
> *An' then, they're all so different, yeh find, before yeh've done.*
> *The more yeh know uv all of 'em the less yeh know uv one.*

Why was Graeme so crazy about this Sentimental Bloke? Did he identify with the Bloke's bumbling self-contained ways, the way he loved his Doreen to bits, long-distance as it were? Why didn't he adore bold women, the Isabella Birds or Anne Morrow Lindberghs of this world; wasn't it obvious that no Doreen in her right mind would even think of taking a tiny boat across oceans?

Mother

We'd been married for a year when Mutti came to visit, staying for a month. After Pappi died her letters got very sad and I had suggested it. *Just come, Mutti, you can stay with us on the boat.* Mutti and Graeme's first meeting at the airport and the drive to Mosman has vanished from my memory, but not the look on her face when she first saw our boat. We had brought *Hope* alongside the marina for the day, scrubbed and shipshape. Her ropes were neatly coiled, the varnish glowing like garnets. The cockpit, sheltered by a new white canvas cover, looked snug, and my heart swelled with pride.

After a long silence Mutti looked at me, the boat, at me again and finally said, '*Wo wollt ihr damit hin?*' – where do you want to take this? Mutti recognised a seagoing vessel when she saw one. I said nothing. '*Wohin,*' she persisted. 'Around the world,' I said softly, adding a tentative 'maybe' when I saw the shock and disbelief on her face. Graeme stood, looking anxious. 'What's she saying?' he whispered. He didn't speak any German then. 'She knows,' I whispered back, and he looked relieved. Perhaps he had expected her to faint or accuse him of not providing a proper home for me as his family had done. There was no chance of Mutti doing that. She not only knew boats, she also knew me, and if I was in this, I wanted to be in it.

I had not expected difficulties over Mutti living aboard with us and there were none. Jinky got a bit haughty over having to share the forward bunks with her, but Mutti soon charmed him into a purring pussycat. Immensely practical, it took her no time to settle in, quicker to grasp the complicated pumping system of our marine toilet than other visitors: open sea cock, let in water, pump the lever, never forget to close the sea cock after you've finished. She didn't. Showers were in the boatshed attached to the marina, and Graeme's mother had offered her place for her to have a bath if she wanted one.

Mutti arrived shortly before Christmas and I was a bit worried how she'd cope with an Aussie Christmas, so very different from our intimate candle-lit celebrations at home. I had only been to one of Graeme's family Christmases before and knew what a strange affair it could be, with thirty or more people milling around screaming, laughing and (using Jean's words) talking ten to the dozen. The women arrived with high-domed electric frypans, the food almost cooked with 'only the gravy to make'.

A big 'come and get it' lunch followed and after a rest and many of cups of tea, everyone got together for the traditional Christmas tree. It took hours for the appointed Father Christmas to hand out countless little presents stacked under the tree, one for everybody. A plant, a plate or a tea towel was given with a funny note attached – in-house family jokes like *to the sister with the curly hair, or to the quiet one in the family.* Hankies, soap or perfume received last year had been carefully rewrapped and were given to another auntie. It didn't matter what the present was, as long as it was *something.* Jean had confided in me that she always had 'spare' presents tucked away in her handbag in case another person turned up or she'd forgotten someone.

I needn't have worried about my chameleon mother. I should have known she would fit right in and bask in her novelty status. Mutti spoke no English and, smiling sweetly at everyone, she soon had a stack of soap and hankies piled up in front of her. I translated her thanks and endless reams of small talk. At the same time, keeping a straight face, I did my best to find answers to Mutti's whispered observations and little asides – *why does that woman wear so much rouge? Thick enough to scrape off*, or *Goodness, that dress looks like a nightie* ...

Mutti was feminine, slim and attractive. She got her way with government authorities, shopkeepers, work colleagues and bosses by being charming and, if necessary, Greta Garbo flirty. Twelve years younger than Pappi, she'd grown up in the Charleston-dancing thirties after the Great War, crazy times when skirts shortened and moralities shifted. The budding sixties weren't as difficult for her as they had been for Pappi. By the time I was 10, all but one of my mother's five siblings had come to the West, escaped Communism before the borders shut tight. I had cousins and uncles again and family parties were cauldrons of emotions, with drinking and fighting, singing and dancing, crying and hugging.

Tante Jutta, my namesake and the oldest of the sisters, would give you the shirt off her back. Onkel Fritz, the youngest, was the wild one; he taught me how to waltz, holding me tight, taking long steps. Tante Martel, the beauty of the family, was reputed to have danced on tables. At one party she entertained me, and my cousin Sabine (barely teenagers), with the story of how she caught her husband cheating on her. It ended with the wicked girl interloper perched naked on the top rung of a ladder leading to the loft, while Martel stood at the bottom calmly pointing a finger at her and telling her to come down and *get out*. I doubt if she threw the girl as much as a handkerchief to cover her nakedness.

Mutti was Martel's younger sister, and stories of their exploits and survival were aplenty. Still of a generation where women were dependent on men, the sisters were brilliant at wrapping men around their little fingers. I know Mutti was because she tried hard to pass such valuable skills on to me, forever coaching me to be more playful and feminine. *Men don't like women that are too clever – they don't have to know how smart you are.*

Playful to her was to have the (male) manager of a shoe store dance around her, fitting her with every shoe in the shop and then walk out with a casual remark that the selection was inadequate. As a child trailing in her wake I'd felt embarrassed, mortified. 'How could you do that, Mutti?' I vowed never to use my femininity in that way. 'You're like your father,' she'd scolded me. 'Far too serious.'

Mutti could see the lighter side of things. She had the knack of skimming over the top of difficulties, was diplomatic enough make things work for her. Her tears were more often those of anger and frustration than of sorrow, her way of letting off steam before getting on with things. But she could make me laugh, better than anyone.

I still get the giggles when I think of the time we trooped off to Graeme's mum's place for Mutti to have a bath. I'd forgotten that Jean liked to clean her bathtub with kerosene, believing that this would minimise scratches and preserve the porcelain. Mutti was used to shiny, squeaky-clean surfaces, and running a finger along inside the tub she begged me to find stuff to clean it with. I told her it was clean, explained about the kerosene, told her I wouldn't insult Jean. 'It's not our house,' I argued. 'Come on, get in… it's not poison, what's a bit of kerosene.' I ran the bath and Mutti got in, resolutely refusing to touch the sides. I sat on the toilet seat, amused at her antics, and seeing me laugh set her off on a pantomime fit for a silent movie. Sitting primly in the middle of the tub, she pretended that the tub surface really was poisonous 'and please darling will you hand me the soap, careful now…'

Mutti hadn't changed and I found myself helplessly pulled back into her orbit, the closeness and intimacy instantly re-established. I was happy for the warmth it generated but it also begun to dawn on me that I might have left home as much for Mutti's overpowering presence as for Pappi's unbending ways. I began to question my belief that Mutti was my saviour, that left to Pappi I would have been forever sober, forever dutiful. Three years apart had given me more adult eyes, and it struck me how central her position had been in our family, how all-consuming her energy had been, leaving no space for a daughter so different from her in temperament.

We loved each other, that would never change, but my leaving home so young and with such finality had separated our everyday lives. I knew little of her friends and the life she was building for herself after Pappi died. It must have been more difficult for her to find me in another country, speaking another language, no longer her daughter but a married woman hell-bent on adventure. We never spoke about it, but by some tacit agreement decided to make whatever time we had together good times, a holiday just for the two of us. I was happy for her to call me *Kindchen*, to be her *little child*, adore her, show her off and laugh with her.

A workable arrangement; Mutti was extrovert enough not to notice feelings of resentment I may have had towards her and I introvert enough to work most things out in the privacy of my head. But despite that a few angry moments did break through, quick like whirlwinds. Taking long walks around the harbour foreshore, Mutti felt she had to tell me how Pappi had died, how they had talked during his illness, for weeks. She wanted me to hear what he'd said about me; how proud he had been of my bearing, my independence and the way I handled work, money and travel. She told me that he'd cherished a photo I had sent from Melbourne in my first year in Australia, proud of his beautiful daughter...

It made me angry to hear it.

Proud, I demanded, 'Why didn't he say those things to me? I was there last year... it's hardly fair to make you his messenger.'

'Kindchen, you know what he was like, he couldn't be any other way.'

'So you want me to make allowances for him, forgive, forget and all that, think warmly of his reserve and his stupid aloofness...'

'Stop, Kindchen, stop, he is no longer with us, you have to make peace with him,' Mutti pleaded.

'Easy for you to say,' I railed. 'I remember the fights you had... very convenient for you to forget that.'

For my entire life it had been Mutti and me against Pappi. I'd been *her* girl, *her* ally, the one to dry her tears and give her total loyalty when Pappi was 'difficult'. Mutti had turned the tables on me.

Your girl no more, I thought angrily.

Deep resentment flared up again at another time, startling and unpredictable. The three of us had sailed up to Pittwater and had had a fabulous time; warm nights under the stars, lots of swimming, champagne at New Year's Eve and the occasional shore excursion. The weather was brilliant until we headed back to Sydney, over 15 miles of open water. We were about halfway home when the pleasant nor'easter behind us strengthened into an absolute howler, a black nor'easter. Graeme and I reefed the mainsail, made the boat snug and got everything moving along nicely. I relaxed and promptly got seasick.

Mutti didn't get sick. Not that I wanted her to get sick, but did she have to flirt and laugh with Graeme using her ten words of English while I had my head over a bucket? I might as well not have been there, and sick as a dog, I became bitterly aware of a long history of my mother sidelining me; always one better than me, slimmer, more charming, her heels higher, her shoes more expensive. I remembered the time when I was 15 and fell in love with a purple bouclé jumper displayed in one of the expensive city boutiques. I saved up to buy it, longed for payday, raved to Mutti how soft and beautiful it was. Sure enough, next day Mutti came home wearing it, and seeing the shock on my face she quickly said, 'Oh, you can borrow it sometimes.' I would have shredded that jumper rather than wear it.

Shredding again entered my mind when I saw the photo which could have only been taken by Graeme. He adored her and had caught her balancing on *Hope*'s steeply leaning deck dressed in my dark blue wind cheater, barefoot, her trousers rolled up, a colourful scarf casually wound around her hair and laughing like the sun. She was pointing at a rope as if to say 'is this the one you want me to pull?' I remember that photo clearly, we had a large print made for Mutti to take home, yet I cannot find it anywhere. Jealous 'little me' must have shredded it after all.

A photo that survived: Mutti, relaxed and laughing on Sydney Harbour.

Yet love for my amazing, annoying, beautiful 53-year-old mother overwhelmed me in equally unexpected ways. Visiting Graeme's mother, she found herself introduced to Mrs Hill, a Jewish woman living next door, 'because they both spoke German'. I came outside to join them and found Mutti crying and thanking Mrs Hill for talking to her at all. Mrs Hill had lost relatives in the concentration camps and it had taken her thirty seconds to have Mutti in tears, guilty and ashamed; my mother, who had fled from advancing Russian tanks, walking west clutching a little boy on one hand and a toddler on the other. I knew how Mutti had suffered, had absorbed much of it. Seeing her standing like a penitent in front of Mrs Hill wrenched my heart and I wanted to hold her, cocoon her with my love and protect her.

Not long after, although unwittingly, I too made Mutti cry. Meeting Mrs Hill had stirred up emotions, and walking along a dirt track towards South Head I told her of a nightmare I kept having; could it have something to do with the war? I described clear images, fragments of train rails shining grey and silver, leaden heaviness, and me stuck to the ground immobilised. *Can't move ... a row of carriages, massive wheels, huge levers.* 'It's a horrible dream, frightening,' I said, trying to shake off the images and stretching my back in the sun. 'Look what a gorgeous day it is.'

I looked at Mutti and she wasn't smiling. 'It's not a dream, Kindchen,' she said flatly. 'It happened.' On our refugee trek westward she had spotted a freight train about to leave from a track at the far end of the rail yard. She and other people in her group began to crawl underneath rows of carriages to reach it, but I had thrown myself on the ground screaming and refused to move. Mutti remembered the day, how she had beaten me, dragging me under first one train and then another, both of us screaming. 'What could I do?' she said. 'You refused to move.'

Listening to her, my heart started beating wildly, the train image suddenly more real than ever. 'But what if the carriage had pulled away when we were under it?' I demanded. 'It would have killed us.' Mutti had checked, had seen that there was no locomotive in front. I had been dragged under lines of carriages shunted onto side-tracks. The stuff of my nightmares had no substance. 'You might have told me,' I said quietly. 'All you had to say was "Look Jutta, no locomotive."' I had known my mother to cry in anger and frustration. This was the first time I saw her cry in grief, for me, for what I remembered.

I have many things to thank Mutti for, and while it would have been good to inherit her cheerful optimism, I'm happy she's passed on at least some of her courage and resilience. The day she left to go back to Germany gives a hint of the fighting spirit we shared. Her ship was to leave in the afternoon, and we'd left early to have lunch in town – dressed up for the occasion, Mutti in a pale blue knitted suit and me in skirt and blazer. A stiff southerly tore through Mosman Bay and it had been a struggle to get us, and Mutti's luggage, safely ashore in the dinghy. The ferry arrived, and settling on the side benches to get a last look at *Hope*, I relaxed, relieved that all had gone well.

As soon as the ferry took off, I knew something was wrong. Instead of travelling her usual curve towards the opening of the bay, she headed straight for *Hope*, tied fore and aft to a nearby mooring. I jumped up screaming 'Stop, stop!' but the ferry kept going and next thing she crunched up hard against *Hope*. I heard timber tearing, and not wasting a thought I leaped off the ferry onto *Hope*'s mast, boom and deck and raced forward to undo her bow mooring. Still tethered to the stern mooring, she swung out of the ferry's way and I watched helplessly as the ferry travelled past and crashed into *Ataruka* behind us.

I heard bells ringing and passengers shouting aboard the ferry, but stranded on *Hope*, I had to rely on Mutti's report of what happened next. Wedged against the yacht moored aft of *Hope*, the ferry captain left his wheelhouse screaming 'What the hell are you doing?' at the engineer working in the open fenced-in engine room in the bottom of the boat. But it seems that a lot more shouting was needed before the ferry finally reversed back towards the wharf. By then Mutti was furious and, grabbing the engineer by his overalls, proceeded to tell him what she thought of his and the captain's competence. It was only when he began answering her in German that Mutti realised that he was German! – lucky for her because being heard and understood made her feel a lot better. Perhaps not so lucky for him, because Mutti had a great deal more to say. Not letting go of him, she made sure that a boat was sent to fetch me off *Hope*. She also instructed him to let the captain know that until her daughter had rung her husband to inform him of the disaster, this ferry was not leaving this wharf.

It wasn't difficult to see what had caused the accident, and everybody knew it. Like most of the ferries on Sydney Harbour, the Mosman ferry was double ended. After reaching the wharf, a mechanism releases the bow to become a rudder while the rudder is fixed to become a bow. On that day, whoever was responsible for making the changeover had failed to do so. The captain, unable to steer a course with the rudder fixed and the bow unstable, had no choice but to plough into us. If I hadn't jumped onto *Hope* to free her from her mooring, the damage would have been considerable. Luckily only the handrails were ripped off, but our claim for repair costs proved unsuccessful. Apparently the wind on that day had been so fierce that the accident was declared an Act of God. Luckily God only acted once, and the second time we left the wharf (after I was reunited with Mutti, my shoes and my handbag) the ferry had no trouble finding its usual path out of the bay.

~

Despite the holdup, we had enough time to get Mutti aboard ship, settle her into her cabin and get back on deck to meet Graeme's mother and sister as previously arranged. It was to be a special farewell with little gifts, perambulating on deck and talking of good times. Jean, a keen gardener, was sure to have brought a small bouquet of flowers but I only remember Helen's present: a nest of purple passion fruit, prettily arranged in a little basket; a bit of Australia for Mutti to take with her.

I'm on edge, in emotional overload, barely present. *Where is Graeme, did he get my message, has he secured Hope? Is Hope okay? ... A huge bump like that could have cracked her hull ...* Helen is trying to tell Mutti that the pips in passion fruit are edible, wants me to translate. I can't, don't know the German word for pips... *Such a strange fruit, Mutti probably won't eat the pips anyway. I know I don't.* To my relief, Graeme arrives just as the first call for visitors to leave the ship comes over the loudspeaker, and yes, *Hope* survived the battering, she is okay, not too badly damaged. I am happy I can tell Mutti the good news before she leaves, she too has been worried, has got to like our stately little ship. *Bon Voyage dear Mutti, travel safely!*

Life examined

I thought I wouldn't miss Mutti, but I did. Her easy laugh and her unquestioning support of our venture had been fabulous. Graeme's mother lived twenty minutes away and still had no idea that we were planning to sail the world. I don't remember her ever coming aboard *Hope*; none of the family ever went sailing with us. How they missed the obvious and why Graeme didn't tell them borders upon the bizarre.

How different our families were, not only in temperament but also in outlook and perception. My family had get-togethers in the truest sense of the word. Graeme's family seemed more like a bunch of satellites circling each other, glancing off each another but never really docking. They talked ceaselessly but nobody listened. Upmanship was the order of the day even among closest siblings. Driving to Uncle Geoffrey's one time, I was jokingly cautioned not to touch anything: 'Could be wet, he'll have given everything a last-minute lick of paint to show off his house.'

Jean didn't find out about our venture until someone from Graeme's old company sent her a staff newsletter featuring us as the 'Sailing Globe Trotters'. We were halfway up the Barrier Reef by then and I teased Graeme how lucky he was to be of age, or else she'd have him hauled off the boat by the police. Her wrath didn't last long though and before long we became validated adventurers, on par with the celebrated Francis Chichester. It was her turn to show off at family gatherings. Family, friends and neighbours got to read our letters and the ladies in her lawn bowling club were allowed to take them home to show their husbands. I was aghast when I found out and stopped adding to Graeme's letters; in my family letters were private, strictly confidential.

For my German and my Australian family to be comfortable with each other would have needed a team of mediating angels. I still think that and have wondered why Graeme and I got on as well as we did. I believe that it was due to an above-average chunk of genes passed down from our respective fathers. Both of them were mavericks, outsiders who left their families early, separate and distinct like rocks dropped from the sky unwilling and unable to return; Graeme's father a silent Scot and mine a stoic and principled Prussian. Whether we liked it or not, we were their offspring.

～

Paying back our debt to Irene and Johnnie Johnson was on schedule, we had set a preliminary date for leaving, and then the unthinkable happened. I missed my period, and two weeks later I knew I was pregnant, furiously and angrily pregnant, crying and pleading *this isn't happening, not now, please ...* For a time Graeme's and my world stopped, and when the word abortion was finally spoken neither of us objected. Our dreams of freedom, and the vision of sailing our beautiful *Hope* to distant places proved powerful enough to overrule every moral argument.

Abortion was illegal, and strangely enough it was the men

in Graeme's office who provided the contacts. A roll of cash changed hands at a city chemist, I was given an appointment at a Kings Cross address and a week later I walked up a narrow flight of stairs next to a busy supermarket. It was a ghastly and humiliating experience and listening to pro- and anti-abortion advocates ever since hasn't helped me to form a definite opinion on the right or wrong of abortion. It would be easy for me to give an impassioned keynote speech at a convention of either camp.

I don't know if Graeme's conscience delivers him guilty reminders, because after it was all over we never talked about it. My conscience does, and at such times it helps me to run a playful script inside my head, a detached little performance that has me arriving in the Milky Way (after I have left this planet that is). I have a list pinned to my nightie tallying up how I've lied and gossiped, stepped on people's toes, cheated the rich, smacked my kids and had an abortion, all of which count as big fat minuses. Then comes the good part. A second column on the list tallies up the plusses, the times when I've been kind, helped friends and strangers, carried spiders outside, regretted wrongful actions; and luckily (on my optimistic days at least) the plus/minus balance doesn't look too lopsided.

Having said that, I will now earn myself another minus and wilfully and deliberately hope that the nurse in the abortion clinic will have a *humungous* minus pinned to her nightie when she has to front up. On my check-up a week later, she literally screamed at me because I had not taken the red pills she had given me. 'But you didn't give me any,' I whispered, terrified. I knew she was lying, but grumbling on full force she muttered '... comes in here all woozy, can't remember a damn thing and tells *me* I didn't give her any pills.'

In my distress I wrote to Mutti, and her reply came by return mail, warm and simple: *I understand, Kindchen, try and forget it now ... many women carry that guilt.* Along with her letter came six boxes of the Pill. I hadn't been able to get them, and she had talked her doctor into prescribing them for me. She kept track of when I needed another batch, and it would await me poste restante in the various ports we called at.

~

Departure time drew closer and I grew anxious, enough for my colleague Richard to notice. Richard was from Switzerland, an artist, musician and a draftsman. We had worked a few contracts together and knew each other well enough to talk about our lives in Australia, cultural differences, families and future plans. He knew about the sailing venture and, seeing me so edgy, assumed I was scared. 'I know I would be,' he said. I couldn't agree with him. 'Not scared,' I said. 'It's worrying about things, there's a thousand things to remember, my mind just keeps going over it, again and again.' Richard knew about worries, he had his own, and suggested I see his therapist. 'Talking helps,' he said. 'Go and see Adrian, he's a good man.'

Adrian was a big man in his late forties, calm and friendly, with offices across the road from Rushcutters Bay Park. Before my sessions I would wander through the park, lean against the seawall, gaze at the harbour and the boats tied up at the Cruising Yacht Club marina and arrive well primed to talk about sailing.

Adrian dealt with my persistent worrying in the simplest and most straightforward way. 'Worry isn't going to change any given situation,' he said. 'You know you will do this sailing business... put all safety measures in place and then let it go.' Glaringly obvious advice, but hearing it spelled it out so clearly made it sink in, and repeating Adrian's words to myself became the magic wand that could stop a downward spiral. And his advice to take every safety measure made it okay for me to figure out solutions for imaginary problems, such as hitting logs floating in the sea. I was not silly; I was a 'Plan B' person, and no more apologies to Graeme.

I liked Adrian; it felt good to talk openly, and before long our sessions moved beyond the cognitive rearrangement of worrying thoughts into deeper layers. Pappi's death had upset me, and my talks with Mutti had made me realise how far the tentacles of my childhood had stretched. Traditionally, the war and its aftermath had been parental pain, adult trauma; it was assumed that we were only little and would forget. Adrian corrected that view, asked questions and validated my feelings. He listened when I told him of my nightmares, of terrifying noises and crazily disjointed scenes... of feeling wedged into a corner, of cold, of something heavy and slippery on top of me... *can't move, can't scream* ...

The train incident I had talked about with Mutti surfaced again and I realised that while I might have been too young to remember the actual facts, my body still contained the terror. I remembered how often, as a child, I had pressed Mutti to talk about what had happened, how much I wanted to hear and feel the horror in my childish attempt to understand and verify my share in it. I knew the beginning of her stories by her sighs and the words *Ach, Kindchen, they were difficult times.*

I know how she had to leave Prussia in the depth of winter to get away from the Russians, carrying what she could. How cold it was, how Pappi had to stay behind 'at the front' and how lucky we'd been to reach Uncle Willi's place on the island of Rügen, 500 kilometres to the west.

She told me that I was a good walker (mostly) that I was a brave girl (mostly) and how frightened she'd been. I cried with her when she told me how her best friend had lost both her mother and her child, shot by snipers from small planes flying overhead. I felt her despair when she told me that Tante Martel had seen our house burn, that there was no going back.

Pappi refused to speak of the war. What I know of his survival also came from Mutti, secretly and in whispers. She told me that after the collapse (as I came to know the end of the war) he'd been captured by the Russians but escaped from a prisoner-of-war column being marched towards a camp. Under constant danger of being re-arrested he walked alone for hundreds of kilometres through ice and snow, arriving at Onkel Willi's house months later. Mutti said he was ill, terribly thin; only the hope of finding us had kept him going. He still had his service revolver and wanted to end all our lives, convinced that there was nothing left to live for.

※

Father came into our sessions a lot, his death still raw and Mutti's demands for me to make peace with him impossible to fulfil. Pappi and I had parted polite strangers, and I was still determined to blame him for it. Adrian pointed out that we had both been equally righteous, equally stubborn, but I found such similarities with Pappi hard to admit. To be told I was like him felt like criticism; it made me remember the many times Mutti had pointed this out to me. The part of him I was willing to align with was the father who took me for quiet walks in the countryside, giving names to trees and flowers and teaching me how to distinguish the flight of a buzzard from that of an eagle. I liked to think I was romantic like him, remembering a freezing cold night and the two of us standing outside our front door searching for Orion among millions of stars. I could identify with the dreamer who painted a watercolour of two sailing boats gliding along on a calm sea, a sea that could only have been the Baltic, because Pappi had seen no other. Reddish-brown sails reflect dark and squiggly in the water and rounded summer clouds convey peace and calm.

Pappi's painting was part of my childhood and I gazed at it often. He painted it in 1952, at a time when all of us still lived a cramped two-room existence. It took adulthood (and time with Adrian) before it struck me how my father, then 52 years old, must have felt being trapped in a coalminer's cottage painting lost horizons. It was possible for me to love the father who painted sailing boats, and there were times when I regretted not having told him about Graeme and our plans to sail the world. I like to think that he would have understood.

❦

My time with Adrian gave me room to talk and cry, turn over the things that puzzled me and clarify assumptions. Finding compassion for my side of the story brought out long-guarded feelings and immense relief. I loved the idea that the mind is pliable and can be worked with. I gained perspective, and realised how silly and selfish I'd been to accuse Mutti for dragging me under a train, for pushing and beating me. *I didn't have time to worry about your soul*, she had said. *I had to save your body.* Without a doubt, things had been bad, but so what? I could deal with it. Compared to what my parents had been through, I was having a picnic.

In one of our sessions Adrian wondered what I might be running away from, not an unreasonable question since at the time I had been travelling almost non-stop for five years and had plans to do a great deal more of it. I thought about my answer for some time and finally conceded that I might have been running away at 18, perhaps even at 20, but that this was no longer the case at 23. Sailing away felt more like running towards something: a greater freedom, space, distance and solitude. I felt invincible and optimistic, almost on a high, and I remember Adrian's goodbye hug at the close of our last session. 'I am sure you'll have a wonderful time,' he said, smiling.

Our day of departure, 18 April 1966 and almost exactly two years since I was carried over *Hope*'s 'threshold'. Graeme has spoken to his mum from a nearby phone booth to tell her that we're off on our Barrier Reef holiday. Jinky is aboard. The Vespa, donated to a work colleague, is parked on the road above the Neutral Bay boatshed, the keys stuffed under the seat. Our friends Ed and Marion arrive to see us off, Marion carrying a cake she's baked for us. Eddie jokingly stows away in the forward cabin, hiding behind a sail bag. Marion, heavily pregnant with their first child, drags him out, laughing and scolding him in her lovely Liverpool accent that he *won't get away with that one, thank you*. A couple of workmen from the boatshed wander down to wish us good luck and we slip the lines, no fuss, as if going for a day's sail. Not yet halfway up the harbour, around Bradley's Head, the momentousness of the occasion hits me, and my elation gives way to total exhaustion. By the time we reach

Sydney Heads I struggle with a migraine and it makes sense to anchor in Quarantine Cove for the night, tucked safely inside North Head.

It will take another day before we head out to sea.

Part Two

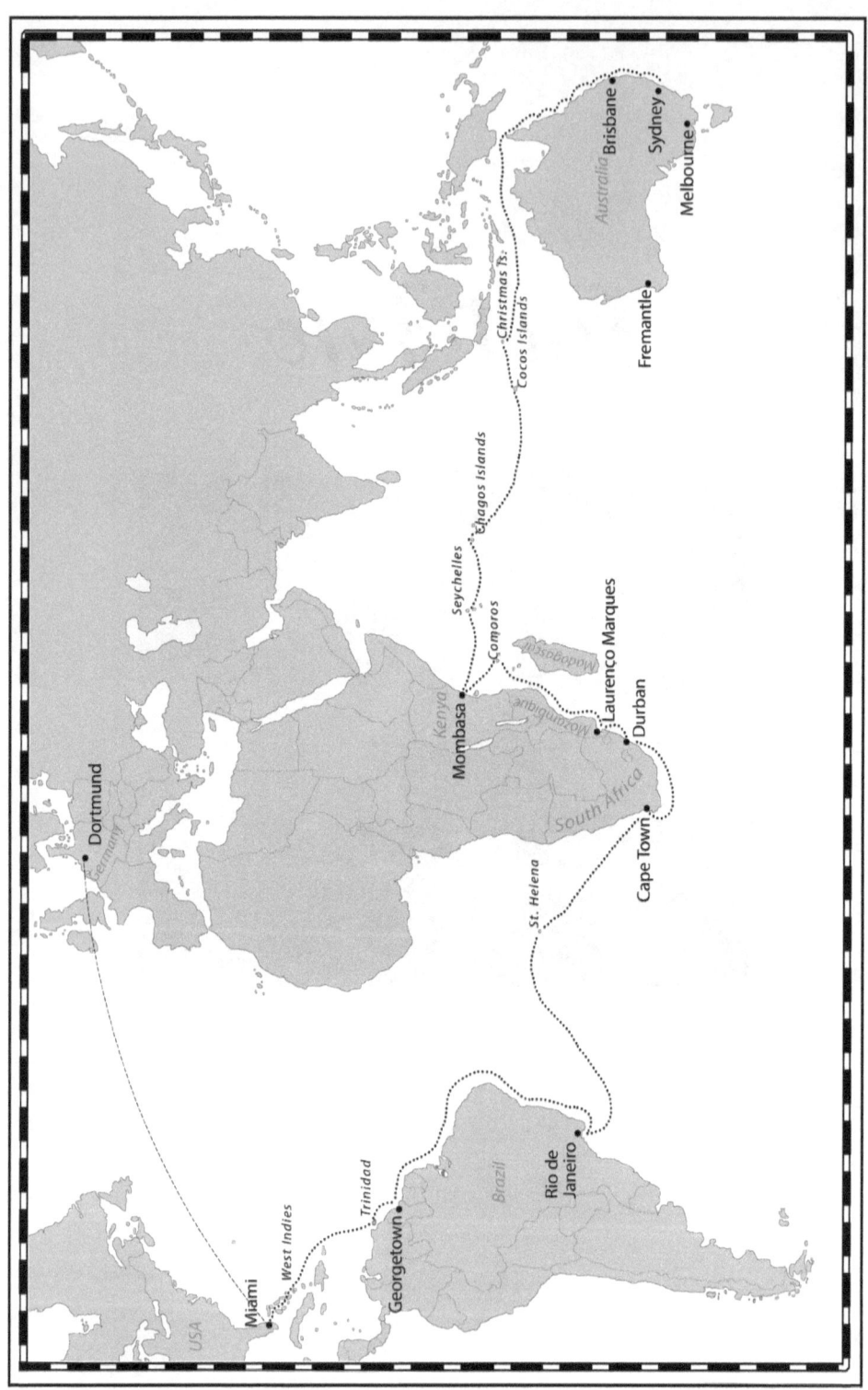

Finding my sea legs

I love the sea and find it easy to forgive her the misery she can inflict. The terror of the wildest night vanishes when a brand-new sun throws diamonds onto the water, when a fair wind blows and the mighty pull of sails makes the stern wake skip and dance. On such days exhilaration and excitement would fill my heart and lungs to near bursting and I'd have to sing, loudly, at the top of my voice. Sometimes it would be folk songs (both English and German); sometimes, especially if the wind was strong, it would be sea shanties; but when things were perfect, belting out 'God Save the Queen' (Australia's then national anthem) was the most satisfying. Not in reverence to the Queen but because the words and tune carry such pomp and weighty momentousness, such an air of celebration that it fitted the majesty surrounding us to perfection.

When we left Sydney I didn't know any of this. I had not yet learned to read the moods of the sea, didn't know when to humbly put up with her nastiness and when to rejoice in her largesse. I had adored the sea as one does a lover in a hot holiday romance, besotted but not wholly sure of my feelings. Cruising, spending years on the water, would transform my love affair into a long-term relationship, a marriage.

Two years of weekend sailing had made us cocky. We were smart. We had the perfect boat, had been to Pittwater half a dozen times, thought ocean sailing was no big deal. Three days of non-stop gale force winds 40 miles north of Sydney spelled the end of our arrogance and to make it worse, we could only blame ourselves for the misery we endured. We'd dawdled around our favourite Pittwater for nearly a fortnight waiting for wind from the south to give us an easy push up the coast, and when a southerly was finally predicted, we simply ignored the severe storm warning attached to it. What the hell, let it blow, we needed strong winds to make headway against the south-flowing current, so we got ready.

A dying breeze took us clear of the land and there we sat, rolling around in an oily swell with boom and sail banging and flapping in the most annoying way. The sky slowly darkened, the Barrenjoey Lighthouse began to blink, and the setting sun rolled out a path of light towards us, glinting oblongs the colour of caramel toffees. It was almost completely dark when the first puff of wind sent ripples across the water. *Heavenly ... wind from the south, at last*, and I volunteered for first watch.

And thus, naively, happily, right at the very start we ran into one of the worst storms of our entire journey; a veritable baptism with enough water thrown onto our heads to initiate or to drown us. I don't know how close we came to disaster out there off Newcastle, all I know is that the storm sank two fishing boats in the region and pushed a coastal freighter aground – strong and sturdy boats with crews far more experienced than we were. I also know that Graeme's and my relationship changed after that storm. Being equally untested as far as ocean sailing went and both of us away from home now (and likely to be that way for years to come) had levelled the playing field. Facing possible death together bonded us, made us birds of a feather, cooperation a given. Individual quirks and idiosyncrasies stopped being the butt of jokes and became something to be accommodated, cared about and acknowledged. One monster storm and two weeks of drying out in Port Stephens afterwards brought us closer than the past two years of marriage had. When we left port again we were truly wedded, to each other and to our boat, a strong triangle and a configuration that suited us both.

Our 'initiation' began sweetly enough. *Hope* was humming along nicely and, happily ensconced in the cockpit, I watched the distant shore lights slip past. But that soon changed and by dawn we had *Hope* reefed down to her storm trysail. Another hour and even that tiny sail pushed her too hard, and she began surfing down the flanks of ever-steepening waves. Spume started blowing horizontally across our decks and before long, green water started crashing aboard. We had never been out in such weather, and my romantic notion that our gallant *Hope* would simply ride over the top of the waves like an avenging angel blew away. Pressured to translate much-read theory into action, we yelled over the top of the horrific noises. *Should we force her head into the seas? ... We have to slow her down ... she mustn't surf ...* But in the end the wise old lady told us what was best. Left alone, she slowly swung her ample bottom into the huge breaking seas, asked for her tiller to be loosely lashed and began riding the seas on her quarter, quite happy.

The next day and the one after were utter misery. There was nothing to do but wait, either wedged in the cockpit periodically drenched with masses of water or hanging on below decks in a wildly gyrating cabin, feeling seasick. Listening to the marine forecast gave no joy either; the storm showed no sign of easing. We heard about the fishing boats being sunk and another broadcast reporting the yacht *Hope* as missing. Graeme was livid, furious, *bloody hell, that's ridiculous*, but who could blame his mother for ringing alarm bells? She didn't know we had dawdled around Pittwater, and had expected a postcard from Brisbane long ago.

A well-built yacht in a storm is safest out at sea, as far away from the coast as possible. We knew this, but fools that we were, we decided to run for Port Stephens. The rubber strip sealing the skylight had washed away; waves crashing over the deck forced curtains of green water into the cabin and everything was sodden right down to the carpet. Three days of being wet, cold and seasick had worn us down. From a distance the harbour entrance, flanked by a strong headland, had seemed clear enough, but as we closed in the huge swells began crashing and falling over each other and we weren't so sure anymore. *Hope* was tossed around alarmingly, spray obscured our vision and with racing hearts we steered into the white seething mess, into what seemed like the most likely passage into Port Stephens.

We were lucky, beginners' luck. Good old Neptune gave us the nod and *Hope* was unceremoniously picked up and shoved at tremendous speed through masses of curling water, past slate-grey razor rocks, past the solid bulk of Tomaree Headland and into the sheltered waters of Shoal Bay. One wave tore loose a plastic bucket tied on deck and shoved it upside down on top of Graeme's head. Ned Kelly in a red bucket, something to laugh about later. Jinky, glowering and triumphant, had held his post in the cockpit. *Never mind wet feet and dripping whiskers, I'm staying* – rows of bleeding scratches on my arms an indication of my failure to push him below decks for his own safety.

Dropping anchor was sweet; we made it... *wow, scary stuff!* The silence in the lee of the land felt eerie. With wind and waves still hammering in my ears I felt removed, in limbo, as if sealed into a decompression chamber. I saw people walking along the street singly or in pairs, children playing near the water's edge, a boy riding a bike, shops in the background; a pretty drawing from a children's book. I had no wish to go ashore, didn't want to talk; couldn't have found words to tell of my knowing how fragile the thread of life can be.

We stayed in Port Stephens for two weeks, rarely going ashore, each day retreating further into isolated bays. We had tasted the life we were courting, had to find new composure and renew the will to move on. Working on *Hope*, replacing rubber seals and drying our sodden gear, little everyday tasks and the restorative power of uninterrupted sleep slowly returned us to equilibrium. Choosing the sunniest, most beautiful day possible, we sailed north once more.

A last duty, almost a mission before we felt free to take off, was to call in on *Hope*'s previous owners, Johnnie and Irene Johnson in Brisbane. The money we owed them was paid back; we wanted to thank them and show off *Hope*. Johnnie would be interested in the alterations we'd made. The cockpit was now self-draining,[2] the galley had a double-burner

---

2 Raising the cockpit floor above water level and fitting drains made *Hope* a safer boat. The cockpit floor on *Hope*'s original design was below the outside water

stove, and we had figured a way of making up a double bunk while in port. *Hope* was as shipshape and cared for as she could possibly be.

In a marvellous coincidence we saw Johnnie on the high seas a couple of days short of Brisbane. Working a casual shift on a merchant ship, he had spotted 'his' *Hope* sailing northward and persuaded the captain to come up close. Recognising Johnnie on the bridge was a great relief for us, an easy explanation for why the freighter had suddenly changed course, heading straight for us. Shouting through a loudhailer, Johnnie blasted us with 'Good luck *Hope!*' and equally excited we shouted back 'See you in Brisbane, see you soon!'

Hope was well known in Brisbane; it had been her home-port before we bought her, and shouts and greetings followed us as we motored up Brisbane River towards Wright's boat-shed. Johnnie had spread the word that we were coming, and it felt weird to be given such a welcome, more like a homecoming than the beginning of a journey.

❦

Our teamwork improved immeasurably over the coming weeks and so did our tolerance of each other. Around the end of May, Graeme made this entry into our informal diary-type logbook – a little undercover love note to his fidgety First Mate and an admission that he was not Mr Supercool either:

Jutta is like a cat on a hot tin roof – checking charts, weather forecasts, pilot book, sailing directions – all to steady her nerves – however my

---

level. Water from waves breaking into the cockpit would run into the bilges and require pumping.

version of it is to be irritable – so we just have to make allowances for each other.

Yes, I was still fidgety, and it would take another mishap, another misery before I would settle down. It happened off Fraser Island, just north of Brisbane. Fraser (now K'gari) is an oblong green mound about 120 kilometres long, the largest sand island in the world and the only place where rainforest grows on sand. The island leans sharply seawards from its southern tip near the coast, as if reluctance to part from the mainland keeps a connection via a shallow sandbar. Storms and tidal flow carve intricate networks of navigable channels into the sand and our book of *Sailing Directions* gave instructions on how to approach the bar, and which markers to follow. It sounds easy, but sandbars shift with every storm and Johnnie Johnson had suggested that the safest way would be to get there at sundown and follow the fishing fleet in. Good advice except that when we arrived, there wasn't a boat in sight. We had forgotten that it was Sunday, clearly the fishermen's day off.

Hope drew 6 feet and had 4 tons of lead on her keel. The thought of running aground on a shifting sandbar at sundown was scary. *Let's do it anyway – can't be that difficult* we agreed, and carefully lining up the markers, one tip of a triangle meeting the tip of another, we headed in. Late afternoon sunlight played on the water and we couldn't see properly, *where the hell is the next marker?* Tide and waves pushed from behind, *Hope* picked up speed and the stern wake began crawling up her transom. Dry patches of sand popped up on either side of us, and a sudden fear that we could be in the wrong channel – a dead end perhaps – made us turn back while we could. Five more minutes of anxiety might have seen us into deep water, but the risk was too great. Disappointed to miss out on a snug anchorage and a couple of days of easy sailing in the shelter of Fraser Island, we were heading out to sea again. We had no choice but to sail along the seaward side of Fraser and round the island's northern tip; a solid 95-mile detour.

The gods should have rewarded our caution; instead at three in the morning we were hit by sudden fierce squall, apparently the norm off Fraser. The jib tore all the way across. Graeme raced to drop the mainsail and next thing I saw him jumping up and down on the deck like a toddler having a tantrum and screaming like a fiend. 'What's wrong?' I yelled, but the only reply was another stream of swear words and more jumping; my competent husband was losing it big time. Enclosed in near darkness and howling wind, it took me a while to figure out why things were so bad, but I caught on soon enough. In the hurry of dropping the mainsail the peak halyard had disappeared up the mast into the night.[3] With our jib shredded and unable to raise the mainsail again, we were as good as crippled. The nearest anchorage was out of *Hope*'s engine range and there was only one choice: Graeme would have to climb aloft at first light and rethread the runaway halyard. Using our precious fuel, we motored out to sea; if we were going to drift for the rest of the night the last thing we needed was a lee shore.

The scene of Graeme climbing the mast in a leaden dawn was surreal, nightmarish. Barelegged to get a better grip on the varnished mast and white-faced with concentration, he inched his way up, letting go of one hand every so often to

---

3   A halyard is the rope that pulls up the sail. *Hope* had two halyards: one pulled up the sail laced around the mast along with the boom attached to the top of it; the second halyard raised the tip of the gaff boom, tightening the sail into its taut oblong shape. It was the second halyard that had come adrift, making it impossible to set the sail.

try and grab the wildly swinging halyard. With the motor running I steered *Hope* directly into the waves to minimise any rolling; the pitching was bad enough. Every wave coming towards us had me screaming 'Hang on... hang on!', terrified that the mast would catapult him far out into the sea, or worse, that he would lose his grip and crash onto the deck. Getting the job done took forever.

'Frigging in the rigging' (Graeme's words) and slow sailing with only the main and staysail – the jib still shredded – tallied up to a twenty-four-hour detour. It was another sunset before we finally dropped anchor off the northern end of Fraser, directly below the lighthouse. We ate half an orange each, skipped dinner and slept for twelve hours straight.

It took me two days to hand-stitch the jib back together, plenty of time to chew over what had happened and put safeguards in place to stop it from happening again. We saw little of Fraser, apart from one peaceful walk ashore, yet the island marks an important internal shift for me. After Fraser (latitude 25 degrees South, longitude 153 degrees East) I became more composed, let go of my edgy vigilance of 'sailing a boat' and slipped into 'sailing as a way of life'. Bad things happen, so what? We'd deal with it.

I had gained my sea legs.

The sea and her disciples

The first person to sail a small yacht around the world was Joshua Slocum. He set off from Boston in 1895 in his sloop *Spray*, and his book *Sailing Alone Around the World* has become a classic. Slocum sailed westwards and took three years to complete the circumnavigation, a good pace for working the seasons, following the trade winds and making stops along the way.

Like flocks of birds, men and women have cruised the oceans in small boats ever since. Adopting Joshua Slocum's three-year formula, Eric and Susan Hiscock were the first husband-and-wife team to circumnavigate the globe in their yacht *Wanderer III*. Setting out from the Isle of Wight in 1952, they got properly hooked and never stopped sailing, rounding the globe twice and pottering around New Zealand in their later years. Eric's first book, *Cruising under Sail*, was the book Graeme had lent me when we first met, and he couldn't have found better ambassadors for cruising.

The Hiscocks were in their mid-forties when they set out on their first round-the-world voyage, equal players in a joint venture and deeply devoted to each other. Their yacht, the same size as *Hope*, was well prepared with every detail taken care of. Eric had a solution for every possible mishap; a 'Plan B' person like me, who made cruising over oceans look as safe as paddling over a millpond. On the many public talks he gave, he was frequently asked why he didn't carry a two-way radio aboard their yacht *Wanderer*. He replied that if they got into any trouble it was up to them to get themselves out of it or perish... he didn't want to be a bother to anyone else.

Eric's sentiment echoed my own, in the adventure stakes at any rate. Admittedly, such boasting was partially driven by the inevitable because back in the 1960s, rescue at sea for a yacht in trouble was unlikely. Communication was via two-way radio, one specific channel kept free of talk for three minutes every half-hour to give clear air space for distress calls. But even if one did manage to get through in the magical three minutes, it would be near impossible to spot a 9-metre yacht unable to give an exact position. Navigation was by sextant, and if the sun didn't shine an educated guess would be the best we could radio through. Armstrong had yet to walk on the moon and Global Positioning Systems were futuristic dreams.

I have happily embraced the technical changes that have come my way over past decades, but when it comes to sailing I am stuck with being hopelessly romantic. I take secret pleasure in having sailed in the 1960s when taking a small boat over oceans still had a touch of exploration; when a whale or a dolphin was a black-and-white photograph in an encyclopaedia next to a block of text, and a colour picture of a coral island became a trigger for dreams; when *National Geographic* had only just begun to publish articles with photographic spreads that astonished and amazed its growing readership; a time before sponsorship had skewed the freedom of adventure, and satellite images, virtual tours and countless blogs began to convey intimate views of people and places from almost anywhere on the planet.

Embracing the social and political changes of past decades is more difficult. Politics, terrorism and piracy, both at sea and in ports, have entered the equation. Sailing the world in the 1960s had a fraction of such heartaches. Red tape was at a minimum; we were given a ready welcome in many places and often celebrated as trailblazing adventurers. It was a guilt-free adventure in a world still buoyed by optimism that two world wars and the horrors of Hiroshima would pave the way towards peace.

And perhaps seafaring adventures deserve celebration still. To take a small boat across oceans will remain a challenge, because for the sailor the sea has not changed. She is and will remain unpredictable, both gorgeous temptress and unyielding boss woman, indifferent to nationality, creed, age or gender. Time has not taken away the risks and the dangers and to embrace her will always need courage, stamina and romantic dreams in generous measure. Sailing *Hope* today would be as thrilling as it was half a century ago. It could as easily end in tragedy.

Threading our way north along the Queensland coast, we met some of the freewheeling adventurers of the 1960s, the seekers, the dropouts, but also the hardworking fishermen always ready to pass on local knowledge about tides and currents, good and bad anchorages and other bits of information not written anywhere.

Hardworking was certainly true for Ian and Elaine, a young couple living aboard their fishing trawler *Josey*. Business wasn't good; Ian was desperate for a change of luck, at least one decent catch. 'We're down to our last four dollars,' he said. Elaine smiled at him reassuringly. Gentle and slight, she looked out of place on their rough old trawler, and I had the feeling she would have preferred a shore life. *Josey* was headed for Great Keppel Island. 'Great place,' Ian said. 'You should call in… I'll introduce you to the Svensons, friends of ours… good people.'

Josey arrived ahead of us. Ian introduced us to the Svenson family – mother, father and three boys – who had lived on Great Keppel for the past sixteen years. A comfortable afternoon followed with food, a few beers and easy talk about the weather and fishing; lovely topics. The oldest Svenson boy, also as a fisherman, skippered a small fishing trawler and planned to join the *Josey* for a time. Ian was pleased, full of hope that teaming up with the Svensons' boat would change his luck. Fishing starts before dawn, and by the time we climbed out of our bunks the two boats had left.

We met *Josey* again a week later, but Ian and Elaine were alone again. Rowing across after dinner to check how the luck was holding, we extended our courtesy call into a long evening. I nearly froze to death in their open cockpit (lit by two hissing Tilly kerosene lamps) while Graeme pitched in with cleaning garfish, little slippery fish used for bait. It involves running a thumb along the bottom of the fish to squeeze out the contents of its gut before chucking the emptied fish onto ice. It's an awful and smelly business that apparently keeps the bait fresh. That night I rowed our dinghy home while Graeme trailed his red stinking hands in the water. 'Don't even think of touching me,' I warned him. My log entry records that *I am glad I'm not a fisherman's wife.*

⁂

A little further north we made friends with Tony, Pat and their baby daughter sailing on *Janis*, a yacht even smaller than

Hope. Tony and Pat hailed from Melbourne and intended to slowly circumnavigate Australia, no fuss and no rush. We liked each other and shared anchorages for a time. Taking turns to provide dinner, we spent the evenings talking about sailing, music and life in general. Tony came from one of the European Eastern Bloc countries; he looked to be in his late thirties and he'd had his share of the war. I admired Tony. He seemed to have found his heaven being with Pat and their baby and sailing *Janis* where the wind took them. His contentment made me question my own restlessness, our pressing need to keep moving. We had committed ourselves to a certain pace, had to catch seasonal Indian Ocean trade winds, and before long *Janis* slipped behind.

There were others like Tony and Pat, happy to be gypsies. Once you owned your boat there was no more rent to pay. Food came courtesy of the sea, the wind cost nothing, and occasional shore jobs brought in enough money for boat upkeep and little extras. Some lucky people managed to make a good living out of their passion, like Alan Lucas on his boat *Rendezvous*. With care and precision, Alan made detailed sketches of anchorages and recorded local knowledge about tidal flows, markers, shops for provisioning and beautiful places to see. His book *Cruising the Coral Coast* would go into many editions and inspire countless nine-to-five workers to take up sailing. We knew Alan from our Sydney days and chanced to meet him again in the Reef doing what he loved best, sailing his boat with his beloved cat Kai-Kai.

Not on par with Alan's sophistication but equal in resourcefulness was an old man living in Pancake Creek, a fair dinkum coastal swagman. Rounding into the creek we noticed a bark hut, a small humpy built above the high tide mark. It looked idyllic; a few chickens scratched around the patchy grass and a couple of dogs watched us put down anchor. The old man appeared at the door but took no notice of us, not a wave of his hand, nothing, just a silent stare. Later in the afternoon we rowed over to say hello and he ambled over, must have got used to us being there by then. Up close he looked ancient, his face deeply lined, his clothes nondescript, the pants tied up with rope. Shy as the mud crab he was catching, it was near impossible to get a word out of him, not even about his dogs or the weather. I tried to imagine his background, what made him live there, was he happy, self-sustaining? Was he married (now or ever) did he have friends, an address ... what would that crazy hut look like from the inside?

He gave us no clues, didn't invite us in, and after a few minutes of awkward silence we rowed off again. He was probably sick of stickybeak city folk in fancy yachts but hours later, he did acknowledge us in his own sweet way. Around dinnertime he rowed across to *Hope*, a shapeless hat pushed low onto his face, and handed me a very large mud crab, mercifully dead. I asked him how to cook it, but 'boil it' was all I got out of him before he pushed off again. I did just 'boil it' but found the supposedly divine taste of Queensland mud crabs unfamiliar, almost unpleasant. At a pinch I could have contemplated living in a bark hut – for a little while anyway – but not if I had to sustain myself on a diet of mud crabs.

⁓

The actual sailing was glorious and miserable in turn. We had crossed the Tropic of Capricorn, the most southerly latitude at which the sun appears directly overhead at noon. This put us officially into the tropics, but warm weather stayed elusive. An out-of-season cyclone stung us with its tail, giving us more sailing practice and a large share of uncomfortable anchorages. Searching out the calmest and most beautiful anchorage became an obsession. It was finally realised in Cid Harbour, a scene fit for a glossy advertising brochure: dark rounded hills, a beautiful yacht bathed in a pink sunset and a young couple marking a virgin beach with their footprints. And all of it a hundred times better than perfect because there was only us, no photographer and no advertising to speak of.

Tourism was in its infancy. A leaflet for the Whitsundays covered all the islands and promised *gay resorts a-tinkle with ice cubes and laughter*, and 'gay' back then did not mean homosexual. Word of mouth among the yachties (either conveyed at anchorages or shouted across the water as we sailed past one another) had spread the information that South Molle Island was putting on a dance on Saturday night. We had intended to sail past South Molle but what the hell, *let's sail over and check it out*. We dug out our party gear, tied up *Hope*'s dinghy to South Molle's rickety wooden jetty and joined the throng. But things had changed for us. Only three months earlier I would have loved that party, now it all seemed too frantic and rushed. It was no longer our scene; we weren't holidaymakers with a couple of weeks off work. We had found a different rhythm, observed a dress code of bare feet, sarongs and T-shirts (if that) and lived by the wind, the sun and the rain.

'Sailing as a way of life' was firmly established. Graeme had minor regrets about missing the Film Festival in Sydney – his yearly treat – and I rejoiced in the fact that it was Census Day and there wasn't a police station in sight for us to register our existence. For a time we sailed in the company of *Renegaat* – sailed by Ted, a Dutchman, his English wife Pam and two Australian crewmembers, and with *Safari Too*, owned by a German husband and his English wife who hailed from Sydney. It was good to have occasional company, do a little lighthearted racing of one boat against another, but meetings were left to chance. We were used to letting mood and weather dictate our schedule. Graeme and I were happy in each other's company; just the two of us and of course Jinky, our furry crewmember.

Jinky had grown into a sleek cat. No more foolish jumps into the water and well in charge of his four sea legs. Rarely on dry land now, we decided we'd treat him to a shore excursion at one of the lonely beaches, let him stretch his legs and have a little run-around, or so we thought. Anchoring just outside the surf line the three of us got into the dinghy. Jinky stood at the cap rail, the way he usually did to see us off, and wasn't at all keen for me to drag him off the boat and into the dinghy. On high alert, he literally *stood* on my lap, watching every move, and as we reached the line of surf (nothing big, just enough curl to give us a good push ashore) Jinky decided that this was *not safe*. It was time for him to make for higher ground, my head as it happened. The scuffle was big but through it all we managed to get the dinghy ashore, jump out and pull it up on the beach. I had a few scratches, my beautiful Voigtländer camera lay ruined in the water, and Jinky sat in the middle of the dinghy refusing to budge.

'Come on you stupid cat,' said Graeme, 'this is your special outing.' Running around the dinghy, we tried to get him to jump out and follow us, but he just sat there glowering. Eventually Graeme lifted him out, but as he lowered him onto the sand Jinky splayed his legs out as if he was about to hit water. Finally realising that the white stuff he was standing on was solid, he began hi-stepping like a wind-up toy and we could almost hear him muttering... *oops I can walk on this stuff*. And we just stood there and laughed; poor Jinks had a lot to put up with.

Getting him toilet trained had been a laugh too. While in port, his toilet box half-filled with sand had sat on deck near the mast. At sea it needed a safer place and we put it underneath the spray dodger beside the hatch. Not the best place, because Jinky managed to kick sand everywhere. The alternative we came up with was to gradually replace the sand with layers of newspaper cut to the size of the box. Jinks tried the old burying routine for a time but caught on soon enough. In the end, a single sheet of newspaper in the bottom of the box was okay with him and fine with us. Whoever was nearby after he'd used it simply tipped the lot overboard and washed out the box in the sea. The only trouble was that Jinks didn't like to get his feet wet in his own wee and when Graeme started calling him Pissfoot he came up with some stunning acrobatics. Accurately gauging the movement of the boat, he planted all four paws in a row alongside the edge of the box, suspended his rear end over it and did his business swaying like a four-legged bird clinging to a tree branch. If a sudden lurch of the boat made him slip in, he was plainly annoyed and raced around the deck afterwards to let off steam and dry his feet.

Toilet arrangements for the rest of the crew were only slightly more refined. At sea we soon gave up using the inboard toilet. When the boat heeled over, the pumping arrangement to facilitate flushing didn't work too well, and sitting in the enclosed compartment was likely to bring on seasickness. Graeme had an easy time peeing overboard; all he had to do was watch the wind direction. If I peed overboard there was always the thrilling possibility of getting my bottom slapped by a passing wave, a bidet with a difference, to be avoided in rough weather. Jinky politely offered me his box when it stormed, but thanking him nicely I opted for a bucket in the cockpit.

The many lighthouses along the way fascinated me. I thought about the people who had given them lovely names like Cape Capricorn, Sandy Cape, Lady Elliot, and I thought about their keepers too, the men who made sure that night after night the same signal flashed across the sea. Alone on a night watch I thought of the keeper alone in his lighthouse sending me coded beams of light. When the sea was rough he became my guardian and I sent him my gratitude for helping me steer a safe course. And on still moonlit nights, the sea awash in pale lavender light, I imagined him my friend, sharing the magic. I would have liked to visit every lighthouse and pay my respects, but getting to the tall white towers can be difficult. Being built in isolated places or high up on cliff tops makes them hard to reach. To begin with Graeme and I tried, imagining what good exercise it would give us, but soon gave up. After the first hefty climb it was easier to find a rock to sit on, have a chat, drink some water and admire *Hope* anchored far below us.

Low Island Lighthouse off Port Douglas was near sea level, and that we did visit. Coral reefs surrounded a sandy shore and right in the middle of the island, set among a tight circle of thick vegetation, stood the red-topped lighthouse, looking like a birthday candle stuck into a round green cake. The tide was very low and anchoring in the lagoon might be tricky, but the island looked so beautiful we couldn't sail past.

Heading for the lagoon, we noticed a group of people moving about on the reef. These turned out to be the Williams family, Lloyd the head lighthouse keeper, his wife and five of their six children. Mum had given the kids a day off from radio correspondence school; it was the lowest tide of the month and the whole family was out searching for one specific shell still needed for their collection. We joined in, although my understanding of shells had not yet gone beyond *oh look isn't this pretty*. One small daughter about 6 years old, dressed in shorts, gumboots and gloves held in place with rubber bands around her wrist, admonished me with an earnest expression on her face that I must be *very careful* and *never ever* touch a cone shell. 'They look really really harmless,' she said, 'just brown and white, but they can kill you.' Her mother joined us and we chatted as we moved about the reef; she told me how much she loved living on the island, *a good life*. The only bitter drop seemed to be the absence of her oldest son, who had to leave for the mainland to attend high school. She missed him terribly.

The Williams family and those of the assistant keepers lived in a tight cluster of cottages hugging the lighthouse. Lloyd took us up into the tower to show us the intricate arrangement of revolving lights and mirrors, which had only recently been expanded to electric operation. But it was the 360-degree view of water, coral reefs and the distant shoreline that got me thinking. I wondered what it might be like to stand in the circular room of a very tall lighthouse, Cape Wickham for instance, 85 metres above Bass Strait... the isolation wouldn't worry me but to be up high in an eyrie totally exposed to howling storms would have to be scary.

A couple of days later we met another isolated family, three generations of Dutch people. Anchoring off the long sweep of beach behind Cape Tribulation, we didn't expect to meet anyone, but rowing ashore a man wandered out from the dense foliage. Introducing himself as Robert, he invited us to his house 'a little way up the track' where he lived with his wife and children. Chatting all the way he told us that the family owned the surrounding land and made a living off felling and sawing timber. 'But how do you get the stuff out?' Graeme wanted to know. No roads led to Cape Tribulation, but 'Hale's launch', travelling weekly between Cairns and Cooktown, picked up the timber and brought in supplies.

We arrived at the house, a modest dwelling half hidden under lush green rainforest next to a creek chuckling away under flowering bougainvillea – a paradisiacal setting. Robert's wife, her fair hair tied loosely at the back and two naked cherubs holding her skirt, looked perfectly at home in the soft shadowy light of the rainforest. We stood in the outside kitchen on smooth brick flooring, the chip stove, table and benches protected by an overhanging roof and lattice walls. I told her how lovely it was, but it wasn't easy to get a conversation going with Robert chatting away, rushing off and coming back with bananas and pawpaws for us to take, rushing off again and coming back with coconuts and limes. He wanted Graeme's opinion on the boat he was building, a big 50-foot boat to a Dutch design; was keen to go cruising. He also wanted us to meet his parents 'another little way up the track'.

The walk up the track took us over a little bridge to a two-storey Hansel and Gretel house, a varnished and polished jewel built entirely of silky oak, teak and mahogany, the only imported piece of furniture a piano for Grandma. According to Robert, getting the piano off Hale's launch had been something else. Grandma and Grandpa spoke little but proudly showed us around. There was not a speck of dust, nothing was out of place and even the lettuces in the garden stood in neat rows, like soldiers, carefully enclosed by animal-proof fencing. Grandma pressed a parcel of lettuce and some fresh parsley into my hands before we left.

With so much kindness offered I felt almost ashamed for wanting to get away quickly. The Dutch family, in contrast to the lighthouse family from a couple of days ago, seemed in strange discord, not entirely comfortable to be with. Robert's wife was German. I have forgotten her name, but I remember her sad face when she told me how much it upset her that Robert wanted to leave and go cruising. 'It's the only place I have ever been happy in,' she told me. My heart went out to her, and I would have liked to know her better. What was her background, how had she learned to be happy in such an isolated place? I would have loved to ask her but Robert's incessant talking and rushing around made it impossible.

I'd had my chance to settle in paradise a month previously, further south on Orpheus Island, and had rejected it. Spending a day on the island we were told it was for sale, or could it have been for lease? A New Zealand couple managed the resort and taking in guests for three months of the year kept them solvent. The island had rustic cabins, no telephone or television, just peace and beautiful diving, and the asking price was twenty thousand Australian pounds; dollars had been introduced earlier that year but our 'thinking currency' was still pounds. I stood entranced in the spacious kitchen, listening to the wife telling me how beautiful life was on the island, how they would miss it, how happy they were here... *but we're getting on in years now, want to retire and go home to New Zealand.*

Stunned by the possibilities, Graeme and I looked around the island and met the only other person living on Orpheus, a retired sea captain, an Old Salt still familiar with square-riggers. A tall and bony man with a sunny regulation smile for visitors, he had found joy in his retirement by breeding geese and chickens. His firm, upright bearing reminded me of my father. Not surprisingly, the captain's charges were equally well trained. We walked up just as the old man had sprinkled food on the ground in separate lots, one spread for the chickens and one for the geese. He opened the enclosures and as his brood rushed out, he talked them into order. 'Come on now... no rushing... heh, Lizzy, behave yourself...' He had names for them all and the animals obediently observed his orders, waiting in their respective corners until they were given the go ahead to step forward and eat. One hungry goose, 'a bit muddle-headed that day' or so the captain said apologetically, toddled over to the chicken feeding area. She was promptly admonished, immediately changed course and hung her head in shame. A goose with a conscience; I knew how she felt.

Late that afternoon Graeme and I sat up on a hill to think things over. What would it be like to live here permanently, and could we make it happen? The Australian mainland stood etched onto the horizon in pale undulating shapes and the air on my skin felt like the touch of a silk shirt. At first, we dreamed a little – and then followed it up with hard calculations. If we sold *Hope* and brought in a partner (and we already knew somebody who would be interested) we could do it. This was probably the opportunity of a lifetime and we were sure to love it. It was painfully tempting, but in the end it came down to a few words.

'Do we really want to sell *Hope* and buy an island?' I said.

A long pause followed, and then Graeme's decisive 'Nah, let's not.'

'That's settled then,' I agreed. 'Let's go.'

We sailed at two o'clock that night, headed for Dunk Island. Full of words not yet expressed, both of us stayed up, sitting in the cockpit to share the night. *Hope* moved along effortlessly in calm seas and gentle offshore winds, and a cool dawn found us gliding along the dark, densely wooded shape of Dunk Island. The rich aroma of damp rainforest wafting across the water opened our hearts and lungs. Breathing, loving and moving along felt good and Orpheus Island was not mentioned again.

☙

Communication with the outside world was via letters, posted and received at post offices in mainland towns. I only wrote to Mutti. My letters, often ten pages or more, were like diaries, added to whenever I had the time or felt like it. The description of the sea captain and his charges on Orpheus Island is in the letters but Dunk Island got a bigger write-up:

> *Dunk Island was our special treat. We had read Ted Banfield's book* Confessions of a Beachcomber. *The author and his wife lived on the island with local Aborigines around the turn of the century. From reading his book we already knew a lot about the island – and made a pilgrimage to visit Ted Banfield's grave high up in the rainforest ... Dunk was more tropical than anything I have seen, the bush so dense one has difficulty getting through it; thick undergrowth with vines and ferns, and dozens of different birds. A coral reef rings the island – it is unbelievably beautiful ...*

Mutti's stay in Sydney, for all the soul-searching it had triggered for me, had brought us closer. I no longer wrote duty letters but wanted to invite her into my heart. And because my letters were also meant for Frank and his wife to read, I sometimes attached private communications, a separate page for Mutti alone. Surrounded by sea I was unreachable, entirely my own person and it felt right and safe to open up to her. Mutti knew about my therapy sessions in Sydney; my 'soul doctor' she called him. I had explained how it had raised questions for me, but judging by one letter I must have slipped in the odd accusation as well. Mutti destroyed the private pages only meant for her but one of my answers, written on Dunk Island, sounds a lot like back-pedalling, smoothing over an accusation I must have made:

> *Liebe Mutti ... I want to protest your undertones of guilt. Neither Pappi nor you have reason to feel that ... to have brought us up healthy and whole in such dreadful times is more than other parents have managed to do. We* [I include Frank into this] *have to thank you for instilling in us enough tenacity, ambition and morality to allow us to live our lives with enjoyment and satisfaction ... I am sad I can't talk to Pappi about this anymore.*

Had I been entirely honest, I would have written that I still blamed her (and Pappi) for a lot of things. Her for having switched sides and leaving me to come to terms with a father I hardly knew. She had claimed me so entirely as her own that Father had always seemed like the outsider. Who was he, where did he come from? As a child I had not thought to ask and when I did want to know, Mutti could only give me snippets of information; that he'd rowed in the Eight of his university team, that he voluntarily joined the army when he was 17, that he'd been married before he met her. Mutti thought it futile of me to want to know. 'What difference does it make? I am not interested in the past,' she said. 'Let it go.' She found it easy to accept that his life had started with her. 'You met him when you were an adult, you're not his blood,' I countered. 'I'm part of him, remember.'

I found it interesting that both Father and I had left home and family at the age of 18. What had happened to him? Why didn't he talk about his early life, why the wilful, almost total oblivion of his childhood and the twenty years that followed it? If I was so much like him (and I no longer minded that) I had little to go by. Who were his parents, my grandparents, what were they like? I imagined Grandfather would have had to be stern, but what about Grandmother? I didn't even know their names, not a single photo of them exists and none of my father before the age of 39, the time he met my mother.

Aboriginal country

I had lived in Australia for over four years but hadn't met a single Aboriginal person. My Sydney friends told me Aboriginal people were said to be excellent horsemen employed as jackaroos on outback cattle stations. Graeme told me stories of their outstanding tracking skills, most famously helping to capture Ned Kelly. It seemed that not many of them were left, most of them killed in the process of colonisation. They had become a declining race whose exit from this world must be aided with care and compassion, and efforts were underway to adopt their children to integrate them into civilised society. Many city people thought it a fine thing to guide a black child into adulthood.[4]

I was curious and my chance to meet so-called 'native Australians' came when we gained permission to visit Palm Island near Townsville, a government-run centre reserved for Aboriginal and Torres Strait Islander people. I don't know what I expected, but seeing the people on Palm Island was a shock and didn't tally with anything I had read or heard. Dark faces withdrew into cheerless square buildings. No life or laughter, nobody spoke to us. The atmosphere felt heavy with an overlay of apathy. Little boys followed us

---

[4] In fact, many children were forcibly removed and would eventually become known as the Stolen Generations.

around showing off their toys made from empty food tins. With tops and bottoms removed and long wires threaded through them, the tins became miniature steamrollers that could be pulled along the dusty road.

Not until much later did I learn that the Aboriginal and Torres Strait Islander people on Palm Island were displaced, detained and forlorn men and women taken away from their families and their land, both central and integral to their very existence. Government maintained control by segregating the sexes, taking children away from their mothers, by imposing night curfews and vetting the mail. Unknowingly we had visited a modern-day penal settlement for 'disruptive elements'; men released from jails, women 'guilty' for falling pregnant to white men, and the unfortunate children of such unions.

Sailing north, we met more Aboriginal and Torres Strait Islander people, happier people going about their business and giving us friendly greetings. It helped to soften the stark images of Palm Island and I began to take notice of the voices calling for a referendum on equal rights, appalled to think that they didn't even have that. But respect for the knowledge and resilience of the traditional owners of this continent came to me via a different route. It came from spending a few days with Fred and Jacob, two Aboriginal men we met in the Flinders Islands.

Needing a couple of days' rest and wanting to get *Hope* shipshape for the last stretch towards Thursday Island, we sailed into the shelter of one of the Flinders group of islands. The idea of rest and solitude vanished as we rounded into the bay and spotted a large white ship at anchor, which turned out to be the *Alpha Helix*, an American Research vessel. *Renegaat* and *Clipper I*, our companions of past weeks, had arrived ahead of us and were anchored nearby.

Aboriginal country

Big hellos followed and the promise of parties to come. A small tent city had been set up ashore to facilitate the fieldwork of the scientists aboard, with two of them reserved for social gatherings. At one party we took a count of the multi-national, multi-cultural community gathered in the middle of nowhere. We counted twenty-two American men, scientists and crew of the *Alpha Helix*. Looking after the *Helix*'s shore outfit were two Aussie outback blokes (Baxter and his mate) and two Aboriginal men (Fred and Jacob). Then there were the visiting yachties: *Renegaat* had a Dutch skipper, his English wife and two Australian crewmembers; Tommy Corkhill, skippering *Clipper I* single-handedly, hailed from New Zealand; and *Hope* was sailed by one Australian and one German (me).

We were invited on a tour of the ship, and the scientists told us a little about their brief to study the filtering system of mangroves. They were a dedicated lot, hardworking and proud of their beautiful laboratory where the lights never went out. Baxter, the Aussie bush bloke in charge of the shore outfit, sourced different mangrove species for them. Laconic and with the driest sense of humour, his opinion of 'the Helix blokes' ran along different lines. Baxter was forever snorting condemnation at the non-practical scientists; 'absent-minded professors the lot of them, useless buggers... got to ferry them ship to shore all hours of the day and night... can't handle a bloody runabout... bloody run over each other.' Baxter was also the shore cook where more snorts let us know that the *bloody* cook on the *bloody Helix* could only warm up *bloody* frankfurts in a stainless-steel galley the size of a *bloody* football field. Baxter's tasty, onion-rich, open-fire barbeques were well attended by everybody – scientists, crew and even the ship's cook.

Fred and Jacob, the two Aboriginal men, supported Baxter,

provided local knowledge and brought in seafood that still wriggled. They didn't join in on the parties but seemed to be always in the background, happy to be looking after their mate Baxter. Fred had the more powerful presence of the two. Neither assertive nor shy, he had an easy authority, the gentlest smile and unshakable calm in his eyes. He told us who his people were, names I could neither pronounce nor remember. His English wasn't easy for me to understand and my knowledge of Aboriginal lore too limited to comprehend his tales of dreamtime, spirits and kinship ties, but when he said 'many cousins... all the time' I felt the tone of his voice change, becoming softer. Fred had family, a community he belonged to; this was his country.

On Baxter's suggestion Fred escorted us to a nearby island for 'better hunting and fishing' and to show us cave paintings. All seven yachties sailed over on Tommy Corkhill's *Clipper I*. Fred sat on deck in shorts and shirt, his spears upright in front of him. Next to him the five sailing blokes, rifles planted in front of them, intending to shoot goat for dinner. Goats had been released on the islands during the 1800s with the idea that they would provide food for shipwrecked sailors. In another of Australia's environmental disasters they had multiplied to pest proportion, threatening to denude the islands of vegetation.

Fred wasn't after goats and needed no gun to hunt. Rowing ashore he suddenly motioned us to stop. I barely noticed the shadow flit beneath the glittery surface of the sea, but seconds later Fred pulled a turtle from the water. Standing up in our wobbly dinghy, he had speared it right through the neck. As the day unfolded he added a good supply of fish in a similar manner, while the gun-carrying blokes managed to shoot a poor old goat. Baxter's famous barbeques that night offered extras: goat steaks tough as boots followed by succulent coral trout and tender turtle.

Before our return to camp, Fred took us up into the hills to show us rock paintings. Following him single file, we walked along a narrow dirt track leading upwards towards a series of wide rocky ledges, formed into open caves by overhanging rocks. Gaining the ledges opened up a sweeping ocean view over the tops of trees and shrubs. And turning towards the rock face, we could study paintings of ships that would have travelled that very ocean hundreds of years ago. One image showed a single-sail outrigger, another looked like a canoe, but the picture of a square-rigged ship, deep ochre outlined in white, intrigued us the most. Was this Captain Cook's *Endeavour* sailing past 200 years ago? We asked Fred but he didn't answer, keeping a respectful silence.

Later, we questioned Baxter but he didn't know either, simply gave another one of his snorts. 'Don't tell anyone you've seen it, not even the bloody authorities... museum blokes are the worst... they'll put bloody fences up and every other bugger has to climb over them.' At the time Baxter's comment struck me as funny, but I've since come around to thinking that in his no-nonsense way, Baxter might have had the right idea. He knew how vulnerable the paintings were, how fine the threads that make up the fabric of Aboriginal cultures. Fred and his mob were Baxter's mates, and he was fiercely protective of them.

Back at sea again, sailing north once again, I mused how easily the American scientists, Australian outback bush blokes and the Aboriginal men had worked together. Individually, only Fred, Jacob and his people (and probably Baxter) would survive in that isolated, inaccessible country. Yet the scholarly scientists would receive most of the accolades. The work of Fred, Jacob and Baxter was unlikely to warrant a footnote.

North from about Cooktown, the Barrier Reef angles close to the mainland, making a challenging stretch of water for any mariner. One can slip through Cook Passage and sail outside the reef, but we decided to stick to the inner channel. It had neither markers nor lights, but the waters were well charted, and provided we put down anchor every night it should be easy. As required, we notified the harbourmaster in Cooktown of our intended route and if we didn't turn up in Thursday Island in a couple of weeks, at least there was some record of where we might be found.

As we sailed along the long spike of the Cape York Peninsula I thought of Fred from the Flinders camp again, not by way of reminiscence but more like an insurance policy. Images of hot and dry country beyond the water's edge played on my mind: no road, no townships, no water – I wouldn't have a clue how to survive in such country. Should we be unfortunate enough to get wrecked anywhere along that lonely and inhospitable coastline, being found by Aboriginal people like Fred and Jacob would be our only chance of survival.

Luckily, we didn't have to face such dangers but for me at least, it wasn't entirely free of trouble. Like the heroes in the fairy tale books of my childhood, I too had to pass a test, a dark night of the soul, literally. It happened roughly 150 miles below the tip of Australia. By then we had established a pattern of sailing until about four in the afternoon, then I'd climb the mast for a better view from aloft and direct us into an anchorage that looked good, both on the chart and from my lookout post. On that particular afternoon all we could find was a sandy patch in the lee of a good-sized reef. The breeze was stiff, but the sea downwind of the reef looked calm enough. It would be rough but, as we told ourselves, it would only be for one night.

Darkness fell, the tide came in and the reef we had chosen all but disappeared beneath the waves. Worse still, the wind piped up to near gale force. Complete darkness added its terror; was the anchor holding, should we let out more chain, what if the wind shifted and the submerged reef became a lee shore? *Hope* rolled so heavily that water began to slosh into the cockpit. Countless times, when the barrage of *what ifs* threatened to choke me, I would crawl on all fours up the companionway and peer out the hatch. I could see nothing, but hearing the sound of the waves crashing over the reef *upwind* of us calmed me. In that night there was no Plan B, no second chance; one wind shift and we would be in very big trouble. At a small hour, seasick, tired and frightened, I wanted nothing more than to get off the boat for good, the same words repeating themselves in my head over and over. *This is it ... I can't do this ... why am I doing this ... this is madness ... I can't do this ... this is it ...*

Four years of thinking, planning and dreaming nearly came to an end that night, the closest I ever came to giving it all away. Ten days of rough sailing and 'that time of the month' had pushed my resilience close to zero. I'm not sure what kept me going. I seem to remember telling myself that I wasn't the first sailor to go through this. I thought of *Renegaat*; they must be anchored somewhere nearby, probably in a similar predicament. Shame flooded me, sailors down through the centuries mocked me ... *come on, pull yourself together, this is nothing, a bit of wind, steady on now.* At any other time I would have found a saucy answer to such taunts, but in that night the torture of being tethered into a wild sea spiked with coral reefs made me obedient and I pulled myself together.

Dawn arrived, the wind still fierce. Skipping breakfast, we made sail immediately, and the reward for keeping my nerve was the best sailing I had ever experienced. Laughing and shouting and bursting with adrenaline, we pushed *Hope* to the limit; at times it was hard to hold her at the helm. Under a reefed mainsail she simply roared through gleaming, aqua-tinted seas. The ordeal of only a few hours ago was history – resolved by the morning light and the magic of our little ship. I had guessed correctly, and *Renegaat* had been in the vicinity. Bigger than *Hope*, she slowly sailed past us with cameras flashing both ways.

A couple of days later we rounded the northern tip of Australia's mainland, barely visible above sparkling seas bathed in brilliant sunshine. The Great Barrier Reef lay behind us and, well pleased, we set course for Thursday Island. We had come through unharmed. Over the past four months we had experienced most of the dangers and delights that come with sailing. We had learned to deal with storms and calms, with cut fingers and toes, headaches and heartaches, good and bad moods and had come through it all, keen to keep moving. My log entry records:

The Indian Ocean has welcomed us nicely and both our thoughts are on times to come. Three cheers for good old Hope!

To which Graeme added his voice:

Three cheers for the crew too! Jutta has turned out better than I could have hoped [adding a more humble] *and I have even surprised myself.*

Thursday Island, or TI as it is known, lies off the northern tip of the Cape York Peninsula: a small island nestled among larger ones. Around the 1880s it was the hub of the pearling industry, with as many as 200 pearling luggers based on the island. The industry attracted thousands of fortune seekers from Asia and Japan. My preference is to stay *above* water, and one look at the ancient diving equipment in the museum made me bolt. The early diving outfits are the stuff of nightmares. They weigh around 200 kilograms and consist of a stiff canvas suit, lead belts and a large copper helmet bolted onto a shoulder plate. The helmet had air driven into it by pumps, hand-operated from the ship above. Solid lead-soled boots added the final touch. Not surprisingly the death rate was high, as can be seen in the TI cemetery, the graves of Japanese divers marked with small rice bowls for feeding the spirits.

Thursday Island has remained the administrative centre of the Torres Strait Islands and is still the hub for all inter-island travel and the touch point for yachts coming and going in every direction. A few square kilometres in size, it had a tarred road, one taxi, a collection of odd houses, a glass-strewn strip of beach and a few dilapidated pearling luggers anchored offshore. For friendliness, acceptance, help offered and impromptu parties it was legendary, and invitations from ashore and from other boats were plentiful. On Thursday Island we again met up with Aboriginal people, although as far as I could make out the Torres Strait Islanders were more exuberant than their cousins further south: easy-going islanders. Graeme, still playing his guitar, picked up one of their songs – pure TI, sung very loudly by the local women, ending with a chorus of unrestrained laughter:

Wasse matter you last night. You never come see mamma,
I tink so you lie-ke me no more, you too much like another girl,
Other pellow [fellow] *lie-ke me too,*
You're number one good looking too much [too handsome]
alo-hah, ha-hah, hah-ha-hah hey ...

And, of course, we didn't miss the Saturday night dance in the town hall, complete with floorshow. Rumour had it that dressing up was required and that the boys had to wear shoes. Graeme found long socks to go with his, and I dug up some modestly high heels from the shore locker. We needn't have bothered; nobody else wore shoes. About twenty Aboriginal women from nearby Darnby Island, wearing feather-decorated masks, gave a fiery floorshow, stamping the bare boards of the town hall to a rhythm kept by wooden instruments. After the Aboriginal dancing there was taped music, and the yachting crowd added to the general chaos by dancing the Twist. The Darnby Island women watched us, helpless with laughter. Supper came last. It cost 40 cents per head and I made several trips to the table, happily filling myself up on cake, an unknown luxury in our days.

⁓

Thursday Island is a good place to count how many yachts travel the world. Almost all cruising boats call at TI, and in the 1966 season there were about half a dozen of us going westwards. Two yachts – *Sandefjord* and *Safari Too* – had already left for Christmas Island, and four of us were ready to sail. The craziest of the bunch was the New Zealander Tommy Corkhill, headed for Durban via Singapore on *Clipper I*, a 26-foot Hedley Nichols design trimaran. I

Aboriginal country

had sailed on his boat a couple of times – a daytrip from Cairns to Green Island and again in Flinders Islands – and found it a scary ride. In my view a boat leaping across the water like a spider at speeds of up to 8 knots was not fit for ocean sailing. Tom disagreed, largely because *Clipper I* was all he could afford. Apparently he'd owned a single-hulled yacht before and sailed it from Yokohama to Indonesia, but returning from a trip ashore in some remote Indonesian island he'd found his boat completely gutted by thieves; not a screw left on it, he said.

Another trimaran, the big 40-foot *Galinule*, was also tied up at the TI wharf, dwarfing little *Clipper I*. *Galinule* was sailed by the Cole family, who had left Kenya after Independence in the hope of finding a better and safer place to live. They had sailed eastwards crossing the Indian Ocean against the trade winds. Sailing against prevailing winds is hard going, but since their initial goal was Australia it made for a shorter route. Aboard were Commander George Cole, retired from the Royal Navy, his wife, two adult children and George's 93-year-old mother. Grandmother featured in headlines worldwide.

Grandmother didn't join the yachting parties, but I talked to her briefly and she seemed contented, happy to be with her family. The sailing part, so important to us, was inconsequential for her; she knitted for most of the way. Giles, her grandson, told me she knew nothing of sailing, and her comments on wind and weather were polite small talk. Giles was the youngest aboard and seemed to feel the pain of losing his Kenyan home more than the rest of his family. He was involved in game-keeping in Kenya's national parks, missed his work and had plans to return as soon as the family was settled.

Famous British sailor Dr David Lewis, the scholar, author,

adventurer and non-conformist, also made a brief stopover. He cruised on *Rehu Moana* (also a trimaran) with his twin daughters and their nanny, Priscilla; his wife had fallen ill and had been left behind somewhere on the mainland to receive medical care. David was obsessed by his desire to prove ancient Polynesian navigation methods and used no compass, sextant or marine chronometer. With a hacksaw and a feather (so the yachting jokes went) he seemed to find his targets, although Priscilla knew how to navigate by more conventional means and had the authority to correct him if things got risky.

Renegaat, companion since the Whitsundays, was tied up alongside us once again. Skipper Ted and his wife Pam liked to keep to themselves, but we had made good friends with their two Australian crewmembers and with Rob especially. He was a keen diver and had made lots of money diving for abalone down south around Gabo Island. Rob had supplied us with fish in many of our shared anchorages. Come dinnertime we'd shout, 'Hey, Rob, how about a couple of coral trout?'

'Okay, no worries, who's coming with me?'

Rob didn't dive alone. He liked to joke that having one other person with him reduced the risk of shark bite by half, three brought it down to a third, four to a quarter... and so on.

After finishing his crewing job on *Renegaat* he planned to set up a diving business and was keenly checking out the trimarans in port; 'all that deck space would be perfect for diving'. In a bitter irony Rob was lost at sea when a large trimaran he eventually crewed on didn't reach its destination. An ache stabs my heart when I think of him. He was the best swimmer I have known, and I almost hope that a very big fish ate him very quickly; swimming in mid-ocean for hours and hours without hope of rescue would have been worse.

Aboriginal country

Cruising folk are an extended family who, generally speaking, share the same 'genes'. Newcomers are introduced, supported and given permanent membership. Get-togethers are easy and party talk is amiable; it hardly matters whether one agrees or disagrees. Having sailed long distances over deep water creates a bond, engenders mutual respect, a willingness to suspend belief, and a tolerance for foolishness one would criticise in one's shore friends. The family grapevine stretches around the globe for generations back.

Meeting another yacht, we had either heard of them before or shared an anchorage with someone who had. Gossip and information travelled readily: 'Did you know that Alan on *Rendezvous* married Nina?' 'Yeah we met them in Mackay. Nina is lovely isn't she... I heard that Alan's cat Kai-Kai got so jealous he kept shitting in Nina's bunk.' Or 'Have you heard that *Sandefjord* is making a movie of their voyage?' 'Yes, Kurt told me... he ran into Mary, she crewed on *Sandefjord* in the Pacific. Apparently they took good footage of her swimming naked with the seals in Galapagos.' 'Wow, that would be fantastic to see, hope they'll get it past the censors.'

The gossip out of the way, discussion usually headed in the direction of technicalities: navigation, charts, books, and the hardware of boats. At one party, Dr Lewis, skipper of *Rehu Moana*, tried to explain Polynesian navigation methods to Commander George Cole, skipper of *Galinule*. Dr Lewis was compactly built and using a lot of hand gestures; tall George, towering above him with calm Royal Navy bearing, listened attentively, but navigation was his profession and he was clearly sceptical. An equal waste of energy was Tom's attempt to convince me of the safety of trimarans. 'They never sink... and even if they tip over you can cut a hole into the hull to get at the stores.' He told me some cruising trimarans had axes fixed to the underside of the boat in case they flipped, a precaution which Tom didn't have to worry about because 'his Clipper would never tip over.'

The 36-foot ketch *La Mouette* was the only yacht permanently berthed at the Thursday Island wharf. Living aboard were Lenny Foxcroft and his family, ex cruising people who passed through TI six years earlier, 'got stuck and loved it'. Lenny knew a lot about sailing, had sailed on square-rigged ships. Keeping to the tradition of ancient sailors, he had a knife strapped to the back of his belt; 'sometimes one has to cut a rope quickly to free a sail or to free a boat.' Alert and moving quickly, he was helper and adviser to the cruising family and organiser of whatever needed to be organised.

Lenny knew gaff-rigged boats, and he and Graeme discussed our difficulty in bringing *Hope*'s mainsail down in wet weather. Ropes tended to get stuck in wooden blocks, and clawing a recalcitrant mainsail and a swinging gaff boom down, especially in rough weather, had given us much anguish and a few nasty bruises. Lenny and Graeme got together and re-rigged the arrangement (taking one block out) and the difference was nothing short of a miracle. *Hope* now had a mainsail that was a little harder to pull up but came down like a window blind. To see a big problem suddenly vanish was an extraordinarily good omen. I was exuberant. A good omen! Everything had fallen into place, and I was ready to tackle the big Indian Ocean.

Rounding up Jinky, who had learned to go walkabout on land and on other boats, we left with the tide. There was a crowd to see us off. Lenny stood on the wharf holding his daughter's hand, his wife Carol in the cockpit of *La Mouette*, their new baby boy in her arms. The yachties still in port waved nonchalantly – they'd be next – and we had cheers from the mixed crowd that usually hung around TI wharf. Bruce, the primary school teacher, and his girlfriend, Beverly, had come down to see us off. Beverly brought me a pearl-shell brooch as a farewell gift and with that my goodbye tears started rolling, and quite a river of them.

A perfect farewell and then we messed up the leaving. *Hope* had been on the dry for repainting and not everything had been put back in its rightful place. The halyard winch handle could not be found and with the wind fully into the half-up mainsail we flapped around like beginners. Ashamed of the shambles we limped off to sort out the mess, sailed a large circle and proudly moved past the waving crowd again, under full sail this time, pushed along by a healthy 15-knot breeze.

The tide pulled strongly, and following the markers we raced along the channel towards open water, leaving us no time for sentimentality. But gradually, as the soft aqua water of the channel deepened into rich deep blue, a quieter kind of excitement overtook us. *Hey this is great ... we did it.* Breathing deeply, we savoured the start of a new kind of sailing, true ocean sailing. Half an hour later Thursday Island was a small dark hump, barely distinguishable from the distant shoreline, and soon that was gone too. We trimmed the sails to take her almost true west and *Hope* quickly found her stride, obediently lifting her stern and surging forward with every rolling wave, each one taking us farther into the vast Indian Ocean.

Thirty days at sea

It has been said that the sea can't sink a good ship, only the land can do that – put differently it means that sailing deep water is safe. There is nothing to hit, no reefs or rocks, clean ocean for miles ahead. Storms are another story but they have to be pretty bad to sink a yacht. Well-built boats have survived pitch-poling (going arse over turkey as the ancient saying goes) as well as rolling all the way around, sideways. *Hope* was well built, she had four tons of lead on her keel and if she ever did turn turtle, providing all the hatches were closed she would eventually come right way up. It wouldn't be pretty, and she might lose her mast in the process, but that's hardly life threatening.

Sailing the Barrier Reef had served as an extended shakedown cruise and we had come through, trusting each other with our very lives. Sailing into deep water was an easy next step, and heading westward we slowly cast off ambition, urgency, thoughts of money, and responsibility to the rest of the world. I ditched my need for perfection along with occasional nagging, and Graeme's dubious jokes and his tough Aussie exterior slipped into our wake almost as easily. Whatever came our way we'd be okay, confident that we could handle it.

It felt like a minor hiccup when Graeme's first attempt at

sextant navigation went wrong, funny rather than serious, a disaster just big enough to satisfy my superstition that something has to go wrong before it will go right. Steadying himself against the dinghy lashed upside down over the skylight, he'd taken his first sextant sight.[5] My job was to start the stopwatch when he shouted 'Now!', recording the exact moment in time when he got a good measure of the angle between the rim of the sun and the wobbly horizon. Satisfied with his reading, he'd jumped below to plot our position. It took a long time, and I could hear terrible bouts of swearing, but finally he emerged, a clear 'don't ask' look written all over his face. Planting himself defiantly on the heaving deck, his sarong flapping wildly around him, he cast furious looks at the sky. Suddenly he jumped, pointed a finger at the sun, swung around 180 degrees and yelled, 'You ... you should be there!' Angry at the sun's audacity to be in the wrong quarter, he stomped below again.

I glanced at the compass. *Yes*, we were on a westerly course, and *yes*, the sun was where she ought to be. Doing a quick bit of educated guessing (officially called dead reckoning) I figured that if we recorded direction, gauged speed, adjusted for currents, watched for clouds and birds and checked water depth, we might be okay without celestial navigation.

---

5   For the technically minded: Before satellites, finding one's position was achieved by measuring the angle between the rim of the sun and the horizon, using a sextant. At the same time as taking the 'sun shot' one needs to record the exact time of day. Books of Sight Reduction Tables show precisely where the sun is at any given time, and collating this with the angle measured between boat and horizon makes plotting one's position an exercise of trigonometry. Without correct time the process is not possible, which is why the development of an accurate marine chronometer was so important. We had the luxury of radio signals to get the correct time, but our sextant was, in principle, the same instrument that had been used for celestial navigation for well over 200 years.

If Dr Lewis could do it, so could we. *Not a good start though, pretty miserable in fact, he'd better sort that one out pretty quick.*

Half an hour later he did, had navigation licked, and flushed with pride he talked of shooting the moon and the stars as well. Chagrined and somewhat low-key, he owned up to his mistake in the log:

> The celestial navigation has settled down ... since I realised that the Sight Reduction Tables are printed for the northern hemisphere, and that is why my calculations were wrong.

All was well and in years to come we never missed a landfall. To spot a low coral atoll from *Hope*'s heaving deck we needed to be pretty close, but invariably the tops of palm trees would appear exactly where Graeme had predicted.

~

Sailing deep water gave me a feeling I can only describe as *this is it*, followed by a deep exhalation. The sea in her enormity and power satisfied a deep longing, condensed my world into the basic elements of life, love and nature. In a strange paradox the vastness of the universe made me feel secure in my insignificance. We were mites floating on a bit of timber; nothing would hurt us. Night watches were seductive. With Graeme asleep below I was happy in my solitude; the world was mine, my thoughts adrift without critique or censure. If wind and sea behaved themselves steering was easy, almost instinctive. With *Hope*'s sails trimmed to keep her on her designated course I didn't need a compass, simply picked a star to steer by or held the breeze on the same plane of my face or neck. Standing in the cockpit I was just the right height to straddle *Hope*'s tiller, steering the boat with my whole body like a jockey riding his horse. *Oops too far past my star* ... a gentle press of my thigh would correct her course ... *now she's heading too far to port* ... another sway of my body and once again she would respond obediently.

Days were unstructured. We didn't set watches and lived the hours of sunlight as they unfolded, taking turns at steering, cooking and cleaning. Guiding *Hope* along was an easy responsibility, a labour of love that had us dipping, cresting and surging along with her. She was a beautifully balanced boat and with a little ingenuity we often had her steering herself, leaving us plenty of free time to read or to just look. I loved to watch wind and water chase us along, to see watery crests curl up into pointy white crowns, to glide down dark flanks of water streaked with white. I watched *Hope*'s slim wake trail behind us, a series of short squiggles and after that nothing more than undisturbed ocean.

On that first long hop across the Indian Ocean, magic was asking to happen to this introvert dreamer and fairy tale reader. Not that I looked for magic. I had no wish to catch up with Davy Jones, rumoured to be the spiritual reincarnation of people who died at sea. I saw no little creatures hanging about the rigging, never once spotted a mermaid, but sitting quietly on deck one day surrounded by sunshine and wrap-around horizon, I swear I saw a little iridescent blue bird flash past streaming a silken banner that read WAKE UP, THERE IS MORE TO DISCOVER THAN EXOTIC PORTS. *Wow, did that just happen – did I really see that?* I have no doubt that I did, because whizzing off again the little winged creature took with it a layer of mist, a thin membrane surrounding me, keeping me separate and distinct. In the space of a wingbeat

I was released into a boundless world, intense and vibrant. Colour and warmth became full and deep and the air I breathed was pure love – not love for anyone or anything but simply there, everywhere. I wholly belonged, intrinsic to the world, undefinable and beyond words.

Looking back, I know that the little bird felt sorry for me. It must have seen a half-opened door in my brain and pushed it all it could. It didn't want me to miss the vastness of the heavens, nudged me along with a little tease, a tiny taste of absolute freedom. Thanks to its swift wingbeat, lightness stayed with me for a time, a gift of enchantment in a tangible world. That night a killer whale swam alongside, the boat heeled right over towards the mighty fish. Awed and wide-eyed I watched the black lacquered curve emerge from silvery water, white markings milky in the half moon. I *felt* his grace and movement and had an impulse, almost a need to reach out a long, long arm into the night and touch it.

Apart from conjuring up ephemeral creatures, the ocean itself offered surprises. I had imagined storms and rough seas and would not have believed that an ocean could get completely, breathlessly calm. A week out of Thursday Island the trade winds became fickle and then disappeared altogether. For reasons unknown they took a rest, and for the next seven days we had no choice but to drift around in more or less the same place. At first we begged and cursed, raised sail for every puff of wind, but the distance travelled rarely made the effort worthwhile. Hoping and wishing for the wind to return kept us watching and anxious for a time, but before long the seemingly unending stillness had us slip into acceptance of what we couldn't change.

Time took on a different measure, offered a different way of living and being. Black-and-yellow sea snakes swam past, tiny crabs swept by in ruffled undulating mini-waves, big and small fish checked us out, and one day a turtle paddled past on its unwavering path. Seabirds tried to land in the rigging, a brazen cheek that nearly drove Jinky insane. Good reception from an Australian radio station had us listening to requests for the boys serving in Vietnam; Johnnie O'Keefe sang 'Will you still love me tomorrow' and Sonny and Cher had us join in with 'I got you babe'. BBC London (we picked up their news daily) told us that two Norwegians had successfully rowed across the Atlantic in ninety-eight days.

I began teaching German to my keen husband, who bravely attempted translating articles from a German women's magazine. 'What is *Mitesser*? And why would you want to beat a wish out of your head?' We laughed a lot and I remembered my early Melbourne days of trying to learn English reading the *Women's Weekly*.

Most evenings, porpoises crisscrossed under our bows, bursting through the surface with noisy puffs. Each one left a trail of phosphorescence, and multiple jumps created fireworks of tiny sparks in the darkening sea.[6] Once we had a huge pod, dozens. We could hear their underwater high-pitched noises and Graeme raced to get his guitar to sing to them; they were said to be curious, perhaps they would stay longer and listen ...

And still the wind stayed away. Graeme began to get

---

6   Phosphorescence refers to the emission of light by bioluminescent plankton. Ninety per cent of deep-sea marine life is estimated to produce bioluminescence in one form or another – mostly in the blue and green light spectrum, the wavelength that transmits most easily through seawater. When bioluminescent plankton is present, it becomes visible with movement. Becalmed in the Timor Sea we could make out *Hope*'s underwater shape as she swayed, and a hand swirled around in the water would glow as if sprayed with fluorescent paint.

impatient but soon scolded himself for being ungrateful. This soliloquy from the log asked was he not – as the Sentimental Bloke would say,

> 'trying to grasp the shining stars from out the sky, calling the world a cheat, and trampling at the daisies at his feet ...' – each night is cool with a million stars ... a rosy sun rises each morning to start a perfect day and sets again with breathtaking beauty ... a year ago this was just a dream as I sat at my desk.

~

CJ Dennis' poetry did have its uses (even I had to admit that) and Graeme telling himself off had results; he got out his woodcarving tools and carved a beautiful fish. The fish done, I took over the tools and recreated a woodcarving I had seen in a museum in Cooktown. A traditional gift from a Norwegian bridegroom to his future wife: a chain with a spoon on one end and a fork on the other carved from *one piece of timber*. I got so engrossed carving my chain that Graeme had to take over the cooking.

And still we did not move. Eventually the ocean became completely flat, the horizon invisible, the pale sea blending seamlessly with the sky. A sphere of blue, calm and safe until one morning I was silly enough to break the bubble, diving headfirst into the sea to cool off. After swimming towards the horizon for about 50 metres I turned around and was instantly terrified. *Hope* was no longer the solid home I knew but a low streak of white brushed onto a milky sea. Sudden images of huge creatures with long tentacles rising from miles of water beneath me had me walking on water back to *Hope* – or so Graeme claimed. Wanting to touch a killer whale was one thing, trespassing into their element quite another. Happy to feel good solid planking beneath my feet again, I made do with the old way of cooling off – pouring cascades of water over myself, lifting it from the sea with a bucket, a rope tied around its handle.

※

Eventually the wind found us again and such are the vagaries of the sea, it came with a vengeance. It quickly blew into half a gale and, putting on wet weather gear, we were off again. And with the wind came heart-stopping anguish when our cat fell overboard. Jinky always looked after himself in storms and we had stopped worrying about him, but rough weather after days of calm caught him off guard. His favourite sleeping spot on top of the spray cover became unsafe, a big gust heeled us right over, and still sleeping on his cushion he slid into the sea.

'Jinky!' I screamed.

We had read enough man-overboard procedures to spring into immediate action. Stunned and silent I crouched on the foredeck – so as not to be flattened by sails and booms – my arm outstretched and pointing a finger at Jinky, never taking my eyes off his black pointy ears and white paws treading water. One blink away would have made it impossible to find him again in the rough sea. I knew I had to keep my finger pointing while Graeme manoeuvred the boat towards the spot I was pointing at. Our first run missed him, we came in too wide, but the second run was perfect. Hanging upside down with my legs curled around the handrail, I was ready to scoop him out of the water when the boat heaved up on a wave and he was unreachable, 3 metres below me. I screamed with frustration and helplessness, but Jinky had a guardian angel. The same wave swept him along the boat, taking him up past the cockpit. Graeme let go of the tiller, grabbed him and dragged him aboard.

Settling the boat back on course came first. *Hope* was okay except for a small hole in the mainsail where the roller-reefed sail had hit one of the running backstays not released quick enough in the frantic manoeuvres. Next came Jinks. He was in bad shape, barely breathing and unresponsive. We dried him off and I wrapped him in a towel and held him, talking to him constantly. 'Come on Jinky, you are a tough little sailor... come on Jinky, be brave... you can do it!' And he did, the little trooper came good. He shuddered hugely, gave a succession of deep painful sighs, and after a long nap below decks, he was up and about again.

To have him with us was a big relief; we were the old team again, happy to sail on. Our week of calm and the nightmare of nearly losing Jinky slipped behind as the trade winds continued to blow strong. For the first time, *Hope* was running under twin staysails;[7] she steered herself and we had all the free time we wanted, happy like kids let out of school. Daily runs of 140 and 160 miles brought Christmas Island almost within reach and when two days of sudden calm stopped us again we complained bitterly; we had done our time, *this was definitely not fair!*

Sitting becalmed once again, Graeme threatened to stick a knife into the mast (Old Salts used to do it to bring back the wind) but nearly in tears I begged him not to, *one must respect omens, please don't meddle with the gods, why stick a knife into Hope, it's not her fault.* He didn't, and that evening Mother

---

7   Twins are two identical staysails boomed out on either side of the boat with lines connected back to the tiller. It gave us a slow rolling ride, but was our preferred rig for running before the trade winds and up to 30 degrees into either quarter. We did not have to steer, and often both of us would turn in for the night.

Nature rewarded us with a present that shamed us both into total acceptance. Watching the drama of the blood-red sun dipping into a calm sea we suddenly noticed a tangerine moon rise on the exact opposite horizon. Looking first at one orb and then the other felt as if *Hope* was suspended in the centre of the universe, brief moments of magic that no camera could capture.

Indian Ocean islands

Christmas Island is a mountain rising from the sea, the top lopped off into a platform of roughly 19 by 14 kilometres. Broad terraces step down from a height of 300 metres, the last platform ending in almost vertical cliffs dropping straight into the sea. A mere 20 metres from shore the water reaches depths of 400 metres. We arrived after dark and tied *Hope* to a huge ship's buoy out in Flying Fish Cove. Sleep was sweet and I woke to the smell of flowers carried by the morning breeze and the sound of roosters crowing back and forth across the valley. After thirty days at sea, the sound of roosters was a novelty and I stood rapt. Graeme, ever practical, ended my reverie. 'Come on,' he said, 'breakfast time... sounds like fresh eggs to me.'

Scanning the shoreline, we saw a large freighter tied fore and aft to massive buoys, hovering under a flexible boom loading phosphate into the hold. The only landing area for us was a short jetty jutting out from a narrow pebbly beach. Heading towards it, we spotted *Sandefjord*, her stern tied up to bollards on the wharf and her bow secured to an offshore buoy sunk into unreachable depths. Helped by *Sandefjord*'s crew we soon had our lines secured in the same way, snug and safe. Apart from the noisy roosters the island seemed strangely silent. Asleep in the middle of Flying Fish Cove, we had missed the Commissioner's Ball, the year's big event. It took time for the day to blink into focus and for the revellers to surface. People apologised later for not guiding us in. 'On any other night we would have spotted you, brought you in, but you know... we were busy dancing.'

Telling someone in the sixties and seventies that we'd been to Christmas Island usually elicited a response of *which one, there are two of them aren't there?* Yes, there are two, one in the South Pacific and one in the Indian Ocean. The one we called at, the one in the Indian Ocean, is well known today. It has become an island of sprawling detention centres, of fierce political debate over boatloads of refugees arriving in the hope of beginning a life in Australia, an island of tears, hopes and tragedy. It is difficult to reconcile the differences of a few decades.

Christmas Island in 1966 was a paradise by any standard. Phosphate mining employed most of the people on the island and provided a living to shopkeepers and restaurants. Living standards were high, there were smiles wherever we went, and Australians, Chinese and Malays outdid each other in kindness. The proprietor of the Chinese photo shop cum general store refused to charge us for developing our films, and whenever I shopped he added presents: a sweet, a postcard or a tiny silk pincushion. Outside his shop stood a shelf loaded with stiff lacquered brown paper umbrellas with wooden ribs, costing a dollar each. Business peaked whenever a tropical downpour swept along the slopes, sending people into his shop to pick up a 'dollar brolly'.

The Malay workers invited us to eat at their canteen by the waterfront. We were shown into the kitchen, pot lids were lifted and I ordered: *some of this would be nice and yes, thank you, some of that would be nice too*. A risky business; there was no menu and I had no idea what I had asked for. A white opaque mound that I had assumed to be sweet pudding turned out to an almost tasteless rice jelly. I was glad for its blandness, because everything else I had selected was unbelievably spicy. Malay meals cooked for their own workers had little resemblance to anything I had eaten in restaurants before. My lips felt anaesthetised for half an hour afterwards.

~

On Christmas Island we began playing the game of *if not Sydney where would we like to live?* and the island got the thumbs up – at least for a spell of money-making. Employees of the phosphate company had good pay, nine pounds a week tropical allowance for having perfect weather, free medical, dental and hospital, free transport and cinema, cheap food, housing and tax-free goods.

We were interested in seeing the phosphate mining sites and Len and June, a young Australian couple, drove us up into the hills to show us around; a rough ride into a bleak surreal moonscape of jagged rocks scraped bare of every bit of soil containing the minerals. For me the ride was made more surreal still by my concern for heavily pregnant June. The baby was overdue, and June had happily volunteered for the drive. 'A bit of jolting will hopefully bring on the birth,' she had said with a laugh.

We would have liked to stay longer, but the weeklong calm in the Timor Sea had spooked us; we were at the tail end of the seasonal trade winds and had no time to waste. *Sandefjord* had already left for their hometown of Durban and a few days later we set sail too, bound for Cocos Island, Australia's most distant territory. Our forepeak was stacked to the deck head with parcels brought down to us by Christmas Island workers keen to send presents to their families living on

Cocos. On the last day a parcel was added, addressed *to the Yacht, from the Cocos Malays*. It contained packets of biscuits and bottles of Carlsberg pilsner, a thank you for our 'postal services'.

The rocky ride over the hills must have helped and June did have her baby before we left. Len came down to the boat to tell us the good news. Thinking he was roughing it at home we offered him a meal, but he declined. He had moved into the hospital for the week, was fed there and (so he said) slept in the bed with June, the baby in the cot next to them. Hospital regulations have loopholes for charming people, and Len was clearly one of them.

Sighting land after a spell at sea is a huge thrill, exciting and overwhelming, and the time-honoured shout of 'land hoooh' arises unconsciously, almost primeval. When I first spotted Cocos from about 10 miles off, my shout must have carried for miles. It had taken a while to be sure that the white wobbly line with a smudge of green above, barely distinguishable from the bright horizon, was definitely land. 'Hey, this is fantastic, wow look at it...' Halfway up the mast I raved on and on, while Graeme sat quietly, pleased with his navigation.

A dot in the ocean for us to explore, and sailing towards it a tantalising feast for the senses. Ever so slowly the white wobbly line sharpens into a beach topped with lacy palm fronds. Water rushes more urgently past the boat and the soft smell of the land begins to reach out. We're close and I'm up on deck now, searching for the lagoon opening, excited and jittery over leaving the safety of deep water, 'Look, there's a break in the surf, quick, give me the glasses, do you think that's the opening? ... Yes it is, it's widening out now.' We sail on another ten minutes 'just to make sure' and then it's 'Ready about!', the sails slap across, *Hope* heels over on her new course and next thing we're over the reef and into calm water.

Safely inside I relax, totally. We glide along, and the water turns from emerald to light blue and finally to the purest aqua. Low sandy islands, pinned down by tall palm trees, circle the lagoon like a glittering bracelet hugging a precious stone. We sail towards Direction Island, towards the Air/Sea Rescue Base marked by low buildings just up from the beach. To my delight, a small mound of sand topped by single palm tree trails off the end of the island, the original model for all shipwreck sailor jokes. The anchor drops and as we row ashore two bare-chested men wander down the beach to welcome us. An elaborately painted sign, nailed above the door to a corrugated iron building behind them, reads *Outcasts Atoll, No Woman Atoll, No Leave Atoll, Nuttin' Atoll*.

We have arrived. The spell is broken. The men introduce themselves, Tom and Brian; they offer us cool drinks and before long laughter and chatting fills the air; *how are you, where are you from, lovely boat you've got there*.

Wandering into the building the men tell us that it's a long weekend (*a long weekend, how strange*) and that the other five crewmembers of the rescue base have gone to West Island across the lagoon to participate in the once-a-year Cocos Island Olympics. Tom and Brian are the only people on the island, left behind as skeleton crew.

'Would you like to go to the Olympics? ... It's always a lot of fun. We'll run you across if you like.'

'No, thank you, we'd like to stay here.'

Too enchanted with what we have found, we have no desire to go anywhere.

Indian Ocean islands

We spent most evenings with Tom and Brian, four of us on the entire island, a perfect number for sitting around quietly and talking. *How are things in Australia?* A bit of cricket, a bit of chat, nothing too serious, let's not get heated, this is paradise, one must respect paradise. Brian told us about a family that had lived on the island when it was still a cable station; he missed their music. The father had taught himself and his children to play recorders, and sometimes the family would sit on their open veranda and play Baroque pieces, the clear sweet sound of four different-sized instruments floating out over the water. My imagination, always quick to run away with me, soon had me sitting on a deserted beach playing the flute for my beloved sea. *I'd love that*, I thought, *a female Peter Pan ... one day, maybe.*

But despite music and paradise, talk did occasionally move towards serious matters, towards politics and wartime experiences. Tom told us how he'd been torpedoed off Singapore and taken prisoner, how he escaped in a Malay fishing boat and how, after drifting at sea for two months, he was picked up by a German raider. A horrific tale, but Tom managed to convey it in comic low-key manliness. His stories of navy life (at least in the way he told them) would have made great material for the Goon show. *Ah, Bluebottle ... and what did you do when the naughty Germans came?*

Graeme, keenly interested, later recorded the detail of Tom's travails in the log, but all it elicited from me was the thought that *men will talk war*. Being one of the 'naughty' Germans, I tended to steer clear of political discussions, and happily slipped away to cook elaborate meals for us all. An easy task with freezers stacked to the rim with supplies flown in to the airport on West Island and ferried across to the base. We even had mushrooms; a change from the mostly tinned fare we had at sea. *Will I cook one chicken or two ... maybe fillet steak would be better ... or how about coral trout ... anyone for more ice cream?*

I was, and there were tubs full of the stuff, in all flavours.

Snorkelling the reef is part of island life, and in Cocos I was finally convinced to try it. I'm not a confident swimmer, and my niggling fear of sharks had fended off all previous coaxing. But Cocos felt different to me, safer; the water was shallow, and I believed sharks to be on the *outside* of the lagoon. Graeme coached me in the use of snorkel and mask, and with him holding my hand we slowly swam out over the reef. Enchanted by the multitude of shapes and colours beneath me, I soon let go of Graeme's hand, happily drifting over coral castles inhabited by swarms of fish in every colour. My delight over what I saw filled an entire page in my letters to Mutti. Knowing she would never experience anything like it, I described my swim in unashamed poetic excess, conjuring up images of butterfly fish parading delicately over fields of bottle-green sea cucumbers soft as velvet, of blue and red sea stars decorating the sand, and of tiny sparkly fish weaving around purple fronds like droplets of light.

Graeme's log entry tells the rest. He writes:

Jutta has caught the bug now and I'm going to have trouble keeping her out of the water.

He was right, and my pleasure in swimming in water so clear as to be invisible never ceased. Even at night the water in the Cocos lagoon remained crystalline, the full moon casting *Hope*'s shadow on the sand below. Swimming back to the boat from an evening ashore I watched my body casting shadows too; an arm reaching out drew a wriggly line, curling into a ball created a shadowy circle. Remembering how Pappi used to make birds fly across the wall by shaping his hands in front of a candle, I tried to form myself into a swooping bird, but wobbling my arms and legs about merely produced a lopsided star.

For a day and a night we shared the lagoon with *Rehu Moana*, last seen in Thursday Island. Rowing over to pay a courtesy visit, we found David Lewis ready to leave again. It seemed that having successfully made landfall using his Polynesian navigation method was enough for him. It was time to make for the next target but suddenly, almost as an afterthought, David felt that perhaps it would be a good idea if his small twin daughters had a walk ashore before they sailed. David's wife was still parked somewhere, not yet well enough to join the boat, but Priscilla, the nanny and back-up navigator, volunteered to get the girls ready. Watching the four of them get ready for a shore walk was nothing short of hilarious. The dialogue went something like this:

David: 'Should we take the girls ashore perhaps, Priscilla, do you think?'

Priscilla: 'Yes, David, I think that is a splendid idea.'

David glanced at the toddlers, naked and tanned to the colour of milk chocolate.

'Should they be wearing their sundresses, Priscilla, do you think?' he asked.

'Yes, David, I think they should,' said Priscilla.

After rummaging around a locker for a while David held up a couple of dresses and began again. 'Priscilla, which dress is Vicky's and which dress is Suzy's?'

By then I had decided that David must be the most

absent-minded person that ever sailed the seas, and it wouldn't have surprised me if his next question had been *Priscilla can you please tell me which one is Vicky and which one is Suzy?*

We left before they were ready, but watching from *Hope* we could see that the girls were duly taken for a walk along the beach. They were wearing dresses but might as well have gone naked; the beach was empty and there wasn't anybody to see them. An hour later *Rehu Moana* had sailed, and once again the most beautiful lagoon in the world was ours alone.

A few days later we also pulled up anchor with me (as always) both sad and happy to be leaving. Tom and Brian would post our mail over at West Island, among the letters congratulations for my brother, now married to his German love and proud father of a son. As a joke we also posted him a coconut, a huge thing that had just fallen off a tree, his address written directly onto the husk and the stamps painted down with varnish. *Sender: Yacht Hope, Cocos Island, Indian Ocean.*[8]

Last thing before we left, I gave Graeme a much-needed haircut. I'd been cutting his hair for years, but it was the first time I had the use of electric hair clippers hooked up to the island's generator. A novel experiment, and before I knew it Graeme had an Autobahn up the back of his head. Keeping my giggles down, I managed to fudge a punk cut of sorts around it. Not one for gazing into mirrors, Graeme wouldn't have minded that much, but when he offered to

---

[8] To the credit of the postal services worldwide, the nut arrived at Frank's place three months later, delivered by a very puzzled postman who had no idea what he was handing over.

cut my hair also, I was quick to get away just in case he did get near a mirror.

Leaving the lagoon, we talked of the people we left behind and of the charmed life they lived ... *not as good as ours but pretty good*. We also wondered why the Clunies-Ross community living on Main Island had been off limits for us. The island, one of larger 'beads' in the bracelet that makes up Cocos, had been in private ownership since 1886 when Queen Victoria granted John Clunies-Ross (also known as King of Cocos Keeling) ownership in perpetuity. His descendants upheld the claim and at the time of our visit John Cecil Clunies-Ross (Ross V) owned the island. Keen to find out more, we had imagined that carrying mail from the Christmas Island Malays for their relatives on Main Island would make a visit to the community automatic, but that wasn't so. Cruising yachts bringing mail was clearly an established ritual, because not long after our arrival a powerboat drew alongside to collect the parcels we had carried. The transfer was done in silence, no invitation was offered and not a word was exchanged. Rumours had it that not all was well in the Kingdom of Cocos.[9]

Cocos, a mere 6 metres above sea level, soon slipped below the horizon, and the sea claimed us once again. Our next port was to be the Chagos Archipelago, 1,487 miles west of Cocos – a distance we covered in 12 days and 23 hours

---

9   Twelve years later, in 1978, rumours of slavery prompted a United Nations investigation into the Clunies-Ross community, and in response to UN recommendations the Commonwealth of Australia purchased the island. I don't know how much it cost Australian taxpayers to buy a paradise from a king; it was sure to be a lot more than the fabled annual peppercorn paid by King Ross V to the Crown.

at an average of 115 miles per day, duly recorded by my keen-on-percentages navigator husband. The wind was behind us and for the first few days *Hope* sailed herself under twin sails, rolling along like a drunk. I got horribly seasick and when that eased up, a migraine followed. I blamed it on good Cocos Island living, ice creams galore, drinks and rich food, which was probably correct. Me (and my bucket) stayed wedged in with cushions on the cabin floor, the area where the motion is least, and for a time I wouldn't have cared had I died.

I surfaced eventually, but the seas continued to be rough. One dark night huge waves from astern began throwing green water at us. Up until then the large spray dodger over *Hope*'s companionway had allowed us to keep the cockpit doors and the main hatch open,[10] but on that wild night everything had to be closed. I didn't like being stuck below, inactive and unseeing and everything shut. Hearing the fierce wind and not feeling it felt weird. Feeling anxious, I tried to let go, let my mind drift beyond our tiny cabin and watch *Hope* from high up, safely carving a path through dark water...

...There she is, brave old *Hope*, confidently surging through wild waters, the light from the masthead streaks her twin sails. Waves crash over her but she marches on, determinedly, her mast sticking out of a sea of foam ... she is good, she is strong. Below decks I make out a dry warm oblong of yellow space and the two of us wedged into narrow bunks, our faces barely visible in the glow of the kerosene lamp, safe from the elements...

My imagery worked for a while, but then the thought of

---

[10] A spray dodger is a custom-made waterproof cover, in the manner of a hood over a baby's pram, arched over the companionway. It allowed us to keep the main hatch open and gave protection from the wind and spray in the cockpit.

leaving *Hope* to battle it out on her own got the better of me. Resolutely putting on oilskins and gumboots I went up and sat in the cockpit, careful to shut hatch and doors behind me. Actually seeing and feeling what was happening, and the occasional drenching, was far better than the inactivity of being locked up below. It must have been a rough night because Jinky, always the first to hold his post on deck, declined to join me. *He is turning into a sook*, I thought – *either that or he has more sense than I.*

Two days later heaven returned. Flying fish jumped clear of the water, gliding long distances on shimmering wings – 50 metres, sometimes more. Every so often one would hit our sails and land on deck with a *plop*. Jinky had learned that *'plop'* meant manna from heaven, and raced along the deck to pounce on his prey before the next wave could wash the hapless creature back into the sea.

On calmer nights, when *Hope* sailed herself and both of us were asleep below, Jinky came up with another trick. Proud of his first catch of the night, he would jump below, drop the wriggly thing onto the carpet and meow loudly until we woke up. Switching on a torch one of us would lean over the edge of bunk, inspect the fish and praise him: 'Wow Jinks, that's beautiful … well done, now back in the cockpit and eat it.' Luckily, praise for his first catch was enough. I have no idea how many more fish he ate in a night because in the morning there was neither bone nor wing to be found, only a very round cat, sleeping.

For a yacht to meet a ship in mid-ocean is rare, but on this leg of our journey we saw two. First, a large Japanese fishing boat spotted us and came for a closer look, the crew lined up on deck waving and taking photographs. We held up our Australian flag to let them know where we had come from, and a lot of shouting and chatter followed. What an amazing sight we must have been, and how sad that we would never get to see the photographs they took.

The next encounter (and possible batch of unseen photographs) happened the day after, Thursday 13 October 1966, late in the afternoon. We were both below, me sewing and Graeme playing his guitar, when he jokingly said, 'Time for our ship, go and have a look.' 'Okay,' I said, and looking out the hatch I shouted, 'It's there! Quick, quick, get the flag book!' A British freighter of about 6,000 tons, travelling in the opposite direction, had slowed down to look. The ship was quite close, the crew on deck shouting. Once again we did the Australian flag routine, having first grabbed T-shirts to cover our nakedness. Graeme flipped furiously through our flag book and deciphered the MKC – BCG message. It meant *do you require – anything?* Immensely proud that we needed nothing, nothing at all, Graeme hoisted our No flag. More shouting and waving, the ship gave a long hoot and took off again. It was hard to settle down again after that. I loved the flags, so beautifully old-fashioned, like sending smoke signals.

Diego Garcia atoll in the Chagos Archipelago, 17 square miles in size, had far more land area than the narrow ring of islands that make up Cocos, but the drama of entering the lagoon, the gentle lift of ocean swell pushing us over the reef, and the invisible water beyond charmed me anew. Our visit was especially moving. News had already leaked out that the island was to become a USA military base, would soon contain an airstrip and become a hub of planes and military hardware. The islanders – willing or not – would be 'relocated' and access to the atoll restricted. We had come at a time when it was still a largely unknown, out-of-the-way place and were well aware how fortunate we were just to sail in, no Customs and no controls, just a few curious onlookers.

But all was not well in paradise. Dropping the anchor off a little settlement, we couldn't help noticing a faintly cloying, acrid smell. Not entirely unpleasant, but certainly not the normal clean, breezy island smell. We found out later that a week before our arrival the copra storehouse near the water's edge had been torched, destroying an entire season's crop – hence the strange smell. Harold, the plantation manager, a Frenchman from the Seychelles, told us that he had locked up the two men accused of the crime. The next supply ship would take the men to the Seychelles to be charged. Harold wasn't sure if the revolt was due to the planned airbase or some other dispute.

Around 1,500 native Chagossians lived on the island, their ranks swelled by 300 workers recruited from the Seychelles and Mauritius to help harvest the coconuts. Harold drove us along rough tracks winding through the plantations to show us around. Huge black men, their arms reminiscent of oversized bronze statues, worked beside mountains of coconuts piled high like medieval cannon balls. With unbelievable speed and accuracy and hands like vice grips the men would pick up a nut (still in its husk) and beat it down onto a steel spike fixed into the ground. Moments later the nut would fly in one direction and the husk in the other. The nuts were loaded onto trucks, and the husks taken away by women and children carrying huge loads in baskets on top of their heads. Each man de-husked as many as one thousand coconuts a day; two nuts per minute for an eight-hour shift without a break. No wonder their arms were huge.

By comparison Harold and his wife, Odette, lived like royalty. That night we were invited to dinner at their house, a cool bungalow with tall ceilings and French-style doors and shutters. After drinks on the veranda, dinner was served indoors, the four of us sitting around a large table for what turned out to be an all-night feast. A male Creole servant brought in the first course on a large silver platter and as the guest of honour I was first to be served. Bending over, the servant reverently held the platter in front of me and I looked at a whole baked fish beautifully arranged on a bed of fried breadfruit. *Lovely, but what do I do with it?* Was this whole fish for me? ... Was everybody getting one like it? ... How was I going to get this thing onto my plate? The manager noticed my confusion and leaning across, he picked up the silver serving spoons, pushed the skin of the fish aside, scooped up a couple of spoonfuls of juicy pink flesh and put it on my plate. After that the platter made the rounds and everybody else did the same.

After the fish came chicken, pork, sauces in different colours; more chicken, another salad and in between, servings of fruits peeled and cut into bite size pieces. Without their skin it was hard to tell what they were, sweet juicy morsels that tasted like melon or papaya. Different wines were served to sustain our appetite and help our digestion along, and by the time we arrived at coffee and liqueurs it was well into the small hours.

Compared to the exquisite food, the conversation was clumsy. Harold spoke in halting English and Graeme's schoolboy French wasn't a great deal better, but augmented with a lot of gesturing, we got to understand the manager's troubles. Too much drink on the island, too much anger, too much discontent, people wanted more... The arson attack had scared him. His wife Odette dared not leave the house. *Could you please take a report to the plantation's Director in Mahé in the Seychelles?* The next supply ship wasn't due for two months.

A couple of days later we got a more candid view of island life when one of the workers came down to the boat to chat with us. We had tied up to a little wharf by then, and sitting on the wooden planks dangling his legs, he chatted away in English; he had learned the language serving in the British army. Native to Mauritius he was near the end of a two-year contract, happy enough because he had his wife and child with him. He felt the pay was reasonable, three-quarters of his wages withheld to be paid as a lump sum at the end of his contract. It was fine with him, would give him a good start when he got home. The workers were given an allowance of one pint of wine per week. Not enough, he said, and illegal liquor was brewed from beans, lentils and even potato peel.

Out for a walk along the plantation road one evening, we stumbled onto a drinking party – men, women and children dancing around a fire to the sound of drums. One of the dancers spotted us, motioned for us to come closer, and threading our way through the undergrowth we joined the group. About half a dozen men played tambourines of different sizes, some nearly a metre across, in a steady hypnotic beat that never stopped. Even when one of the players temporarily moved away to tighten the drum-skin over the fire, another man would step into his place or someone within the group would fill the void with a powerful solo.

Our presence seemed to make little difference although

the women, suddenly self-conscious, began to withdraw to the outer circle. But the men kept playing and dancing, trying to get us to join in. Men were teaching small children not yet old enough to walk to pick up the steps, guiding them with arms grown huge from husking coconuts. I thought of the manager's fear, the burnt copra store, and felt uncomfortable. Silver dishes and imported wines one night and naked poverty the next. What would these people be thinking of us? They didn't seem angry, a little sad perhaps, but on one score the manger was right. Everybody was drinking and with a meagre allowance of one pint of wine per week, this was sure to be home brew. *So what*, I thought, on that night at least all it seemed to do was bring out their immense capacity to laugh and be carried away by their music.

We left Diego Garcia knowing that hundreds of years of settlement would soon be over, and its people dispersed. No more coconut industry. No more dancing and laughing. The plantation manager and his wife were hoping to emigrate to Australia, and we wished them well. As a farewell present they had sent us a basket of fruit and vegetables and in return we gave them a photograph of *Hope*, a thank-you note written on the back of it. And at the last minute, ready to cast off, one of Odette's servants rushed down to the wharf with another present: a roast chicken and a dish of millionaire's salad – the salad called thus because a young palm tree must be felled for its 'heart' to be cut out and prepared in coconut milk.

I love living in the 21st century as much as I loved living in the 1960s, and sitting detached on my flying carpet I have excellent views of both. I can see how extraordinary it was to sail *Hope* at the very edge of an era that would bring instant communication and computers that link up just about everything. I can see how today's global outlook has fuelled competition among adventurers, how one achievement is weighed up against another. Satisfying the commercial interests of corporate sponsors has entered the equation to help adventurers achieve their daring feats. And while money does not provide the courage to climb a tall mountain, or sail a nutshell across an ocean, it forces a strong outward focus onto the adventure. The explorer trades freedom for accountability, the need to report, and possibly accept instructions. It would have destroyed much of what was precious to me. I liked setting my own course, free of expectations and responsibilities. It would have spoiled the secrecy and snug isolation of the two of us alone on a tiny boat, trusting and relying on each other totally. Time took on a different meaning. Long stretches between islands and continents gave a hint of a Robinson Crusoe existence. Questions could wait for answers and 'keeping in touch' was strictly on my terms.

Graeme and I had our disagreements, but I believe we never fought at sea. Out in the deep blue, *Hope* and the sea ruled; we were merely servants and whatever was demanded of us made up the framework of our daily lives. We had few rules, we didn't need discipline; love and tolerance did away with notions of entitlement or prerogative. In the daytime we looked after things as needed and the hours of darkness were divided into four watches of three hours each. I liked sunsets and Graeme preferred sunrises, which automatically had me take first and third watch. It gave me an easier deal because Graeme would often stay up to watch the sunset with me. Sitting in the cockpit in gathering darkness, we cradled mugs of tea or coffee and talked until darkness took over. I read one account of a couple crossing the Tasman Sea in a tiny boat and like me the wife got horribly seasick, yet her husband insisted that she'd take her turn. If she could manage half an hour, her husband would take half an hour; if she managed fifteen minutes, he would take fifteen minutes. I felt sorry for both of them; they had clearly missed the lesson of give-and-take so amply taught by the sea.

I didn't mind night watches. The time might go fast or slow, happy or sad, a bit of a lottery really. Three hours alone with the sea gave my thoughts the freedom to wander. The third, middle-of-the-night watch was especially intimate. A dream I had before coming on watch might linger and have me wondering what it meant. I'd sing to myself, make plans, 'talk' to friends or mull over half-forgotten incidents.

One night I thought of the time when, as a 10-year-old, I was asked to recite Friedrich Schiller's *Die Bürgschaft* in front of my entire class. The scene slid into focus with surprising clarity, the smell of chalk, the teacher standing by the tall windows, everybody looking at me from row after row of wooden benches. I loved that poem, knew it by heart but did not want to share it. I knew I would cry at the end, when it gets sad...

The poem is about the deep friendship between two men. One gets caught trying to assassinate the cruel king and is to be hanged for his crime. Brought before the king for sentencing, he begs for three days of freedom to facilitate the marriage of his sister and offers to leave his best friend behind as bailsman. The king agrees. The man takes off to absolve his honourable duty. Three days later he rushes back to release his friend, but everything turns against him. A storm hits, a river turns into a torrent, a bridge is swept away, robbers assail him, but finally, at sundown with only minutes to spare, he reaches the market square. The hanging rope has already been put around his friend's neck and, crying, he rushes up to embrace him shouting 'Stop, it's me that has to be hanged!' The king can't believe his eyes and, deeply moved, pardons the friends and begs to be included in their friendship also.

Predictably (as the 10-year-old me had correctly guessed) I had begun to choke up when the friends embrace each other, but I managed to race stony-faced through to the last stanzas and quickly sat down. Now, out at sea, I decided to give Schiller his due and do a proper recital. It needed a couple of nights to piece the many verses together, but finally I had it all in order. Speaking aloud into wind and sea I began:

Zu Dyonys, dem Tyrannen, schlich Damon
den Dolch im Gewande

...and this time around, when I got to the end the 10-year-old in me cried openly, while the 24-year-old woman I had grown into was happy for the reminder that integrity carries its own reward.

Daylight invariably wiped away the dramas of the night. *How is the bread holding out ... should I make pancakes for breakfast, do we have enough eggs left? Must check on the water...* but at night, like an addict climbing into different realms, I would again allow myself to dwell on scenes and incidents buried deep within me. Since my sessions with Adrian, I no longer fought off dark images but went along with them and actively tried to piece together information, match visions and voices.

On the way to Mahé I thought about my family a lot. My brother, in a letter to Cocos Island, had asked me to be godmother for their son ... should they wait with the christening until we got there? His question meant that rather than hinting at it, I now had to own up that we had changed our plans. We would not be sailing to Germany via the Suez Canal and the Mediterranean, as originally planned, but would sail south around the Cape of Good Hope and then on to South America. Instead of arriving in two months' time, it was likely to be another two years before we would meet again. I knew Frank would be okay with it – somebody would stand in for my godmotherly duties – but Mutti might be upset.

In one of my night watches I wrote to her, crouched in the cockpit by the small light of the compass. I gave her many reasons: we didn't want to leave *Hope* 'all on her own' in England for the winter; our original idea of taking the boat through Europe's inland waterways was impossible because *Hope* had too much draft; the Arab–Israeli conflict was building up, threatening to close the Suez Canal; selling *Hope* in Florida would free us to spend more time in Germany; we might even work there, stay a year, or longer.

All valid reasons, but I left out the main one: I didn't want to go home. I didn't miss Mutti, not yet, not then; if anything it was the opposite. In my nightly reveries anger for Mutti had boiled over more than once. The serious, overly responsible child in me had become my fellow traveller. I listened to her, gave her a voice, allowed myself to remember Mutti's frightening rages, her tears, threats and frustrations. How, after her fights with Pappi, I had helped her pack things into cardboard boxes 'to go away', shaking with fear that she would leave me behind. How an hour later she'd calm down and I would help her unpack again with both of us crying; her in frustration and me with relief because she had nowhere to go. Pappi was *so difficult*. I was *her girl*, her confidante, she said things I couldn't understand, told me that she couldn't go on ... had nothing more to give. Sick with fear I worried that she would kill herself; she'd threatened it often enough. The man next door had hung himself on a washing line tied to a stairway just like ours... the neighbours said he couldn't go on any more ... When Mutti was upset I stuck to her like a shadow and watched her constantly.

In dark nights, afloat on the ocean, my adult brain understood that there was no more need for my childish anguish. I recognised how long ago it had all happened, how difficult those years had been, but taking so much care in writing my *sorry we're not coming* letter to Mutti made me realise how responsible I still felt for her, still her keeper, still worried about her survival. I loved her, tried not to blame her, but I was no longer willing to override my hurt, nor the righteous little voice within that bellowed the occasional *how could she do that to a little girl?* I wanted more time, more distance and a lot more of the freedom I had tasted ... distant horizons and sailing where the wind took us. Africa would be great!

~

And here is the voice of the Captain, written up in the log after one of his night watches:

Monday 31st Oct. 1966
I am in love with the world, and very, very happy and content with my lot. We have been steering these last two nights and will be until we get to Mahé ... but even this is enjoyable with the cool nights, soft wind and the full moon. Little Hope *is averaging 4½ knots with almost no motion at all – just enough to soothe the feelings, a gentle swinging motion.*

Reading his entry in the morning I hugged him, loved him; happy for him, happy for me and happy for us.

※

With my heart open and so much love swirling around, it wasn't surprising that the little bird streaming silken banners came to visit me again. We weren't far off Mahé when it happened and this time it carried no banner, gave no message but simply overtook me with a huge gust of lightness, a jolt and a mighty *whoosh*. It happened on a sunny morning; a good breeze had *Hope* rolling along over blue seas decorated with white curly tops when suddenly without warning my mind became profoundly still, slipping easily into a dimension free from thought, bare of wanting, judging or feeling, not blank but vibrant with a different intensity, wide open to unending space. I was sitting on deck at the time, washing tea towels in a bucket, and neither frightened nor amazed I continued my task, totally absorbed into a world that had lost all markers and margins.

The experience lasted five, perhaps ten minutes, it's hard to know, but it felt as if for a small space of time I tasted heaven, not offering more but simply suffusing me with total and absolute knowing that everything is perfect exactly as it is. I can only define those minutes as a glimpse of what I imagine Enlightenment might be like. It changed me, triggered my search for meaning and my need for a spiritual dimension, all the usual terms we humans use to try and describe the way we go about satisfying a longing for union, for freedom and peace within.

The Seychelles

Sailing towards Port Victoria, on the main island of Mahé, felt like travelling into an over-the-top film set. The night had been calm, the sea dark and still, and *Hope* moved along gently in the faintest of breezes. Befitting the mood, dawn lit up a cloudless sky in gentle watercolours ranging from clear dove grey high above us to the deepest apricot near the sea. Small and large rounded islands stood black against the richly coloured horizon and to haunt us further, less than a mile away a three-masted barquentine crossed our path, moving effortlessly under full sail.[11] *Were we in the right century ... were we dreaming?*

Enchantment vanished with the rising sun. The wind disappeared and flapping sails and banging booms soon had us annoyed and frustrated. Mahé was close, clearly visible, and suddenly impatient we motored the last few miles into Port Victoria. Racing around I made everything neat and tidy; bedding rolled up, dishes put away, wash down the decks, put on clean clothes. We took pride in arriving shipshape, boat and crew alike. Dropping anchor in the outer harbour,

---

11 A sailing vessel with three or more masts, with a square-rigged foremast, gaff-rigged for mizzen and any other masts. Barquentines were popular at the end of the 19th century.

our yellow quarantine flag hoisted up at the crosstrees, we awaited the authorities for Customs and medical clearance.

It looked a snug harbour, with lush green hills dotted with low, red-roofed houses rising gently around the more densely populated harbour foreshore. Looking through binoculars we picked out coastal ships, trading schooners and a few yachts tied up to large timber wharf. The doctor was the first person to step aboard, ferried across by a port worker in an open motorboat. He briefly looked at us (two fit and tanned sailors smiling from ear to ear) insulted Jinky by asking if we had rats on board (of course not) and the medical clearance was done. After ticking the boxes on his forms he let go of officiousness, relaxed and got chatty, *how had our trip been ... where were we headed ... what was Australia like?* Still curious about the barquentine we had seen a few hours earlier, we asked him whether such a ship had left port that morning. He wasn't sure but suggested it may have been the *Verona* from Panama. Graeme and I looked at each other: we hadn't been dreaming, how marvellous to have seen it.

With a friendly salute the doctor made way for the customs officer arriving in another motorboat. *Hope*, like the *Queen Mary*, was a British-registered vessel, her Ship's Papers documenting her homeport, tonnage, passenger list, and so on. As Captain and First Mate of the ship we required no visa and simply had our passports stamped. The ship carried no duty-free goods, but we declared our firearms. Graeme had felt it necessary to have a pistol and a rifle aboard and both were duly sealed into our duty-free locker. To appease conventions and obey the rules we had selected one of the forward bunk storage areas as our duty-free locker, our private little joke because although the locker had a door to seal, it was also accessible by lifting up the bunk boards above it. 'What's the point of locking up a pistol?' Graeme said. 'We're not gonna use it at sea, are we?'

At one of the Thursday Island parties George Cole from *Galinule* had described the Seychelles as 'a very beautiful place where old Englishmen go to die'. My English, fluent enough by then to tackle books in that language, had conjured up images of jolly old men and their well-dressed wives sitting contentedly in cool houses with wide verandas drinking tea, or perhaps an early finger of Scotch, reading an old *London Times*. We found no such scenes, but to give George Cole his due, distinguished English retirees may well have been resting far up in the green hills.

A British colony since 1812 and under French rule before that, the Seychelles were a busy crossroad for sea traffic with ships (and yachts) heading to and from Asia and the Suez Canal or west towards Kenya. In contrast to other places we'd called at, we weren't wined and dined; everybody was busy. French influence was undeniable, the population a mix of English- and patois-speaking Seychellois, the previously mentioned English expatriates and well-to-do French.

Delivering Harold's Diego Garcia arson report to the copra plantation manager gave us a glimpse into the upper echelon of French society. After introducing ourselves and explaining the situation we had expected some reaction, a bit of dismay perhaps, but he seemed unconcerned, disinterested, worlds away from harsh copra-harvesting reality. Briefly flipping through the report before passing it on to his secretary, he turned his radiant smile on us and invited us to attend a cocktail party at his house that very evening. 'I will send a car for you,' he added in his heavily accented English.

'How lovely, thank you.'

I was excited. *What on earth will I wear to a French cocktail party?* We were duly picked up in the early evening, but the party turned out to be a dull affair and a most uncomfortable evening for me. The manager's home was large and sumptuous with low couches, low tables, huge flower arrangements and beautiful Persian rugs. Wide windows framed postcard scenes of tropical splendour. People moved about chatting animatedly, while looking elegantly bored at the same time. The women wore daringly short, slinky cocktail dresses; some had opted for long trailing gowns. I felt – and was – totally out of place, an exhibit for simple wholesome living, dressed in a simple linen shift, pink-cheeked, under-made-up, my hair untamed and sun-bleached. On top of it I was mute. I didn't speak French, and apart from the manager nobody made an effort to try their English. Servants brought endless trays of food, bowls of julienned breadfruit, deep-fried like potato chips, among them. I loved those but must have taken good helpings off the champagne tray as well. Apart from my acute discomfort I remember little of the evening.

Hanging out with other yachties, swapping stories and making trips into the lushly forested hills was a lot more fun. Still without an airport, Mahé was largely free of the modern fixtures so much part of the tourist trade. Women offered to do our washing, to be soaped and slapped over the rocks of a nearby stream. And while Mahé must have had running water, the outlying areas certainly did not. Walking high up into the hills, we came across a remarkably efficient network of water pipes made of split bamboo. The water ran along one length of pipe before dropping down into the next, little guided waterfalls, each one bringing water further down the mountain. I didn't even question if it was safe enough to drink; I just knew it was.

Renegaat, last seen in Thursday Island, was also in port, ready to head off for the Suez Canal. Jim and Rob, the two

Aussie crewmembers, were still aboard, still grumbling about bossy Pam. Not long now, England was close. Jim, an architect, had a job lined up in London and Rob, still keen to start a diving business, would look for another crewing job. One morning *Barlevento*, a 65-foot American yacht more than twice the size of *Hope*, arrived. Her powerful engine and large crew stretched the concept of cruising yacht, yet three of her crew, Nick, Jeanie and Tom, turned out to be true yachties, seasoned travellers hitching a ride on whatever yacht would take them. We became friends and would go out in a group, happily fielding the noisy banter from Seychellois streets vendors. *Oh, you come here and eat, best food for best sailors ... good fish curry ... very fresh.* The food was delicious, variations of rice and curry in a delicate blend of spices, often cooked in coconut milk.

Growing up in Germany, followed by migration to Australia (where the 'White Australia' policy was still in place), had kept me in the company of white Anglo-Saxon people. Apart from reading about it I was a newcomer to colonial life, surprised how readily goodwill was extended towards rulers and visitors alike. Happy-go-lucky islanders, their risqué jokes and easy laughter, were new to me, a new experience.

But walking towards town one afternoon I wondered whether I might have got the 'goodwill towards visitors' wrong. Standing by the side of the dirt road were three women chatting, one of them carrying a small baby. I was about to stop, offer a friendly hello and admire the baby, when one of the women began to urinate. She wore a loose cotton dress and peed standing up, her legs apart, the vertical yellow stream sinking into the sandy verge of the road. Deeply shocked, I hastily walked past. *Can anyone really be that uninhibited as to simply pee whenever the need arises, or is this an insult?*

But when someone told me the story of Angie, I decided that the woman by the roadside probably just needed to pee.

We'd already met Angie, a very pretty Seychellois woman hanging out at the marina, enamoured with visiting yachtsmen. She wasn't a prostitute – one of our sailor friends moved in with her for the time of his stay and she never asked for money. Angie wanted a good time, to be adored, and our friend must have filled that need perfectly. I know, because when his yacht left, Angie was heartbroken. It took half a bottle of our medicinal brandy to dry her tears. Sadly, after the brandy afternoon she attached herself to us, following us wherever we went. A solution was offered by one of the local men. 'Just slip into the Coco Bar on your way to town,' he said. 'She's not allowed in there.'

Angie was barred from the Coco Bar not for reasons of race or colour, but because she had misbehaved. Apparently, she had started an argument, could not be silenced and was finally asked to leave. 'Okay,' she had yelled, 'I'll go!' Walking tall on high heels she'd marched to the middle of the empty dance floor, raised her skirt, squatted down, peed, and left in silent protest. What a statement! My German mind, crammed with propriety and well-mannered upbringing, boggled.

And still we hadn't met any Englishmen, not in the hills, nor trading on Main Street, but finally, on our last day, one appeared and this person I would rather not have met. Ready to sail for Mombasa we had posted our letters, topped up the water tanks, stacked our supply of fruit and vegies and had obtained port clearance for *Hope*. Last thing we hauled the dinghy aboard, to be lashed upside down over the skylight. Everything was almost done when, suddenly, a man came running down the marina telling us not to leave because a hurricane was on its way. Having delivered his message he disappeared again, leaving us perplexed. *A hurricane, really?*

Unusual for this time of the year. Who was this man? We had seen him before, an odd chap, living on a run-down boat further down the marina. Just to make sure, we went ashore to check with the harbourmaster, but everyone started laughing. 'You must have been talking to Hurricane Harvey,' they said. 'If there's a hurricane somewhere he'll find it.' Harvey was an amateur radio buff who loved to track hurricanes.

Graeme thought it funny, but I wasn't amused. *Not a good omen*, I thought, *silly man nearly scared the wits out of me*. Reassured (or semi-reassured in my case) we got ready once more. Always an exciting time, and like any other boat leaving port, *Hope* invariably drew a crowd of onlookers. Children seemed to come from nowhere and people we'd never met offered to undo our mooring lines. *Renegaat* had already left for the Suez Canal, but our Californian friends from *Barlevento* wandered over to wish us fair winds, drawling a casual *see you in Mombasa*. Jinky, quick to pick up on the 'we are leaving' vibe, had installed himself in the cockpit, proud and impervious to any comments. *Here, Puss Puss* wasn't for him. Our little sphinx was looking ahead, calmly ignoring the shouts of good luck following us down the harbour.

But luck did not come our way, and the last leg of our Indian Ocean crossing was dismal. There were times when we would have welcomed a mini 'Harvey' hurricane to get us moving. An unseasonably early shift of trade wind had us sitting in the doldrums – the calm belt between trade winds – and it took 28 days to sail 965 miles. We had been becalmed before, notably the long spell in the Timor Sea on our way to Christmas Island. Back then we had managed to make 'not moving' into a relaxing time, a pleasant experience with little turtles paddling past and the two of us toasting beautiful sunsets with glasses of wine. Inching our way to Kenya had nothing peaceful about it. The sea was confused, often grey, didn't know which way to run and formed itself into little peaks like the tops on a meringue pie. Strong currents against us halved our sailed distance and total calm alternated with fierce 30-knot squalls. One night it rained so hard that a plastic bucket left on deck filled up with water. At one point, wet and dripping from the last near-horizontal onslaught, Graeme worked out that we needed another sixty-eight squalls to cover the distance to Kenya. I'll let the log speak:

Friday, 18th Nov. 1966
We have little wind ... but a choppy sea, then a squall comes: down with the Yankee jib, up with the small jib, maybe roll a reef or two in the main, close the hatch and the skylight. The squalls are generally 30 knots from the west, i.e. straight on the nose. We sail like hell for half an hour, wet and cold, and when the thing is past we have made good maybe three miles. For the first time since we left Sydney we are both getting depressed. Here we are, 12 days out of Mahé, and have made a bare 270 miles.

Jinky, our little comedian, did his best to cheer us up:

Flat calm [again] we doused all sail and went to bed – but had not been there for more than half an hour when there was a commotion up on deck ... I was halfway out the hatch when I collided with Jinky coming down with a bird twice his size in his mouth. The bird escaped in the cabin and we had quite a chase until Jutta captured Jinky, I threw a blanket over the bird and got it outside again ... Jinky sulked the rest of the night.

The Seychelles

Saturday 19th Nov. 1966
Today's run was 16 miles, Hurrah! At this rate we might have the good fortune to spend Christmas at sea between Mahé and Mombasa ... we have beautiful trade wind clouds all around us, but no trade winds. But as Jinky suggests, one can't have the bird and eat it.

Monday 21st Nov 1966
We just can't get any westing. The wind is against us, the current is against us and our daily runs never seem to add up to more than 20 miles. For the last 4 days we have been running through 'funny' waters. Every few miles or so we sail through a choppy belt of water that looks as if it's boiling. We can't quite figure out what it is ... there does not seem to be a system, or explanation.

Thursday 24th November 1966
Conditions are still the same ... Yesterday was the worst of all. From boiling hot sunshine to wet and chilly, from flat calm to squalls that required 3 rolls in the main all was on the menu. Today the only thing gone wrong (so far) is that all of Jinky's food has gone mildewy and now the poor cat is lying on the forward bunk crying. We'd better trail a fishing line.

Wednesday 30th November 1966
We have been at sea for 16 days now and I don't know where the time went. We seem to exist in a world of calms, squalls, rain, gales, current against us, long and miserable night watches, more squalls and more rain ... but it does not get us mad any longer. We have started to collect rainwater and also keep a very thorough watch on our food so that we won't run out of too many things. Sugar, flour, metho [for lighting the Primus stove], *eggs will be short. All fruit and vegetables are finished ... the tinned stuff is rationed, as*

well as the five remaining bars of barley sugar ... I have started to occupy my time with wood carving again. This time it's a little box of teak, a present for Graeme to keep his cufflinks in ... a ridiculous thought, white shirt and cufflinks on Graeme ... I can see him sitting in teeming rain, his oilskin deep over his face ready for the next squall.

Thursday the 8th of December 66
At sea for 24 days. We are 68% of the way there and have 300 miles to go ... Today is Mutti's birthday. Poor Mutti will be worried. I wish there was a way of letting her know that things are all right ... Conditions on board are getting a bit low. My rash is getting worse and is spreading down my legs, and Graeme has [sun] burned his bottom and can't sit down. The stores are low on the more pleasing things and also on some of the essentials.

Hope has been a good girl. She has steered herself nicely on a broad reach under full main, one of the twins as a staysail and the yankee. Two nights ago at 0200 in the morning we saw a freighter ... almost on collision course ... he must have seen our topmast light and altered course. We are very pleased because we have often wondered if ships would see us at night.

And finally, after nearly a month at sea:

Monday 12th of December 66
Land ho!! And a lot of land it is too, a whole big continent ... Great plans are being made aboard, the most important one being that we will eat out tonight, if at all possible ... Our food rationing has been well organised and discipline was held on both sides. Graeme will have the last spoon of sugar in his coffee this morning. We could afford half a pint of milk each with our porridge and sweeten it with the last of the honey ...

Africa – a whole new continent

Our arrival in Mombasa coincided with Kenya's third anniversary of Independence. We had sailed into a national holiday and the party of the year. Everybody was out celebrating and until we realised what was happening it was almost scary. *Why were there so many people about?* As soon as we stepped ashore we were surrounded like celebrities, with everybody keen to meet us. And to top it off we had *almost* received an even higher welcome. As we rowed ashore, people in the yacht club had watched President Jomo Kenyatta travel down Kilindini Harbour as part of the Independence celebrations. Spotting *Hope* anchored of the yacht club, flying her red ensign and the Kenyan courtesy flag high up off the crosstrees, the captain slowed the presidential boat and brought her alongside to hail us. It was assumed that President Kenyatta must have wanted to meet us. It was as well that we weren't there to meet him, I doubt that under the circumstances we would have recognised him.

The yacht club, still very British, awarded us honorary membership and food and drink appeared as if by magic. Being such 'jolly fine sailors' made it implicit that we were looked after, constantly. Everything was arranged for us and after sending a short telegram to my mother (ALL OK STOP LETTER FOLLOWS) we were free to dive into the pre-Christmas social whirl.

Tom, Nick and Jeanie, our friends on *Barlevento*, arrived a few days later. Our atrocious crossing still vivid in our memory, we were keen to find out how their trip from the Seychelles had been; how had they fared in the difficult conditions? *What difficult conditions?* A naive question. *Barlevento* had a powerful engine and large diesel tanks and had motored through it all in a matter of days. A flash of jealousy hit me, but it only took a moment's reflection to return me back to an even keel. *Hope* was my boat. I did not want to travel on a huge yacht motoring noisily through the oceans when the wind ran out, wouldn't enjoy sailing in the company of a rich American family, their precocious 10-year-old son, a permanent Tongan crew and a changing guard of men and women sailors picked up in ports along the way. I liked the closeness, the intimacy of our journey; let it take time, we had time and plenty of it. Graeme and I had crossed an ocean entirely under sail. We were a team, captain and first mate, husband and wife, happy with each other and our valiant *Hope*. As the Australian saying goes, *I wouldn't want to change it for quids.*

Just in time for Christmas two more yachts arrived; Peter and Roger aboard the Trimaran *Nimble Days* sailing home to South Africa from England, and Ken, a Rhodesian whom we had briefly met in the Seychelles. Ken had lost his crew in Mahé and had no choice but to sail on single-handedly. *Good*, I thought nastily, *and may you sail single-handed forever*. Ken wasn't my favourite person after he told me how easy bachelor life had been for him in Rhodesia. He'd had a servant who cooked, washed and cleaned for him. 'A good worker,' he boasted, 'but by God she was ugly ... I couldn't stand looking at her and paid her extra to be out of the house by the time I got home.' *Arrogant bastard*, I thought, *look who is ugly.* Every family has a black sheep, and the cruising family is no exception.

The visiting yachties (minus ugly Ken who was above such things) pitched in to organise the yacht club's children's Christmas party. Taking *Hope* around the point, where the children couldn't see us, we dressed the boat in all her flags, got ourselves dressed up too and slowly motored back and dropped anchor off the club at the appointed time. Father Christmas (Graeme) in traditional red fur-lined outfit rowed ashore in one dinghy, followed by a fleet of dinghies carrying King Neptune (we had fashioned a marvellous gold paper-covered staff from a boathook) and a band of bearded pirates. Jeanie and I were in mermaid tails, fashioned from tightly wound sarongs, and had to be carried ashore, giggling and huge-eyed with iridescent eye shadow and lashes painted to the eyebrows. Pirate Kaeli, a big Tongan man crewing on *Barlevento*, looked the most striking. He was a very large man and Jeanie and I had covered him in lipstick scars and tied little red bows into his jet-black beard.

About forty children and their parents clapped and cheered as the fleet landed and made their way up to the yacht club lawn. For a time even the big kids seemed baffled; they didn't recognise any of us, hadn't met us before ... *could this really be Father Christmas?* King Neptune (Nick), magnificently dressed in white cut-off jeans and an array of multi-coloured sarongs, frightened the smaller kids by using his knife to make cuts in the corners of Father Christmas' mouth – the white flowing beard didn't leave enough of an opening for Santa to drink his beer, which *Ho, Ho, Ho*, he badly needed, coming all the way from the North Pole. The first beer had not reached his thirsty lips but had cascaded down behind his fake beard, frothing cold and tickly down his bare chest; the mermaids were not the only ones to giggle. The pirates did an excellent job of pulling everybody in line, fiercely demanding to know if behaviour had been good. Then Father Christmas got tough too and wouldn't hand out presents until 'Jingle Bells', 'Away in a Manger' and 'Rudolph the Red-nosed Reindeer' had been sung. I got a fair idea what Graeme's childhood Christmases must have been like; he was clearly getting his own back.

Beyond the boundaries of the elite yacht club, in the streets and shops of Mombasa the atmosphere was equally buoyant. Kenya's independence had brought a new order and wherever we went Kenyans shouted a beaming *'Jambo Bwana'* – a greeting we returned in the same laughing way. Even though the Mau Mau revolt (eight years of insurgency by Kenyan peasants against British colonial rule) was finally defeated in 1960, it had taken large troop numbers to do so. There was little doubt that sustained rebellion had hastened Kenya's bid for independence. We were told that Jomo Kenyatta, a conservative and moderate leader, did not expel former white rulers and actively encouraged side-by-side living, but since he was a member of the Kikuyu ethnic group (which had made up the core of the Mau Mau revolt) the question of whether he could be trusted hung in the air.

The years of unrest had rattled everybody, and Europeans were beginning to move out. George Cole and his family, sailing *Galinule* to Australia, had made that decision. For others a wait-and-see attitude, a languid detachment, seemed to have set in. One family invited us to their home for Christmas drinks and Helen, wife and hostess, told me how she dealt with her anxiety over an uncertain future. 'When worry gets to me,' she said, 'I take the car and spend a day alone in the game parks. Sitting quietly watching the wildlife brings life into focus ... giraffes are so beautiful. I love the giraffes.' Looking at the comfort and opulence of her home, her elegant dress and her team of servants silently moving about made this difficult to imagine. Why would she choose the discomfort of rough roads, heat and dust? Yet I believed her. I too had learned how the simplicity and beauty of nature feeds the soul. I found peace at sea; for her it was the wildness of the African jungle and the company of tall, graceful creatures.

One invitation came from Ray Mayer, born in Sydney. He must have spotted us from his sprawling bungalow on the other side of the river, opposite the yacht club. Terribly excited to find a yacht from his hometown in port, he and about twenty of his mates, all of them high on drink, came charging across in a tinny and circled the boat singing a noisy 'Waltzing Matilda' *And of course you must come for Christmas lunch, bring all your friends.* Christmas lunch was to be at his place; *we'll pick you up.*

Six of us went, and with around forty guests already there, most of them Ray's extended family, a few yachties barely extended the party. Celebrations seemed to run along Australian lines and the highlight for Graeme was the annual Christmas cricket match played on the grounds surrounding the house; the 1966 variation was Yachties versus the Mayer family. Still ignorant of the rules of cricket I can't comment, but judging by the banter, us yachties were well ahead when the ball disintegrated and discussion over who should be declared the winner was adjourned to the bar.

My party highlight came when the round-faced black cook,

swathed head to foot in white garments, came to show off her grandchild. The chubby baby girl, dressed in a nappy as white as her grandmother's apron, was happy to be handed around. I held her for a long time and she lay perfectly still, never taking her eyes off me. Perhaps she was as fascinated by my round blue eyes as I was with her round black ones; we just couldn't stop looking at each other. Reluctantly I handed her back to her beaming grandmother, shocked to find that I wanted a baby. *Wow ... come on girl, get yourself a drink, this is not on.*

Ray Mayers farmed sugarcane and bred cattle. Keen for us to see his adopted country, he offered us the use of his bush camp in Voi, about a hundred kilometres inland from Mombasa. His brother-in-law, one of the seventy remaining (now happily extinct) White Hunters of East Africa, also used the camp. 'If you like you can take the camp's Land Rover and have one of the drivers if you want.'

Was it okay if we drove ourselves... no driver?

'Of course, whatever you want.'

Ray had business inland and was happy to drop us off in Voi. There were six of us, a mixed bunch of yachties. Nick, Jeanie and Tom from *Barlevento* joined in. Unfortunately, ugly Ken did too – I had not forgiven him his chauvinistic comments – but having Jeanie along more than made up for it; another woman sailor, at last. I liked Jeanie; she and Nick had been travelling companions for years, the perfect couple except for Nick's reluctance to marry. Nick's steadfast refusal to commit to the relationship had become a running joke but he stuck to his guns... Jeanie was too nice a girl, I thought, to be stuck with someone like him. The cruising grapevine told us that they did eventually have a 'commitment ceremony' (an unofficial hippie marriage) on some Hawaiian beach. They would have looked beautiful, tall and slim Jeanie with flowers in her long blond hair and burly Nick in a sarong, or more likely wearing his favourite cut-off white jeans.

Last in the party was Tom, also from *Barlevento*, a modern-day minstrel. Tom was an excellent guitar player, described by one of the newspapers as 'the Californian singing and sailing his way around the world'. He liked to wear his shirts inside out and enhanced his full blond beard with a carefully waxed moustache. Women loved him and he had made Gordon Lightfoot's 'That's What You Get for Loving Me' his song. Later, in the Durban Mayfair Supper Club, I heard him sing it to his sweetheart of the day, crooning to her about not being the sort of man to hang around. The ease of the sixties was well on its way.

Driving inland after months of slow sailing felt strange and hypnotic, like viewing a fast-forward movie giving quick glimpses of thatch-roofed villages, people walking by the roadside, wide fields of farmland and flat-topped umbrella trees stark against the horizon. It was hot in the car and I was happy to tune out, let the scenes glide past and keep quiet. Ray drove and the men talked politics, cattle farming and the camp we were headed for – easy chatter.

༄

Ray's bush camp was a grander affair than the name implied. Tents and huts clustered on a sandy bank above a shallow river gave it more a feel of a small village. Servants welcomed us, food was prepared and we were shown more-than-adequate sleeping quarters. Ray gave instructions for getting the Land Rover ready for us and took off again, a busy man.

Away from *Hope* for the first time in three years, sleep did not come easy that night, not even with the obligatory nightcap of Scotch. Rustling sounds and piercing bird cries kept me awake for hours, eyes open and watching the full moon play shadowy games on the mosquito net. Finally asleep, I slipped straight into the watercolour pictures from my brother's African adventure books, part and not part of an endless line of people wading through a yellow river, guns and parcels lifted high above their heads. Pinned into my dream by the noise of the river running past the tent, it was hard to wake up, and it took much vigorous splashing in that selfsame river for me to return to a world of friends, sunshine and breakfast.

~

The Land Rover had two seats up front, two behind and a flat area at the back. A canvas roof and canvas flaps gave an illusion of safety should any of the big game decide to check us out. With six of us travelling, two of us took turns at bouncing around in the back on top of our luggage, sleeping bags, food and drink. It didn't matter, we were happy, knew how to rough it. Our combined charm and possibly the sight of the Land Rover (recognised by game wardens and lodge keepers as belonging to Ray Mayers and his White Hunter brother-in-law) earned us friendly waves along the way and, once inside the game parks, tips on where to find a pride of lions or black rhinoceros.

Nick, ever inventive, taped a *National Geographic* logo cut from a magazine cover onto the doors of the Land Rover and that opened more doors still. In one very expensive lodge the manager made the extraordinary concession of letting all six of us stay in a hut meant for two, our sleeping bags rolled out on the floor. That evening we joined safari-dressed men and women in starched khaki outfits sitting on large verandas sipping sundowners and watching game through binoculars at the watering hole below. Our jeans and crumpled T-shirts made us a raggedy gang by comparison, but our laughter must have been magnetic. An exuberant bunch of young people travelling on little money still passed as a novelty, and it didn't take long before drinks and invitations to join other parties were sent to our table. Travelling on yachts, we were used to moving in well-off circles and differences in dress or individual wealth rarely fazed us. Money was okay for some but we stubbornly refused to let it define us. If anything, we showed off with how little we could live on. *The wind is free isn't it?* We were ocean sailors, had come from afar, and rich and poor alike had told us many times over how they envied us our freedom.

A couple of days later we stayed in more modest lodge, built like a village with different-sized square huts, the low walls topped with thick thatch roofs. Graeme and I took a small hut with one window and a door that led into a single room. A dimly glowing light bulb suspended off a wire gave enough light to make out the bare thatch roof sloping darkly up into a point almost directly above a big bed. Exotic surroundings but it was the huge bed that charmed us most, the first really big bed we had ever slept in, infinitely bigger than *Hope*'s double bunk. It may have been queen-sized, king-sized perhaps, maybe bigger ... a football field where King and Queen rolled around every which way, laughing a lot and having a great time.

Morning brought more amusement. None of the rooms had cooking facilities, and servants made the rounds in the evening to collect the food we wished to have cooked and delivered for breakfast. We handed over four eggs, requesting them to be scrambled *and could we have them at seven o'clock please.* We later found out that breakfast was akin to a lucky dip. Handing over four eggs and wanting them a seven o'clock didn't mean it would happen. It was equally possible that we would get somebody else's baked beans at six o'clock, or if one was unlucky enough, a bowl of lumpy porridge at nine. The system of numbering the food to match the huts was clearly not working but nobody complained; this was Africa. We were lucky and did get eggs, *somebody's* eggs, although not scrambled but fried. Cold porridge might have been a bit of a stretch.

It was a quick trip – a holiday within a holiday – yet amusing scenes and still images have remained vivid in my mind. Early morning squabbles among us travellers disappeared in the breathlessness of seeing snow-topped Kilimanjaro in pre-dawn light, a sacred image and a luminous backdrop for a herd of zebra, black-and-white shapes moving silently through sheets of mist. The discomfort of roughing it and unbearable noon heat stand tiny against seeing untouched country, wild animals roaming free and the tantalising spice of a little danger.

Rushing to make camp before sunset, we turn a corner and almost drive into a large herd of buffalo. Viciously applied brakes stop us in time, just metres away from a battery of lowered heads and horns. A huge image: raw power in a halo of late sunlight and airborne dust, the stillness disturbed by the occasional noisy snort. In a tense standoff we back off inch by slow inch, the Land Rover suddenly shrunk to the size of a toy.

Stories about what animals could do circulated in the camps. One told of a giraffe stamping a foot right through a car roof, killing the driver; another of a Volkswagen driving into the back of an elephant, who then had little choice but to sit down on the bonnet, flattening it completely. We also had an elephant story and this one is true, I know, I saw it.

It happened when we spotted a large single elephant bull high up on a hill, sharply outlined against a clear sky. It was an image worth photographing but Graeme thought it too boring, wanted an action shot of the beast charging. We shouted, jumped up and down, beeped the car horn but nothing fazed the elephant, he remained a statue planted at the edge of a lava flow.

They don't like walking on lava, I suddenly remember, *it hurts their feet* ... 'I read it somewhere. Look, he's stuck.'

'Brilliant,' says Tom. 'Go ahead, walk right up to him, throw something at him ...'

'Okay, I'll do it ... back up the Rover just in case.'

Graeme, camera slung around his neck, scales the lava flow until he is as close as he dares, David against Goliath. We watch his arm go up ready to throw a big lump of dirt when suddenly there is the mighty noise of the elephant charging, tusks down, stomping *right over the lava flow* straight at his assailant. In one smooth action Graeme turns and runs, followed by airborne gazelle-jumps down the steep lava flow, the last massive leap ending in a dive under the back flap of the Rover. 'Wow only just made it! Lava flow indeed ... where on earth did you read that?' and naturally I am teased for wanting to kill my husband.

Leaving the game parks and threading our way towards Nairobi, we chanced on a group of Maasai walking by the side of the road, the open savannah stretching into the distance behind them. We slowed to a stop but they did not wish to be seen, each person instantly flicking a long cape over their head and body, covering up completely. All was still and guarded, not even the children peeked and until we drove off again the group remained mute, rigid and unmoving like painted totem poles.

But always, and more than the people, I remember the

animals, the charm of curved eyelashes on a dark-eyed giraffe bending down to munch on a thorny bush, the easy unhurried gait of a lioness and the sight of many little hippopotamus ears flicking randomly above the surface of a river. I recall my childish delight in patting a spotted baby leopard in the Nairobi animal orphanage. About twice the size of Jinky, it purred as low and as deep as a diesel engine. It hadn't occurred to me that wild cats purr.

After delivering the Rover back to Ray's camp we hitch-hiked back to Mombasa, back to the yacht club just in time for the big New Year's Eve celebrations. The club was crowded and busy and once again we were welcomed. Everybody was keen to know if we had seen 'their' beloved Africa – *where did you go, how was it, did you like it, where did you stay, did you call at my daughter's place in Nairobi? Yes we did, yes, we loved it, everything was wonderful … a beautiful country.*

When we rowed out to *Hope*, Jinky's welcome was in stark contrast. Arrogantly flicking the very top of his long tail, he stalked off. He was not pleased to have been left behind. 'Come on Jinks be reasonable,' I pleaded with him. 'You wouldn't have liked the Big Cats. Believe me, they'd eat you for breakfast… oh, okay then… sulk away if you must.' I was happy to be back aboard, my much-loved ocean only a sniff away.

Kenya did not ensnare me. I was a sailor, wouldn't let it happen, but I did get a taste of the country's depth and mystery, understood why the friends we made didn't want to leave, not then, not yet. The heartbreak Africa would become was still in the making, and three years of independence had barely shifted the realities of master/servant relationships. We too had travelled the white man's road, hadn't learned what aspirations Kenyans had for their newly independent country.

Perhaps the closest we came to feeling Kenya's pulse was to learn a Swahili song that Graeme had picked up along the way, a bittersweet declaration of love for a girl called Malaika or 'Angel'. First recorded by the Kenyan Fadhili William in the 1950s, the last lines hint at the pain of the dispossessed, as the singer laments that he can't marry his sweetheart because he has no money.

A fleet of private boats sent us off, everybody shouting and sounding foghorns. We were given presents, a bottle of champagne, a Khanga[12] for me, and Jinky had a tin of sardines to look forward to, given to him by the woman who had looked after him while we travelled inland. As we made for open waters, I felt the lift and swell of the ocean, new, exciting and yet daunting all over again. Three days of miserable oilskin weather reset the gauges and blew away my sadness at saying goodbye to friends we had made and were unlikely to ever meet again.

Everybody on board took turns at getting seasick – and everybody this time meant three people. Tom from *Barlevento* had asked if he could come with us as far as Durban; *Barlevento* was going north and he wanted to go south. Both Graeme and I liked Tom and it was agreed. We were now sailing along busy shipping lanes, needed to keep a twenty-four-hour lookout, and having Tom aboard was a welcome unexpected bonus. Three people on a 9-metre yacht didn't leave a lot of room, but we soon found a workable routine.

---

12 An African garment, a large piece of cotton cloth, one metre by one metre fifty, printed with one pattern often with a surrounding border. Khangas are mostly worn by women.

The only concession Tom asked for was that his guitar, his closest companion and his meal ticket, would be stored safe and dry up forward, out of harm's way. No problem, Graeme was happy to let him use his knockabout guitar, and long and happy song-swapping sessions in the cockpit followed. *Hope* was the smallest yacht Tom had sailed on since leaving America, and switching from a 65-foot luxury yacht to 29-foot *Hope* drew the occasional grumble, especially when our engine refused to work – which it had a habit of doing.

Jinky was the only one aboard not pleased. Tom wasn't a friend of cats, would tease him and flick his ears, but Jinky knew how to look after himself. Whenever Tom raced past him to haul in a sail or fetch something that was needed in a hurry, Jinky would casually reach out a paw, claws unsheathed, and inflict bloody streaks along Tom's bare legs. In return he got more ear flicking but soon the contest stopped being physical. A truce was reached, and like boxers in a ring the two combatants took to glaring at each other. Jinky had coolly and casually established the respect he deserved.

Tom playing the guitar, singing Mason Williams's songs about moose goosers and lunch toters, and another miserable bout of seasickness eased my disappointment over having to sail past Zanzibar. My innocent childhood dream of visiting the island of Zanzibar and sharing drinks with traders in some smoky bar (my brother's African adventure books again!) would have posed a huge risk for *Hope* and her crew. The 1964 Zanzibar revolution – attempting to end a century and a half of Arab and South Asian cultural and economic dominance – was far from over. Several thousand Arabs and Indians had been killed and thousands more had been expelled; it was clearly no place to indulge in dreamy fantasy.

We decided instead to call at the Comoros Islands, a French colony made up of a group of islands situated between Madagascar and the African mainland. Six days out from Mombasa we approached the capital, Moroni on Grand Comoro, but one look through binoculars made it clear that it would be a most uncomfortable anchorage. The port was on the windward side of the island, open to the sea, and the only shelter we could make out was a small area behind a jetty curving outward like a breakwater. Never mind, we were here now, and provided the already vigorous onshore wind didn't get any stronger we'd be okay. Rowing through the line of surf to get to the town was a wet business and Graeme's comment that this was *the bloody stupidest place to put a harbour* spoke for us all.

Our troubles continued when French authorities refused to give us clearance and ordered us to leave the island within twenty-four hours. *Hope* was a British-registered vessel and her expulsion breached international shipping law. We argued, insisted on our rights, but communication was difficult, more so when Graeme tried to explain that we were having engine trouble and could not leave within twenty-four hours. Not speaking French, Arabic or Swahili, I added a shoulder-shrugging German '*kaputt*' to the debate. That seemed to be understood and finally a compromise was reached.

Not having a motor made us 'unseaworthy', and the visa we didn't need in the first place was extended to four days. I have no idea what caused the trouble and can only guess that an Australian, a German and an American citizen travelling on a British yacht posed unsurmountable administrative problems; it was probably easier to try and get rid of us. And in the end the French authorities had their way; a small *Expelled from the Comoros Islands* was entered in our passports, a mean little line that caused much trouble and endless explanations in ports to come.

My shoulder-shrugging kaputt wasn't a lie, but not having a workable engine hardly made us 'unseaworthy'. It simply meant that we couldn't charge our batteries, had no topmast light and had to put up with the nightly hassle of rigging up kerosene navigation lights. We had hoped to find a mechanic in Moroni and a silver lining on the cloud of French bloody-mindedness appeared when the captain of a Southern Line coastal freighter, unloading at the jetty, came to offer his help. Smiling cheerfully, he said 'We'll make that a "foreign order"' and sent one of his ship's engineers to help fix our engine.

The engineer was a Cockney, as cheerful as his captain but impossible for me to understand. He, Graeme and Tom, filthy to the elbows, stripped down our recalcitrant monster tucked behind the companionway steps in a space no bigger than a kitchen cupboard. I had the good sense to make myself invisible on the foredeck, crossing fingers and toes and gazing at the township beyond the line of surf, *perhaps this is the only view of Moroni I'm going to get*. The wind still gusted strongly and leaving *Hope* yanking at her anchor chain a few hundred metres off a lee shore wasn't an option. *I'd love a walk ...*

Tall mosques, their stark white shapes muted by overcast skies, stood among a jumble of boxy-looking buildings. Beyond the narrow fringe of buildings, dark green slopes rose gently at first and then more steeply until they disappeared into heavy grey clouds. I knew that the notoriously active 2,360-metre-tall Mount Karthala stood within those sodden layers of grey, but the way things stood we were unlikely to see the top of it. We had hoped to see a little of the island and its unique bird life and perhaps learn something about the famous catches of coelacanth fish, thought to have been extinct for millions of years. There'd be no tourists I thought, how would one find out?

Wishful thinking and crossing my fingers must have helped. The men got our engine running, the wind eased, and we were ready to admit that perhaps Moroni wasn't such a bad place after all. During the night the wind eased further still and by morning it was calm enough to risk a few hours ashore. Letting out a bit more anchor chain 'just to be sure', we rowed ashore. We had obviously been watched, because as soon as we stepped ashore a young couple came over and introduced themselves. Phillipe and Claire were French but spoke good English, working in Moroni on an eighteen-month work contract, he as an engineer and she as a schoolteacher. They liked it well enough but felt isolated, Claire especially. 'It's not easy here for a Western woman.' She smiled. 'I'm glad we're going home soon.'

Phillipe and Claire showed us around town, and without their explanations the strange atmosphere would have baffled us. We had arrived at Ramadan, a holy time of fasting and reflection for Muslims. Continual prayers were chanted from the minarets, and rows of men dressed in long white caftan-type dresses, bowing and praying, spilled out onto the steps of the mosques. All other activity seemed at a standstill; even the men dressed in European suits walked around silently, their hands on their backs. The faithful took neither food nor drink during daylight hours and did not even swallow their own spit to relieve their thirst, hence a lot of spitting on the ground.

Walking through narrow alleyways we saw women in colourful khangas contrasting sharply with solemn Muslim women covered in black garments. Their faces were invisible under black veils yet many of the women deliberately turned their backs on us, did not wish to be seen at all. The children, some dressed in gold brocade like princes, others completely naked, were curious and would have followed us had their mothers allowed it. I was glad I hadn't brought my camera ashore, wouldn't have wanted to point my camera at staring children, mute women and dark doorways. It was enough for me to walk along, offer a smile to the women who accepted it and *feel* the ambience of a world so very different to mine.

Claire pointed out shops displaying exquisite gold filigree jewellery hand-made by Indian and Arab craftsmen, intricate necklaces and broad armbands to be purchased as wedding tokens by prospective husbands. Trade was good, she said; up to four wives were permissible under Muslim law. She explained that in exchange for the gold and money offered by the groom, the father of the bride supplied the house for the newly-weds. This usually meant putting another storey on top of his house, or adding an odd-shaped extension onto the side of it; many extensions indicated many married daughters.

I have no idea what judgements were passed on me as we walked through the streets; a woman sailing on a boat with two men was unlikely to be deemed a good woman. Careful not to offend, I had put on a long-sleeved shirt and a knee-length skirt, but I found out that there were other ways I could offend. On our way back to the jetty I sat on the low wall surrounding a mosque to shake a stone from my sandal when a man dressed in white rushed up to me. Obviously furious and using violent hand gestures he demanded that I get up – *I was not allowed to sit there*. Shoe in hand I quickly jumped up and motioned a silent *sorry*. I don't know if sitting on a wall surrounding a mosque was forbidden for everybody or only for me as a woman and non-believer.

~

That night the wind piped up again. Tom, wishing to give us privacy, had bunked down on the Southern Line freighter (whose engineer had helped us repair our engine) and didn't realise what was happening until dawn. By then it was blowing a full gale and *Hope* was taking green water over the bows at anchor. Tom had to row hard to get through wind and rising seas to reach us. Heaving the dinghy aboard and lashing it down over the skylight took only minutes, but then our devilish engine refused to start – again! A gaff-rigged boat is not the best rig for sailing off a mooring and straight to windward, and we had some anxious moments clawing our way away from a shore barely 300 metres away. It's the kind of breathtaking excitement I don't wish to have ever again!

With *Hope* picking up speed at last and deep water under her keel once more, we gave a lusty thumbs down to French officialdom. We had our passports but had left without a harbour clearance, *not much they can do about it ... to hell with them*. Our only regret was that we hadn't been able to say goodbye to Claire and Phillipe. We had planned to meet again for lunch and hoped they'd understand. Clearing the island, we sailed south for a day to an uninhabited island within the same archipelago. The anchorage was snug and with a few days of lazing around, a bit of swimming and diving, drinks and music at sundown, the world looked new again. Even our temperamental engine decided to come to life again; one push of the button and it started the way it was meant to.

Ocean currents have become visible with photographic images taken from outer space, but even with today's modern technologies accurate mapping of such currents remains a work in progress. The Mozambique Channel, between Madagascar and the African mainland, is particularly erratic. About 200 miles at its narrowest, it can be a veritable witch's cauldron with huge anticyclonic eddies adding devious little extras to an already strong southward-flowing current. Heading for the Island of Mozambique, tucked close to the Portuguese East African coast just off mainland Mozambique, we sailed hard across the channel hoping to pick up a free ride on the current. Graeme's sextant sights confirmed that we had; in one twenty-four-hour run we covered 350 miles, an unheard-of distance for a 9-metre gaff cutter. *Wow, at this rate we'll have to be careful not to shoot right past the place.*

Elation got a damper when the sun disappeared; no more sextant sights reduced our navigation to guessing current-speed and direction and adding it to the mileage recorded by our trailing log. All we could do was cross our fingers and hope that one of the famous anticyclonic eddies wouldn't push us off course. Eventually the African mainland appeared low and flat, hidden in a smudge of mist. It gave away no identifying landmarks, but Graeme felt sure that – give or take a few miles – we were off the Island of Mozambique. And so we hove to until nightfall,[13] hoping that a lighthouse would reveal our exact position. Keeping a gaze on the darkening land, we sat in a boat as unmoving as we could make it, keenly aware that we might well be travelling along at a good 3 knots of current. It was decided that if we had been swept past our intended destination

---

13 'Heaving to' is a way of adjusting the sails to slow down the boat with a minimum of drift.

we would simply head out to sea again and sail on; nobody aboard was keen to backtrack *against* the current, running strong and unstoppable all the way to the southern tip of Africa.

Darkness fell and it was a relief to pick up the Mozambique lighthouse, group flash four every ten seconds and only slightly north of where we hoped it would be. Not usually keen to enter port after dark, this time we did, and precisely at midnight we dropped anchor in what looked like a reasonable anchorage, a mass of dark walls and an outline of a cathedral barely visible beyond the pale strip of beach. A cup of tea and a Happy Birthday song followed; Graeme had turned 27.

Morning revealed a low island about 3 miles off the mainland. A group of men squatted on the beach near the water's edge, their sarongs rolled around their waists. The beach served as communal toilet to be cleaned by the rising tide. It looked a relaxed and companionable scene and with so much manhood on display I was tempted to cheer. Tom's response was more practical. 'I am not getting into that,' he said, abandoning his habit of swimming ashore in the places we anchored. 'I'll wait for the dinghy.'

We were in no hurry to launch the dinghy ... *let the locals get on with their ablutions.* For now it felt good to be at anchor, to have woken from a good night's sleep and to savour the morning. Sitting quietly on deck we watched the flotilla of dhows sailing from the mainland towards the island, a charming and peaceful sight. From a distance the boats looked like single brushstrokes painted randomly onto a pale sea, graceful little commas all curved in the same way. Up close they lost some of their picturesque charm, looked rough and dirty, sections of the mast tied together with rope, the sails patched and the hulls in need of paint. Some were little bigger than a dinghy sailed by a couple of men; others had larger crews and were clearly big enough to travel offshore. As they sailed past us we could see how calmly and efficiently the boats were handled, the men raising a single hand in a languid greeting as they slid by. Perhaps the serene dawn was responsible for the magic, but I heard none of the shouting so much part of Western coming into port.

Life ashore felt different, perhaps a little softer than other places we'd called at. An attitude of live and let live seemed to have eased the divide between conquerors and their subjects. The Portuguese, who administered the Island of Mozambique, weren't as controlling and organised as the British or the French, who built ports and railways and exclusive trade networks (and toilets) in their colonies. They built churches instead. The Chapel of Nossa Senhora de Baluarte, built in 1522, is said to be oldest European building in the Southern Hemisphere.

It's not hard to imagine why the Island of Mozambique became an important outpost for Portugal's empire. Five hundred metres at its widest, three kilometres long and about the same distance away from the mainland, it was easy to guard, the township safely contained within massive stone walls and watched over by the Fort of Sao Sebastiao. The island evolved into a major trading post for gold and spices and later, in the 18th century, as a centre for the infamous slave trade. Situated about halfway along the east coast of Africa, it was well placed as a convenient stopover for trading routes to the East.

The island was still a marvellous hub of activity. The dhows we had watched earlier had come to sell their produce and the market square was crowded with people. Trade seemed to be mostly local, but for all I knew the groups of men of African, Indian or Arab ancestry in various headgear, clustered under arched colonnades, may as easily have struck secret deals of contraband shipments. Women, some covered and veiled, others simply wrapped in colourful khangas, sat on the ground guarding fruit, vegetables and strange-looking foodstuffs piled in heaps. Some of the young women wore chalk-white make-up, pale ghostly faces seemingly afloat above dark throats and ebony limbs.

It was difficult to see who sold what, how much it cost, even what kind of food it was, wrapped up in plain paper parcels or spread out over plant leaves. Pointing to it and offering some coins in my open hand was the best I could do. Venturing into one of the shops tucked under the arcade, I found a shelf stacked with tins of fruit and corned beef from Australia at four times the price we had paid in Kenya; a practical lesson in the fickle seesaw of supply and demand. I figured that the tins could only have arrived on the island by dhow, but from where? India, England? Not that it mattered (we had enough food aboard to get us to Durban) but the incongruity of finding Australian tinned fruit in the remotest part of the world I had ever visited had me wondering.

These idle musings were soon replaced by the very real question of how to obtain plain old drinking water. The island had no running water and with three of us aboard now (and unable to fill up in the Comores Islands) our water tanks were getting too low for comfort. After much talking, the harbourmaster finally surrendered the key that gave us access to a fenced-in water tank at the far end of the island. To fetch the water our only choice was to take a jerry can each, hire three rickshaws to take us to the tank, fill up the cans, ride our precious cargo back to the beach and ferry it aboard by dinghy.

My rickshaw ride was both comical and absurd, more so because an earlier experience had made me determined not to ride a rickshaw again. As long as I was able to walk, I would not let some poor fellow strain his heart and lungs for me to sit back and do nothing. On the Island of Mozambique I had no choice: there was no public transport, and I could not have walked 2 kilometres in searing heat lugging a jerry can full of water. Pretending not to care, I sat back in a low-slung carriage as my thin brown 'chauffeur' (a head smaller than me) pulled me along through a network of tree-lined streets, past arched colonnades and rows of houses built of thick stone, their rough surfaces streaked with washed-out pastel colours. Passing a secluded courtyard gave a glimpse of a curving stone staircase with black wrought-iron railings leading to an upper floor, an almost European vista. We passed slim dark women swathed in sarongs, blouses and head cloths walking in groups, invariably carrying *something*: a basket, a bundle of sticks or a baby. Totally charmed by the exotic backdrop, I still managed to notice that the only other persons riding rickshaws were large, respectable-looking European matrons holding small handbags. *What lives would they be leading in a tiny township 3 miles beyond the edge of a huge continent?*

My jerry can 'handbag' filled with water was a hefty weight. The rickshaw man quoted five escudos for the ride back, ridiculously cheap, and watching his thin sinewy calves working and his bare feet slapping onto the paved road had me renew my promise not to do this again. It seems I wasn't the only one because after heaving three cans of water aboard the decision to make do with one water-fetching trip was unanimous. A 5-litre bottle of Portuguese wine enclosed in wicker cost a mere 70 escudos[14] and we would stock up on wine instead. Drinking imported wine rather than the murky water we had extracted from the ancient stone tank would have to be safer; at least that's what we told ourselves.

~

A few days later we set sail south again, happy enough to leave the strange little island behind. The wind was fair and we were hoping to cover the 800 miles to Lourenço Marques (now Maputo) in double quick time, courtesy of the monster current. But instead of giving us a straightforward push southwards, the current pulled us into one of the notorious anticyclonic eddies, unseen cauldrons of slowly moving water revolving in circles of up to 150 miles in diameter. Our next lunchtime position put us off course and out to sea by *a whole 100 miles* in a 24-hour run. Graeme refused to believe it, kept taking more sextant sights, checked and rechecked his calculations but it was true. Once again the sea had given us a mischievous reminder that she was calling the shots, she was in charge.

And she hadn't finished with us yet. As we sailed back towards the coast, patches of mist begun to engulf us, the wind chopped and changed and finally dropped altogether. The misty patches turned into densest fog and by nightfall we were wallowing in a monochrome, muffled world. Perhaps the huge eddy that had whirled us offshore was now serving us a storm to match. The milky silent calm felt eerie and ominous.

I didn't like it and, skipping dinner, I took my cup of tea into higher reaches, gliding, swimming on air, watching *Hope*

---

14 Less than one pound sterling at the then exchange rate

drift in a soup of white... more poised than me, serene and unworried. Thin light from a half moon had her floating on an invisible sea, held softly in a hazy bubble... her spars dark and solid, her sails a mere gleam of white... a charming pencil sketch from an ancient book, unreal, timeless. I admired her strength, her beautiful lines, watched the grey figures on deck... waiting, refusing to turn in... They knew a storm was brewing, had sailed long enough to know. Condemned to waiting, deep male voices assaulted heavy air: 'where's the fucking wind?', 'come on you bastard'. Too superstitious to insult the gods, I kept my distance and my silence.

Insults or not, the scene remained static for a whole five hours and then the storm hit. It punished us with ten hours of wet-weather gear, hard work and a wild ride, but luckily the wind blew in the right direction.

Lourenço Marques, with its broad streets, wide mosaic footpaths and green watered parks (and public toilets), looked like Lisbon's little sister, worlds away from the primitive Island of Mozambique that we had left behind. Beautifully dressed European men and women enjoyed life in nightclubs and restaurants. Cafes on broad tree-lined pavements offered huge selections of fancy cakes, and tables were occupied until late in the night. The baking African heat and the presence of black servants working for low wages was distinctly un-European. Harmony between masters and servants was clearly strained. The Mozambique Liberation Front had been active for some years, and three Portuguese warships permanently stationed in port indicated that not all was well.

Politics in general and war topics in particular were among my chosen blind spots; as the child of a nation held responsible for two world wars it was easier that way. I wanted nothing to do with soldiers or warships but made a willing and grateful exception for the Portuguese Navy, and for good reasons. Leaving *Hope* anchored in the river off the township, we rowed ashore to try and negotiate a berth in the small inner harbour alongside fishing boats and other small craft. For reasons not explained to us the harbourmaster refused us entry. The tiny yacht club offered us membership but had insufficient water depth to accommodate *Hope*, and the big game fishing club next to it wanted cash payment in pounds sterling, which we didn't have. All options exhausted, we were discussing the possibility of moving on to Durban as we wound our way back to where we'd left the dinghy. Then horror struck: *Hope* was gone; the river was empty.

Frantically scanning the shoreline, we imagined her aground, washed up, even sunk, before finally spotting her tied up against one of the navy frigates. *Why the navy, have we been seized, arrested? What's happened?* Our questions were soon answered. While we were ashore looking for a berth the tide had turned, the wind had strengthened, *Hope*'s anchor couldn't hold her in the soft sludgy riverbed and she slowly began drifting seawards. The sailors on the frigate had watched her, intrigued by her size, her red ensign and the Portuguese courtesy flag flying at her crosstrees. Noticing her slow drift, a tender was sent out and she was towed alongside. *Hope* (and her crew) had been spared untold misery.

Our luck held and we were invited to stay alongside the frigate for as long as we wished. Navy officials dealt with the uncooperative harbourmaster, and we had the safest anchorage in all of Lourenço Marques. Treated like honoured guests, we were free to use bathroom and laundry facilities. An unending flow of food and drink was handed over the rail and best of all, *Hope* was dutifully watched over whenever we 'took shore leave'.

Navy shipboard life was an all-out male environment. It wasn't fitting for me to join in, but Graeme and Tom reported fun evenings with the crew, the language gaps bridged with alcohol and laughter, with singing and guitar playing. I was happy to catch up on sleep, and Jinky had a pleasant time exploring, made obvious by trails of oily paw prints left on our scrubbed teak decks. To reassure me he was safe, late one night he jumped into my bunk purring his head off, filthy and soaking wet right down to the tip of his tail. How he got out of whatever water he fell into remains a mystery.

Shore excursions were my treat when with a touch of European gallantry, sailors stood by to respectfully help me ashore if need be, a novel change from being one of the 'crew' able to look after myself. I like to think that I managed my exits with feminine grace, not easily done because it involved a non-ladylike climbing up *Hope*'s ratlines to a height that would allow me to step across the frigate's handrails and jump onto the ship's deck. Crossing the two ships was an obstacle course through narrow doorways and along bare corridors, ending atop a narrow gangplank where a white-hatted sailor saluted our leaving. A short walk across the fenced-in navy yard and another salute allowed us passage through the security gate. No papers, no passports, no signatures, no fuss; everybody knew us; everybody was briefed.

The shops in the 'European' part of town seemed like a bright island in dark Africa, the city benefiting greatly from a steady traffic of well-to-do South Africans hopping across from Durban for spending-spree holidays. The European shops offered luxury goods, shoes and clothing at high prices, the early beginnings of designer boutiques and my first brush with luxury for years. I have inherited my mother's eyes for beautiful fabrics and chic attire, but I dutifully told myself that I didn't need fancy things, that it was fun to just look. Besides, money was an issue, but good intentions vanished on our last day in town. Perusing one of the expensive city boutiques, I found a mortar and pestle crafted from solid ebony wood. Beautifully shaped and inlaid with tiny dots of ivory, it rested heavy in my hand. We did not buy souvenirs, but this was *not a souvenir*. It was functional, useful and expensive. I couldn't let go of it, really, really wanted it and quickly put it on the glass counter to buy it.

Graeme looked at the price. 'Too much,' he said, turning away to leave the shop. 'Can't afford it.' And right there and then we had a major argument, our first fight in a very long time. Instantly furious, I told him he had no right to decide what I spent money on. What had got into him? He could hardly call me frivolous... did I carry on when we bought ropes, pots of paint or expensive tins of pipe tobacco for that matter?

The shop assistant looked away, embarrassed. I was livid, angry to the core but suddenly, like a punch in the chest one particular scene of Mutti and Pappi fighting over money slid into my vision, *a stairway, a door kicked, Mutti's tears, her screaming, Pappi's stoicism, my own utter lost-ness and fear* ... The ghastly flashback and the ache of long ago silenced me in an instant and I made a quiet resolution to never fight about money. But anger rose again and I made another resolution; I would not allow anyone, and especially the male of the species, to patronise me. Condescension was out! Smiling stonily at the sales assistant I handed her the mortar and pestle. 'I'll take it thank you, would you please wrap it up for me.'

Nothing more was said and uneasy silence stood between Captain and First Mate. Only later did I realise how much the events both past and present must have been playing on my mind, because I failed to do my usual checks before leaving port. Amid the shouts of leave-taking and taking in the mooring lines I suddenly realised that Jinky wasn't aboard. We were about 50 metres away from the warship when I heard him howling most dreadfully, his little black-and-white face pushed between the legs of the Navy boys leaning against the rails. It took only minutes to turn *Hope* around to fetch him, but getting the lines ready to bring her alongside proved unnecessary. As soon as we came to within a couple of metres, Jinky took one huge, streamlined jump onto our deck followed by a zigzag dash below. I went after him to pat him and apologise but he wouldn't have it. Retreating into the forward bunk he punished me with withdrawal and narrow-eyed haughty looks. But by then I'd had enough of male sulking! Giving him dirty looks of my own I left him to attend to his injured superiority complex.

The joy over my mortar and pestle was severely tainted yet amazingly, my jet-black, tough little vessel with its tiny dots of ivory is still with me. I like to travel light, find it easy to part with things and have given, traded or bartered away truckloads of belongings at different turns of my life – why not the mortar and pestle? Still susceptible to omens I wonder if it holds some message for me still... surely I have fulfilled the resolutions I made because of it... or have I? Sensing the long tail of emotions attached to it makes it hard to believe that its only purpose could be to grind up herbs and spices. Although I have to admit, it's the perfect vessel for doing just that.

Durban

We arrived in Durban on 7 February 1967, late in the afternoon. The yacht club's welcoming routine was well-oiled and before we had a chance to secure the mooring lines, many hands were pushing foaming glasses of cold beer at us. Dr Hamish Campbell, patron saint of visiting yachts, had a standing agreement with the port's signal station that he was to be notified when a foreign yacht entered the channel leading into Durban harbour. Once the call came through the race was on, and the first person to put a cold beer into the hands of the arriving sailors would be declared the winner. The system worked famously. After the beer came fresh bread and milk, a quick dash to the post office to collect our mail, and two hours later I was soaking happily in a hot bubble bath at Hamish's place.

Well fed, squeaky clean and all talked out, we were returned to *Hope* well after midnight, but the highlight of our arrival was yet to come. Sometime during the night I was woken from deepest sleep by a huge thunderclap. Instantly upright and ready to jump, I felt *Hope* shudder beneath me as fierce gusts tore at her rigging. Rain hit the decks like drumbeats and the noise was horrific, but it took only seconds for me to realise that we were safely in port. Relief flooded through me in a warm current and I slid back to the horizontal, happily snuggling up against Graeme. He hadn't even stirred and soon after, I was back in dreamland too. Morning revealed the ferocity of the storm. Uprooted trees and flooding rain had caused havoc. Cars had been swept away, roadways were blocked and houses damaged; I had not been dreaming.

~

Hamish, head of the welcoming committee and tireless organiser of all manner of events, was in his middle forties, a practising medical doctor, confirmed bachelor, keen sailor, birdwatcher, music lover and party fiend all wrapped up into one lovable, hyperactive and generous personality. On weekends he raced his Flying Fifteen, a two-person keelboat he had named *Ffootsack*. The extra f in 'footsack' made him clear winner of the unofficial competition to name Flying Fifteens using two F's, more inventive and cheekier than calling it *Firm Friend* or *Fiery Fiend*.[15]

Hamish's home was known as 'the sanatorium', a sprawling bungalow filled with sails, boating equipment and beds for those who wanted to stay awhile. In defiance of the apartheid laws that forbade black and white people sleeping under the same roof, his old Bantu servant (who had also been his nanny) lived in his house and helped him care for his charges. Communal breakfasts served on his outside veranda, shaded by trees and dense creepers, were a treat. We would tuck into large quantities of food befitting hungry sailors while Hamish, valiantly battling overweight, would restrict his intake to a piece of toast, a poached egg, and grapefruit hot from the oven. He felt that grapefruit helped

---

15 Footsack is Afrikaans, meaning originally 'Forward say I' but had urbanised into 'get lost' – the 1960s not yet comfortable with the f— off version of today.

him lose weight and claimed that a little baking took away the bitterness.

To make up for his austerity he occasionally slipped in an 'eat-the-lot day', claiming as medical fact that one could not gain more than 2 pounds of weight in one day. To be with him on one of his '2-pound days' was awesome. Trailing him, I ate two lobsters, one for lunch and another for dinner, plus the requisite entrees and desserts at each of the meals. 'To hell with poverty, give the cat another canary,' he would declare, waving the waiter over and smoothly ordering another side dish, another bottle of fine South African wine or a round of coffee and cognac.

~

We had planned to stay in Durban for three months, plenty of time to take a break, look around and be off again. *Hope* had to be repainted, and if we could raise the money we would replace her standing rigging in stainless steel. Not that there was anything wrong with the galvanised steel rigging she had (coated in white lead and tallow in the traditional way) but Tom, our Californian friend and crewmember since Mombasa, had warned us that while Americans might buy a gaff-rigged cutter for its romantic appeal, they would baulk at galvanised steel rigging.

Our plans to sell *Hope* in Florida still stood, and thus stainless-steel rigging seemed a necessity. Things fell into place for us when Graeme, beard trimmed and decked out in his old suit and tie, landed a well-paid job as a structural engineer in one of the consulting firms in downtown Durban. He was 'tickled pink' (his words) and a week after arrival an almost urban existence began for us. The alarm would go off, Graeme would wander towel in hand over to the yacht club for his shower, I'd get breakfast ready and then he'd be gone for the day.

I had never 'not worked', and being at home, cooking, cleaning and doing a bit of painting and varnishing barely satisfied my inbuilt Prussian industriousness. An odd statement for someone who had been cruising the high seas for the past year, but contrary to what some people believe, cruising is not idleness. Sailing deep water in a small boat is a twenty-four-hour-a-day, seven-day-a-week occupation where survival depends on alertness, on constantly assessing a multitude of variables and getting them right. It's a demanding job, although one of the best. *Hope* surging through high seas courting the wind, her strength and her unceasing movement had proved balm for my restlessness. I was her servant, busy helping her in her task even if I sat perfectly still, lost in the beauty of a sunset. Durban was idleness by comparison. No longer tied to the demands of the elements, it was up to me to put meaning into the hours.

Luckily I had fellow 'sufferers', my immediate neighbours Pat and Leiv, two boat-wives whose husbands had also found work. Pat was English, sailing *Safari Too* with her German husband Kurt. Like us they hailed from Sydney, and we had shared anchorages before, the last one at Christmas Island before they sailed to Durban along the southern route, stopping in Mauritius. Leiv on *Kelea* was a new friend. She had sailed from Vancouver with husband Henry and their 12-year-old son Curtis. Curtis was booked into school for a term, our husbands were working, and the three of us teamed up to explore Durban, have coffee, swap recipes, go to the beach, attend yoga classes. Leiv had a sewing machine aboard which I happily borrowed. Unusual for a sailor, Leiv was also keen golfer. Her clubs travelled with her and it didn't take her long to find a golf course, but all her efforts to teach me the game were unsuccessful.

Our three yachts, big *Kelea*, *Safari Too* in the middle and small *Hope* on the outside, were moored against the yacht club marina, which gave us front row seats for weekend races and club events. Helping out Hamish, we appointed ourselves members of the welcoming committee for visiting yachts. Durban was touch point and last port for all yachts rounding the Cape of Good Hope, and at times it got busy. During the 1967 season I counted about twenty international yachts.

Tom Corkhill on his spidery 24-foot *Clipper I*, last seen in Thursday Island, arrived safely. He flashed me a cocky grin and said, 'Told you so, trimarans are safe.' Knowing a bit more about ocean crossings myself now, I admired his skills but still thought him crazy. He must have had barrels of luck to come through. The cruising grapevine told us later that his trimaran did eventually flip over, 150 miles off Cape Town en route to the Caribbean. It was reported that he tied himself to his barely visible, upside-down boat. Half-submerged, he floated for fourteen hours before being picked up by an Indian freighter. It seems that the ship had already passed him when the cook spotted him while throwing a bucket of vegie peelings over the stern. He was taken to India, and I have heard nothing of him since. Tom, a daring offbeat adventurer, sought no fame, and his incredible travels are only known to a few.

The opposite in media attention was Robin Lee Graham, the first teenager to sail around the world single-handedly. Like Tom Corkill, Robin Lee had not sought fame either, but it changed when he accepted *National Geographic* sponsorship. I don't know the terms of his contract, except that he needed to complete his around-the-world journey single-handedly and that *National Geographic* had exclusive interview rights. The latter became blatantly obvious when he was whisked away minutes after he had tied up his 24-foot fibreglass sloop, *Dove*. Apart from that first brief glimpse we saw little of him, and he did not become part of the rambling yachting scene with its impromptu parties.

We found out later that there may have been other reasons for his isolation, far more pressing than his pledge of exclusivity to *National Geographic*. In one of the ports along his journey the poor chap had fallen in love with Patti, his dream girl, but in keeping with his contract she could not sail with him. Everybody knew when Robin Lee was expected because Patti would be there, had flown ahead of him to wait for him. She was waiting in Durban but didn't talk much either. Special permission for under-age Robin Lee to marry Patti arrived in Durban, and the newly-weds took off on a short honeymoon, touring South Africa on a motorbike. Soon afterwards Robin sailed again, leaving his new bride behind, his two cats Flotsam and Jetsam his only company.

Another sailor who would eventually make fame and continue to sail and write many books was Wilfried Erdmann, the first German to sail around the world single-handedly. He arrived in Durban on *Kathena*, an old wooden centreboarder. Nearly on his home stretch, he seemed distracted, absent-minded, telling me repeatedly how eating raw onions had kept his teeth strong. Deeply concerned over the safety of his *Kathena*, he begged us not to knock the centreboard case as we squeezed into the tiny cabin; he was unsure how far marine borers had eaten their way into it.

After the three single-handed sailors, very much alone with their individual problems, it was a relief to greet a wild bunch of six Aussie blokes who had sailed from Melbourne.

They arrived one fine day in June, in the middle of winter, on the 52-foot *Winston Churchill* en route to Newport to watch the America's Cup races between Australia and America. We heard them more than we actually saw them, their laughter and exuberance reverberating across the marina at all hours. It seems that they painted the town red, and their blazing send-off a week later proved it.

About fifty people, mostly pretty girls, crowded the marina. The Aussie sailors, oblivious to the cold and high on drink, were naked to the waist, showing off chests and backs covered in biro autographs, messages and lipstick hearts. To keep the show going, when the *Winston Churchill* had moved about 50 metres away from the wharf, one of the crew jumped overboard, splashing wildly, pretending to swim back to shore, shouting 'I'm staying... I love her!' Cupid must have aimed well because no sooner had his mates dragged him back aboard when his sweetheart for the week, equally high on champagne, jumped off the wharf, gasping and trying to swim after the boat. 'Come back, take me with you...'

But cruelly, the boat sailed on. Dressed as she was for winter, in jumper and jeans, it took a few strong men to haul the waterlogged woman out of the water, no doubt well and truly sober by then. Pat and I were watching from our boat and Pat reckoned the girl was pushed.

Graeme made friends at work and our social life broadened out, away from boats. I remember a weekend staying with Graeme's boss and his wife at their beautiful house at the foot of the Drakensberg, quiet drinks on the cool veranda and being attended to hand and foot by servants, right down to having cups of tea brought to our bedside first thing in the morning. Our hosts barely seemed to notice the efficient running of their household, servants were a part of their life, but I had to keep check of my urge to jump up and help with dishes and things. Servants in a restaurant was one thing, but quite another in a private intimate setting. It would not have been appropriate to ask, but I wondered where the servants disappeared to at the end of the day, what different roofs did they sleep under... would they return to their black reserve for the night? There wasn't a chance to ask them either, not for reasons of propriety but because they simply kept clear of us.

Hamish had an easier, almost cavalier attitude to apartheid. When he took us birdwatching he simply ignored the laws that forbade white people to enter black locations. 'Birds don't observe such division,' he claimed as we walked unhindered through green undulating country and thatch-roofed villages. Hamish talked to people in their dialect, laughed and joked with everyone. Driving past one of the villages he told us that one of the elders of the kraal was a Bantu man with an Oxford degree, happy to return to his village and settle back into his old way of life. We found this hard to believe, but Hamish claimed it was not unusual. Yet even Hamish stopped short of walking into the kraal and introducing us to this wondrous man.

On another trip (once again through a black reserve) we came across a group of black women washing clothes on the edge of a river, standing knee-deep in swiftly running water. Surrounded by piles of colourful clothes stacked onto boulders, they sang as they worked, their fused voices forming strong haunting rhythms. Catching sight of us they stopped singing, but Hamish, ever the joker, struck up an opera singer's pose and serenaded the women with a nursery rhyme sung in Zulu. He looked a sight, dressed in shorts, topped by his white short-sleeved doctor's jacket with a row of pens pushed into the breast pocket. We thought it amusing, but the women in the river thought it hilarious. Pushing each other and pointing at The Doctor singing their songs, they laughed so much that I thought they'd all end up in the river.

A little later Hamish went hysterical himself, an 'ornithological hysteria' as we came to call it. He sighted a red cardinal bird and could not settle down. 'Did you see that?' he whispered. 'Give me the glasses quick, quick ... really, did you see it, I mean really ... did you ...? Amazing ... did you see it, did you?' I loved birds, but seeing Hamish dissolve into total delight over sighting a little red fireball of a bird increased my pleasure of birdwatching a hundredfold.

My birdwatching trips with Hamish had made me keen to visit Krüger National Park, and my chance came when Bianca, journalist, wildlife photographer and friend, planned a fortnight's camping trip to Krüger, happy to take me with her. Her impressive array of cameras and lenses carefully laid out on the backseat of the Mini, our clothes, tent, bedding and food stuffed into every available space, we took off, leaving a waving Graeme behind.

Krüger is a slice of make-believe country that aims to mimic Africa's ecology from long ago. Normal animal migration is curtailed, and careful monitoring determines how much wildlife certain areas can sustain, how many prides of lions, how many herds of elephants, what needs to be culled, what can be hunted. It was first set aside as a reserve in 1898; the native human population was 'removed', hunting was restricted and in 1927 the first motorist entered the park for a fee of one pound. We came forty years later. I can't remember how much we paid, except that the entry fee (plus the petrol to get there) made up most of our expenditure.

Krüger is huge, roughly L-shaped, spreading over an area about the size of Wales in England. Bianca knew her way around, had been camping in Krüger many times before, although she had warned me that she did not actually camp out. She would sleep in the car with the front seats taken out and the space levelled out with pieces of foam rubber specifically cut for that purpose. I wasn't particularly worried, figured myself braver than that, but once inside Krüger sleeping in a tent didn't seem such a good idea to me either. Less so when I was told of a woman who had failed to zip up her tent flaps properly and had her nose bitten off by a hyena.

Taking great care to zip up the tent, I settled for the night, but sleep wouldn't come. I knew that animals found their way into the fenced-in enclosure, could hear endless rustling, and a waft of blue nylon didn't seem enough to shield me from the wild. I lasted until about midnight before I made a dash for Bianca's car. 'Been there done that,' she laughed, moving over. Luckily both of us were skinny, and I had plenty of practice sleeping in a ship's bunk only 18 inches wide. Without the front seats and with the gaps filled with foam rubber, it was a comfortable enough space for two. The tent held our gear, and a mosquito net thrown over the car allowed us to keep the windows open as much as we dared.

Our aim was to take photographs and, aligning ourselves with the pace of the wild, time slowed to a trickle. It was nothing to sit for an hour waiting for the light to change or for a group of elephants to move closer. We stayed for days in specific camps because lions had been spotted, or a nearby waterhole promised the chance to photograph giraffes drinking. Patience is not my strongest suit, but waiting for giraffes was okay with me. I loved the way they moved, their towering height and their apparent gentleness, and one evening I was rewarded. As we waited in the car as so often before, this time a dreamlike scene unfolded in front of us, the fading light slowly transforming the image into a motionless sepia of browns and yellows: a mother and her baby drinking deeply, their heads mirrored in the water, their front legs splayed at odd angles.

On another day, in the hottest noon heat we came across a pride of lions at their mating ritual, a big-maned King of the Jungle surrounded by his harem. Every twenty minutes or so one of the lionesses would wander over and bump heads with him, and then roll around in front of him as if to say *come on mate, my turn*. If he didn't respond she would tease him a bit more, or as a last resort back right up against him until she had finally roused him. He would do his duty, bite her on the neck, give a loud roar, roll over and be back to dozing in seconds. The mating took less than a minute. 'Hardly romantic,' said Bianca. *Is it any wonder*, I thought. *Imagine doing it every twenty minutes* ... Later we talked to one of the gamekeepers about it and he told us that the mating ritual lasts up to four days. King of the Jungle indeed.

As expected, birds were varied and plentiful, always present and a welcome distraction when game stayed elusive. We watched green pigeons with yellow thighs and the distinct yellow oriole with its black head, easy to spot, not only by its outrageous colour but by its beautiful, almost liquid-sounding call. I took endless photos of ostriches and eagles, spoonbills wading in riverbeds and kingfishers dashing past showing bits of brilliant blue. My favourite bird was one lilac-breasted roller who did me the favour of sitting still long enough to capture him on film. The photograph shows him sitting on a leafy branch framed by blue sky, a shining prince dressed entirely in aqua and lilac. Every now and then he opened his strong beak, stuck out his chest and gave a loud and lusty *zaaak*. Another time we overtook three large black birds walking by the side of the road in single file. I don't know what kind they were, but they got stuck in my memory as the three nuns walking to church, unflustered, their heads bent in silent prayer.

But invariably the big game made the greatest impact. Coming face to face with a creature many times bigger than oneself shortens the breath and demands unquestioning respect. Sometimes even prayer might be called for. I certainly felt like it when a crashing noise woke us from deep sleep one night. Encased in the small tin can of Bianca's car, we peered out the window and saw solid round legs and a bit of swaying trunk, unbelievably huge. 'He shouldn't be there,' I whispered. 'How did he get in?' We had been told that big game was kept away from the inner enclosure by a strong trip-wire fixed above ground, but this elephant had obviously stepped over it. Both of us sat transfixed, watching the dark shape move around us, wondering if we were in his way, silently begging him to move on. He did, eventually, the sounds of cracking branches slowly disappearing into the relative calm of the night.

'Wow, imagine the headline,' said Bianca sleepily. 'Two Girls in a Mini Kicked Along by Romping Elephant.'

'Better than "Elephant Flattens Two Girls in a Mini".' I chuckled, relieved.

Filthy but happy, we returned to Durban. Bianca, keen to get to her darkroom to develop her films, dropped me at the yacht club. I headed for the shower and then to the yacht club phone to let Graeme know I was home. Fifteen minutes later he turned up, told the boss his wife was back, *I'll take the afternoon off, see you tomorrow* ... For the past year we hadn't been apart for more than a couple of hours and he'd missed me. 'Two weeks,' he laughed. 'Almost a divorce.'

Working out our money situation one evening after dinner showed a disturbing deficit. If we wanted to get to Rio de Janeiro for Carnival we would have to leave Durban by October, not possible on our present income. *Hope*'s new made-to-measure stainless-steel rigging had been ordered from England. That was expensive. The boat needed slipping and repainting, we had to stock up food for a year, and more money was needed for a self-steering arrangement Graeme had designed, presently being manufactured in a local steelworks. We weren't keen to stay another season and neither of us was willing to compromise on what *Hope* needed; we wanted the best for our stately lady. And so, I joined the working ranks. The consultancy employing Graeme had a vacancy for a draftsperson, and for the next three months both Graeme and I clambered barefoot over the boat rails, sat on the wooden piles of the marina to put on shoes and socks, and walked to work.

I could not have guessed how enjoyable work would become for me, how it would prompt me into playing my favourite *if not Sydney where would we live?* game. My previous work as a contractor for many years had given me insight into many companies, big and small, but my time in the Durban consultancy proved the most enjoyable.

For a while Graeme and I worked in different departments

and didn't see much of each other, but that changed when the tender for a large sugar terminal in Brazil got dangerously close to the deadline. In an 'all hands on deck' move every draftsperson that could be spared was put on the job, including me, and for the next three weeks it felt as if a fever had swept through the office, some unshakable bug that wouldn't let us rest until the job was done. Working long hours seven days a week kept us focussed. In a rare experience of perfect teamwork we coordinated, helped each other out and laughed and joked plenty. There was neither meanness nor upmanship, and to support our efforts management brought in caterers on weekends, serving us three-course meals in the boardroom.

Graeme was one of the design engineers for the Brazil tender. It was the first time we had worked together since the time we met five years earlier, and I was fascinated to see the changes in him. He was no longer the happy-go-lucky larrikin, the office joker, but a dedicated engineer passionate about his work. Back in Sydney it used to infuriate him when Australian agencies sought 'overseas expertise' for engineering projects. Now that he was 'overseas', he would show them how good Australian engineers were. What hadn't changed was his total lack of diplomacy. He thought nothing of calling someone a fool if they couldn't see his point of view. He got away with it because his work was good, but I teased him about it, told him he would have to tone down his tough Aussie defensiveness if he wanted to work in Germany as planned. Calling a superior *Dummkopf*, rightly or wrongly, would create quite a sensation in the formal German work environment. I knew I would love to be a fly on the wall if that ever happened.

Our teamwork paid off, the Brazil tender was finished on time and a large roll of drawings was sent off to Brazil, touched by everyone for good luck. The mood was buoyant and time off followed, sweetened with a generous bonus. An artist's impression of the sugar silo, a huge round building standing near the water, had been added to the swag of drawings. On Graeme's suggestion the artist had sketched a little yacht into his drawing, a tiny gaff-rigged *Hope* sailing towards Rio de Janeiro. With a much-improved bank balance this was now a clear possibility.

The company tried hard to keep us, offering advancement for Graeme and more money for me. But for all the temptations, in the end South Africa wasn't for us. The apartheid system was hard to stomach. Racial segregation had been in place for twenty years and white folk did not seem to notice it anymore. For us it was a shock to see separate entrances for hospitals, post offices and government buildings, to find lifts in city buildings and even park benches labelled to indicate which one was for white people and which one for coloured people. Even the beaches had signs: *Under section 37 of the Durban by-laws this bathing area is reserved for the sole use of members of the white race group.*

The rules were rigid; once a person was 'classified' as Black, White, Indian or Coloured (Coloured meaning of mixed race), they had to live within the bounds of that decreed status. Complicating things further, South Africa had two official languages, English and Afrikaans, the mother tongues of two ruling races that did not particularly like each other.

For me the one big advantage of living in South Africa was its closer proximity to Europe. It would be easier to visit my family, but not even that was enough to sway me. Life for South African women was too different for me to embrace it. Few white women worked commercially. Servants did the housework, leaving wives free to study at university, rehearse for the drama group, work out at the gym, play golf, or simply lie on the beach. Yet the easy life was exceptionally tough on marriages. South Africa held third highest place in the divorce statistics, almost on par with Hollywood.

⁂

Hope's new rigging arrived from England, and with the help of many hands, *Hope* was de-masted, slipped, repainted, re-rigged and back in the water more beautiful than ever. We were ready to sail, and our farewell rounds began. Saying goodbye to our friends on *Safari Too* and *Kelea* was the easiest; we would meet them again in Rio for Carnival. Saying goodbye to new friends was different. For the most part it was unlikely that we would ever meet again, and a simple *it was good to know you* and a heartfelt *thank you* was all we could offer. Hamish generously restocked our first aid kit and bequeathed us 'Queen Victoria', his red-white-and-blue striped spinnaker that miraculously fitted *Hope*.

Bianca came to the boat with a farewell gift, a beautiful copy of *The Rubaiyat* by Omar Khayyam, a modern interpretation with soft, almost erotic watercolour drawings of men and women in desert scenes. Suddenly aware that this present was not for me, I tried to recall a single time when we, alone or in a group, had ever discussed Omar Khayyam, and casting a sideways glance at Graeme I wondered, *has he been drinking wine, quoting verse and singing in the wilderness beside thou, oh Bianca?* Not a nice thought ... *but perhaps I've got this one wrong ... or have I ... my antenna is usually pretty good.*

Now I was definitely ready to sail, but departure was delayed once more when we received an invitation to attend the world premiere of *Sandefjord*, a full-length movie documenting the Durban-based yacht's circumnavigation of the world. We couldn't miss that; for all we knew we could be in it, having shared an anchorage with *Sandefjord* at Christmas Island.

It promised to be a big night out; the 'Press', half of Durban and the entire yachting crowd were invited. A grand occasion deserving of a new outfit, and Genevieve and I went shopping. Genevieve, a vivacious French woman, had only recently arrived, sailing with her English husband Barry and their baby daughter. I had been quick to make friends with her, drawn by her lightheartedness, almost carelessness. She seemed like a casual passenger on their yacht, wasn't weighed down by my overdeveloped sense of responsibility, my need for equality. 'Barr-ry will do it,' she'd chime happily.

Genevieve was the perfect companion for trawling Durban's boutiques, her decisive 'yes', 'maybe' or 'no good' reducing dozens of outfits to just a few. Finally I ended up with the one: a long sleeveless dress in cool linen, patterned in light and dark blue shapes suggesting tropical flowers. A white linen ruffle ran down the centre from neck to the hem, stitched down with a broad sky-blue ribbon, an unusual detail, a special touch. Seeing myself in a full-length mirror was rare these days and I kept turning and looking. Living on the water had given me a golden tan and made my eyes bluer, or maybe the dress did it.

It was a Hawaiian import and there was no doubt that it suited me, but looking at the price tag had me reeling. My sweet shopping companion, Genevieve, had no such qualms.

'Go, go, you buy it, buy it, you look wonderr-ful, fabulous, ver-ry good—'

'Genevieve have you seen the price? I can't, honestly, I can't spend that much money on a dress...'

'Whew, not imporr-tant, you buy it... buy it.... You'rre not worried about your 'usband, arr you?'

I tried to tell her that it wasn't about my husband, but that my own morals got in the way of spending that much.

But Genevieve didn't hear me, she was on a roll, unstoppable. 'Neverr mind your 'usband, serve him right to marr-y Continental women. I tell Barry when he gets mad ... you are Continental ... no?'

Genevieve's all-out femininity and persuasiveness suddenly made me think of Mutti. Little wonder I liked charming lovable frivolous *Continental* Genevieve; she reminded me of Mutti. The two of them would have made a perfect pair chanting a chorus of *buy it, buy it*.

And so I did, a crazy extravagance. I was Continental, wasn't I?

The *Sandefjord* premiere was a success, with a great deal of clapping and cheering at the end. How could we not like a full-length documentary of two brothers, Patrick and Barry Cullen, skippering a traditional wooden gaff-rigged boat around the world?[16] It was a dream made into reality, beautifully filmed and edited, both funny and emotional. Thinking of the scene recording *Sandefjord*'s homecoming still stirs my emotions.

An onshore camera had been set up to await the boat's arrival. Panning the huge crowd, it zoomed in on Patrick's wife standing near the edge of the wharf, her hands nervously gripping and releasing the hands of her sons, one boy on either side of her. *Sandefjord* had been away for three years and her husband and the father of her boys was nearly home, had returned safely. And as the boat slowly slid alongside, huge, black-bearded Patrick reached out strong arms and swept her slight form over the top of the handrails, holding her in a tight embrace. Everyone laughed and cheered, but the camera also caught the two little boys left standing on

---

16 Sandefjord was a 48-foot Colin Archer design ketch.

the wharf looking bewildered, the smaller one crying. *Who was that strange man hugging his mummy?*

Most of us yachties had got to know *Sandefjord*'s captain and crew during our Durban stay. We knew what it had taken to transform three years of random filming into a coherent movie, knew of the sums of money swallowed up by the process. We wanted it to succeed, were sure it would, but much depended on what the critics wrote about it. And so, we partied until pre-dawn, waiting for the papers to come out. Happily all the reviews were excellent and Barry, Patrick and his beautiful and devoted wife could breathe easy again.

But for all the laughter and excitement the day ended sadly. Here is Graeme's log entry:

Sunday 8th October
Last night one of the crew signed off. Jinky died and in doing so left a void in our cruising plans, which will be impossible to fill. On coming home from the world premiere of the Sandefjord *film he was found apparently asleep on the wharf – but he was dead. We wrapped him in a sheet of canvas and lowered the weighted body into a deep part of the harbour, the fitting burial for a game seaman. Jinky was a real personality in Durban – known and loved by all the cruising yachtsmen and many others as well. He was certainly no ordinary cat but showed a personality, which was almost human. We will both miss him very much. Perhaps it is fitting that Jinky lies beneath the main yachting channel …*

Rowing far out into the bay to bury Jinky was dreamlike, nightmarish. Graeme rowed and I sat in the stern dizzy with shock and tiredness, Jinky's body, wrapped in canvas and weighted with a rock, heavy in my lap. Lowering Jinky into the cold dark water was awful, and I couldn't stop crying.

Our little comedian, he was part of the crew. *We can't leave without him*. What could have happened to him? He looked so peaceful, asleep on top of the wharf posts, his tail curled around him, the way he always did. Crazy notions of him not wanting to sail around the Cape with us popped into my head. It was a difficult stretch of water, I knew, *but did Jinks know something I didn't?* Arguing fiercely against my foolish superstition I reassured myself that he wasn't a piker, he wouldn't skip out on a tough bit of sailing; he'd lived through worse.

I thought of the time he fell overboard in the Timor Sea, how bravely he had swum, hanging in there until we managed to drag him back aboard. And the time he disappeared when we first arrived in Durban, turning up again a week later in the middle of the night, crazily jumping over all the boats, meowing until he had everybody awake. *If he'd wanted a cushy shore life he could have signed off then.*

And still my thoughts kept churning. Could he have been bitten by something, eaten some slow poison?... But no, there wasn't a mark on him, no frothing at the mouth, nothing...

I would never know.

In the end it soothed me to think that the travelling life must have been too much for him, the heat, the storms, fighting with birds, the excitement. He must have lived out his nine lives and simply died, peacefully, in his sleep, dreaming of flying fish. But when we left Durban and *Hope* sailed over the place where he lay buried, my tears flowed all over again.

The cape of storms

South African coastal waters are among the roughest to sail. Winds can be fierce, but that seems minor compared to the treachery the strong Agulhas Current can conjure up. Roughly 60 miles wide, the current runs south along the coast, slowly decreasing in strength before turning eastward to join the Africa–Australia currents. Britannica describes it as the fastest flowing surface current in any ocean, with estimated speeds of up to 5 miles per hour. It's hardly surprising that when the strong current begins to clash with massive swells marching up from the Antarctic, conditions become wild and unpredictable. The phenomenon is unique to the area and descriptions by researchers (and survivors) range from rogue waves to 'holes in the sea capable of swallowing up ships'.

∼

Not a nice thought, and on top of that we had to worry about heavy commercial shipping. The 1967 Arab–Israeli war had closed the Suez Canal, forcing the entire world's shipping around the tip of Africa. Keeping twenty-four-hour watches was essential, and we were happy to take on a crewmember. Peter, a tall and lanky English schoolteacher, was on the lookout for adventure, said he'd taken a job in Cape Town and would love to come. He had some sailing experience and we agreed, expecting the trip to be a week to ten days at the most.

It began badly. Primed for strong wind and huge seas, the last thing we had expected was dense fog, a three-and-a-half-hour ordeal and the worst experience of all my travels, *ever*. Barely out of Durban, not yet past East London, the wind suddenly eased and as if crossing an imaginary border we slipped into deepest, greyest fog. One minute the sky was clear with reasonable wind, and in the next the wind died and we were enveloped in a dense mass of zero visibility. It had happened to us before, off Beira in the Mozambique Channel a thousand miles north, but this was different. Off Beira the fog had been a nuisance, a waiting game with me happily floating above the events, marking time. Sitting off East London in the middle of a shipping lane was nothing less than a nightmare. Before the fog enclosed us we had counted as many as a dozen ships at any given time. We knew that (unlike us) they wouldn't stop, would still be travelling full steam ahead guided by radar. We also knew that the likelihood of us showing up on their radar screens was next to zero; a small wooden boat with a fold-up radar reflector at the crosstrees simply wouldn't. We were in the hands of the gods.

Sound carries differently in fog and the *thump, thump* of passing ships seemed to reverberate all around us, eerie and non-directional. Barely able to see *Hope*'s bows, the three of us sat on deck listening, hushed and helpless; there was nothing we could do. Too terrified to let go, to detach and trust my fate, I fought ghastly visions of massive steel bows slicing the blinding whiteness towards us. Everything in me wanted to scream, become a human foghorn warning the ships away, drown out the incessant *thump thump*. I didn't scream, couldn't, needed the silence to listen and to concentrate, to 'force' unseen ships away from us by sheer willpower, to make them slip past us. Even my blackest vision would not permit a ship to come at us dead centre, *we would have a chance to push Hope out of the way, surf off the ship's bow, survive ...*

Three hours of torture. Night closed in, another half-hour of murky greyness and then total darkness. Then, as suddenly as it had begun, it ended. Powerful wind gusts hit us, and fifteen minutes later the fog was gone. The monstrous ships became visible, their green and red navigation lights showing us which way they were headed. East London lighthouse gave us a bearing and the ordeal was over. The wind promised to be a howler but I didn't care how hard it blew, force 12 if it wanted to.

It may have been our luck that the unusual calm and the horrible fog saved us from worse, such as rogue waves or 'holes in the water'. The current was slowing down and nearly in our wake now, and riding the huge Arctic swells gave us more than enough excitement. Known as Cape Rollers, these giant waves can reach heights of up to 30 metres[17] and to sail them is exhilarating, spectacular. Steering from the cockpit I'd see a huge oil tanker one moment and seconds later the entire tanker had completely disappeared, hidden in the trough between waves; literally a case of now you see it, now you don't.

It's scary to think of waves twice the height of *Hope's* mast,

---

[17] Conservative South African oceanic research has determined that ocean swells travelling two thousand miles up from the Southern Ocean can reach heights of up 16 metres, getting bigger still as they hit shallower waters. Another 5 metres may be added for local storm waves. Some documentation (pravda.ru) puts Cape Rollers at heights of 30 metres, thought to be the case when two coherent waves join up and become one.

but in reality even the tallest swell tends to be nicely spaced apart, at least in reasonable non-stormy conditions. Sailing up and over them is marvellously exciting, first the long slow ride up the face of it, and then a safe enough roller coaster ride down the back of it. The fun stops when gale force winds heighten the waves and shorten the distance between them, and they begin to topple over and break. The worst-case scenario is for a boat to shoot down a steep wave, for her to 'bite' her bow into solid water and then be thrown stern over bow, pure horror known as pitch-poling or more colloquially as arse over turkey. In theory, the best way to survive such waves is to slow the boat down, making it float up and down in the water, a bit like a surfer refusing to catch a wave coming towards him. Getting a yacht to float up and down in hurricane force winds is not as simple as it sounds. Even with all sail taken down, a real howler can put enough pressure on mast and spars to push the boat into unsafe speeds. Yachting lore talks of trailing a sea anchor[18] or streaming loops of rope behind as effective measures to avoid 'surfing' or 'breaking' the wave. One boat rounding Cape Horn reported streaming their motorcycle behind them, a rope fastened through each wheel.

We weathered one four-day storm where the waves became huge, dark, almost vertical walls of water crashing towards us with unimaginable force. Wedged tightly into the cockpit, a towel around my neck and oilskins covering all but my face I stood transfixed, frightened and reassured in turns. I'd feel tiny *Hope* lift up on waves as high as a house, see her decks awash and the dark mast sticking out from layers of white spume ripped off the water. Next thing she'd reach the top, deftly lift her big bottom over the breaking crest like a dancer swinging a hip, and plummet down into the trough

18 A large open canvas bag like an airport windsock but broader and shorter.

beyond. A brief rest, a shudder and then she'd do it again, bravely tackling the next mountain of water. Sometimes a rogue wave would break before she'd get to the top, punch her down, drench her (and me) completely, but throwing off sheets of green water she would right herself, buoyant, ready for more. For all its terror it was beautiful to watch, a riveting drama, each passing wave a relief and a declaration that *Hope* wouldn't let us down.

It took thirty days to reach Cape Town, half of that time stormbound at sea or battling to windward, and the other half sheltering in ports along the way. Peter, our uncomplaining and competent crewmember, fitted in well. It was good to have another strong body aboard and an extra pair of eyes to watch for shipping, but it also had its drawbacks. *Hope* was simply too small for three people almost continually in wet weather gear. I missed the easy intimacy Graeme and I shared at sea, the two of us snug in the cockpit, our discussions, reassurances and joint decisions, more so after our long spell of shore life in Durban. With a 'foreign' crew aboard, Graeme became the captain giving orders. It needed to be that way, but it made the trip different for me, lonely in a way.

An unexpected bonus for our long and difficult trip was that the South African coast, for all its ruggedness, offered us safe and beautiful anchorages. Knysna harbour with its narrow entrance stands out as the most spectacular. *Hope* beating through a rough morning sea towards the narrow gap in the tall rocky shore must have looked fabulous. We saw about a dozen people standing on the cliffs above us watching as we slipped into the channel, over the sand bar, past the sunken wreck of a ship and into the calm lagoon hidden beyond. 'They've come to watch us get wrecked,' said Graeme with laconic Australian humour.

But had we come to grief, we couldn't have been in a more hospitable place. People living on rugged coastlines know what a wet and tired sailor craves, and all of it was provided in abundance. We stayed for a week in the calm, landlocked lagoon, woken by bird song in the morning and feeling blessed. Kind inhabitants offered daily outings, food and drink and when we left Knysna, people once again stood on the cliffs. But now we knew who they were, they'd told us they would come to watch us leave, had wished us fair wind.

Yet in spite of the good wishes it took barely a day before rough seas and persistent headwinds had us running for shelter again; this time into Gansbaai, a small fishing village nor far from Cape Town. Rounding the breakwater under sail we suddenly faced a tiny harbour overcrowded with rows of pilchard trawlers tied fore and aft to moorings. Yachts don't have brakes, but quick thinking, fast work and a lot of luck had us race between two rows of trawlers, round up behind the last one and drop sail before we bumped into anything. *Whew, some entrance, like a drunk falling into the house through the front door* ... The 'boat with the sails' and her crew seemed to have made quite a hit with the locals. We were greeted wherever we went, and a report of our travels was duly published in the *Cape Times*.

I had begun writing long letters to my mother again. Our Durban correspondence had been patchy, more so after Mutti found one excuse after another for not coming to visit us. Hamish would have been happy to have her stay in his house, and with Graeme and I both working the airfare was no problem. When Mutti spent her holidays in Majorca instead, I had an inkling that a new relationship might be behind it. She certainly wasn't cross with me (always my default assumption) but simply doing a better job of letting go of me than I of her. Keeping her in my thoughts and sending her long letters would hold me, keep me safe. I needed her to keep an eye on me, wanted her to put marks on her atlas in search of her runaway daughter...

Gaansbai, 4th December 1967
Liebe Mutti ... happy birthday to you and sorry we are missing another one. I wish you could be with us to see the amazing scenery, more beautiful than any I have seen. There are steep cliffs that always seem to be tinged with a little blue, generous open bays and hidden small fishing villages – and if you look out to sea there is nothing in the way all the way to Antarctica. We are early in the holiday season and there is not a single tourist in sight. Here in Gansbaai we are known as the 'boat with the sails' and young and old make pilgrimages to the harbour to look at us. It is surprising how folks can live so isolated with Cape Town only 70 miles away by road – and 85 miles by water. It's good that we like it here as much as we do, because today is our sixth day. The wind is still from the wrong direction and we had to weather another storm here at anchor. I'd had enough and slept ashore – I had three houses to choose from. We get on particularly well with one family. Every day we walk up to their place and often stay for dinner. The husband works on a new harbour [for Gansbaai] *and has lived alone for the past two and a half years, but now his wife has given up their farm in Cape Town, she has set up their daughter (19) and their son (21) to live independently and joined her husband. They have rented a Hänsel and Gretel fisherman's cottage and are content. The cottage is delightful; small rooms with raw wooden ceiling beams, leaning walls and crooked doors. In the backyard is a toilet outhouse with a little heart cut into the door. From the front one overlooks the harbour, the sea and the lighthouse. The husband is from Poland and his wife has German*

ancestry and for the past few nights we have discussed art, music, politics, weather, people and much else besides.

Graeme wrote his impressions into the logbook, and a bit of social history besides:

What a place! This whole area is the most beautiful part of the world I've ever seen: it is cool and salt smelling – beaches and rocks backed by tall, rugged, folded mountains, which always appear very blue ... Gaansbai is a terribly interesting place. It is, everybody tells us, the last white fishing Bay in South Africa – all the others are run by Coloureds (half-caste). These people are largely Africaans – a type we did not understand before – but find these people to be very friendly. ... the village is a tangle of dirt roads and very old houses, a lot of them made of mud-daub! But here the hospitality is the tops – we haven't had a moment to ourselves – yesterday for instance, the manager of the 'de Kelders' hotel – 2 miles away had us for lunch afternoon tea and dinner.

I remember the day, hours of sitting around the dining room table, chatting, unhurried and warmed by food and wine. I felt mellow and content, the sea beyond the windows beautiful, gorgeous, positively benign. Bright sunlight blazed onto crashing waves and scores of gulls wheeled through clean crystal air. The barometer was on its way down and it was a gift to escape yet another beating, we could enjoy the show from a distance; watch it like a movie that didn't include us. Late in the afternoon, still sitting at table, still drinking wine, the manager told us about water-filled caves beneath the hotel.

'Go and have a dip,' he said, getting up to fetch a key and a couple of hotel towels. 'It'll make you hungry for dinner. You'll stay for dinner, won't you?'

Of course we would.

The caves he'd described weren't easy to find. We backtracked a couple of times, tried to remember the directions we'd been given and eventually found the opening hidden among the scrub. Unlocking the steel gate and leaving wind and sunshine behind, we wandered into a cool angled space, a triangular gateway into hidden passages. Unseen forces had eased rocky slabs upwards into huge steeples, like a house of cards put together by a giant. Unseen cracks in hidden places shone beams of light onto pools of milky green water deep, large enough to swim in. I'd had been drinking Grünmädchen (my favourite South African wine) in enough quantity to imagine kings and fairies beckoning us, *Wow, let's get in, swim in further* ... Getting our clothes off and jumping in took seconds; it took considerably longer to get our breath back. The water was freezing, liquid ice, instantly sobering and a few quick dolphin dives was all we managed. Graeme got out first. Shivering in his nakedness and trying not to drip water on the camera, he took some hurried pictures capturing some but not all of the magic. That belonged to the moment.

❧

The fishermen made it their business to give us daily updates on their perception of the weather, and finally it looked good enough for our last hop to Cape Town. We left in the morning, a lively nor'easterly breeze behind us and the barometer rising, but by lunchtime the joy was over. As if to tease us, the wind swung to the west once again, dead on the nose. Bowing to the inevitable we patiently beat to windward for yet another day before we passed the Cape of Good Hope, looking stark and beautiful in shades in blue and grey. Now our course took us northwards and at long last the sou'westerly, our foe for the past weeks, became a fair wind. Cheering and laughing we hoisted extra sail, and *Hope* raced towards Cape Town as if to embrace a dear friend. A sense of relief, and a flash of pride at a job well done ran through captain and crew. 'Goodbye, Indian Ocean,' I whispered quietly, followed up by a silent *thank you*.

We'd had a rough month, and I was happy to have at least one really fabulous day tagged on the end of it, a day in which to forget all miseries. Sailing was at its best and I kept apologising to our luckless crewmember; *look Peter, look, this is what it's like to sail Hope* ... Adding more magic, the colder waters of the Atlantic seemed to have populated the sea around us. Dolphins swam alongside and we saw penguins and seals by the dozen. The seals were especially charming; rolled onto their sides with one flipper folded under they looked absurdly like mermaids tucked into bed. If one lay in our path I'd race up forward to shout and warn it, 'Hey you ... watch it!' Startled, it would dive, only to appear seconds later looking at me with button eyes and dripping whiskers. Some must have followed us, because that evening two of the lovable creatures played around our boat right inside Cape Town boat harbour.

Cape Town is both beautiful and interesting, but it never had a chance with us. I cooked a goodbye dinner for Peter, he thanked us with a wonderful recording of *Carmina Burana*, the three of us took the cable car to the top of Table Mountain (as one must) and on 22 December, after refusing half a dozen invitations for Christmas dinner, we set sail for Rio de Janeiro. We wanted to be on our way and if Christmas brought warm trade winds, manageable seas and an end to watching out for commercial shipping, that would be the very best of all presents.

The ocean of the seven feasts

Wind charts show trade winds as two broad bands of wind blowing obliquely towards the equator. One band blows from the northeast quarter, the other from the southeast. The general direction is westward and where the two bands converge the wind stops and nothing much happens, and you are in the doldrums. In reality, neither wind bands nor doldrums run in neat straight lines but meander up and down as currents, continents, water depth and out-of-season storms dictate. Occasionally, however, trade winds behave according to the book and when that happens, a yacht sailing westward will get a fabulous downwind ride, 'connoisseur chocolate box sailing'.

After three days of hard sailing with every sail piled on, we reached the edge of our longed-for South Atlantic trade wind belt and to top it off, on Christmas Eve, we got our present. 'Come and look at this!' Graeme yelled. I raced up the companionway and flying above us, perfectly framed in azure sky, was a red-beaked tropicbird, his long thin tail feathers streaming behind him. 'Happy Christmas!' we said at the same time, laughing and hugging each other. *Hope* surging along under her striped spinnaker, a white tropicbird circling above us and Graeme and I holding each other put me in the middle of blue and white heaven. The bird was happy too and extended our Christmas cheer, flying around us for a long time. Tempted to capture the moment I pointed my camera skywards and clicked away, but when I saw the photos months later, only one little square of film held the bird looking down at me, cocking his head slightly as if to tease me ... *silly girl ... want to hold onto magic do you?* He must have humoured me, kept still long enough to allow me that one picture; a gem in a box of colour slides showing squares of azure sky.

~

German Christmas is celebrated on 24 December, and powerful memories are indelibly painted within my heart: a fresco of heated rooms, a table of special foods and Mutti, Pappi and Frank glowing in an aura of yellow candlelight. Even the smells have stayed with me: marzipan, rich chocolate, and the indescribable aroma of one very special Christmas treat, one yellow smooth-skinned orange right in the middle of my plate of sweets.

Rolling along on warm trade winds put me far away from such memories. I loved our different and unusual Christmas but in spite of it, tiny bits of homesickness did creep into my letter to Mutti:

Heiligabend 1967
Liebe Mutti, of all the Christmases I have had this must be the most unusual. I am sitting on deck in brilliant sunshine, not a stitch of clothing on me, and the radio is playing one of Offenbach's overtures. The sea is the deepest cobalt blue with teensy crowns of white foam on top, and Graeme is making plans for what he wants to eat for Christmas dinner tomorrow. I am not sorry that we left Cape Town; out here it feels much more like Christmas than in a crazy crowd ...

we are now exactly in your time zone and it is easy for me to imagine what you would be doing right now. You would be getting dressed ready for Frank to fetch you. Frank will admire his beautiful Christmas tree and Helga will no doubt have her hands full with their excited little boy.

Australian Christmas came the next day and Graeme entered his reminiscences in the logbook:

Christmas Day 1967 17.15
A peculiar sensation to have Christmas alone with Jutta, no Christmas tree, no presents, no relatives or friends ... There is not a lot of motion – the radiogram is on the gimballed stove playing excerpts from the 'Magic Flute' – Jutta is beside me in the cockpit reading William Golding's 'Lord of the Flies', I'm smoking my pipe – Peace!

A digestive pipe was needed. Christmas dinner had been sumptuous, with tinned ham and lots of fresh vegies. William, a farmer crazy about sailing (surely a conundrum!) whom we'd met briefly in Cape Town, had arrived at the last minute bringing us a case of peaches, a sack of oranges, six dozen eggs, plums, potatoes, carrots, tomatoes and two very special bottles of wine. His generous gifts sailed with us, and eating yet another lush peach I never forgot to say *thank you William, delicious.*

~

One of the treats we invented for ourselves was to have thousand-mile dinners on long ocean crossings. The sailing distance from Cape Town to Rio added up to roughly 4,000 miles, which meant three feasts. For the South Atlantic crossing we added four more: one each for Christmas, New

Year, Graeme's birthday and the unique and momentous occasion when we crossed the longitude of Southampton, the port from which *Hope* had begun her journey to Australia six years earlier. Graeme had taken care to pinpoint the precise time when this would happen. The Australian David Guthrie and his crew, Nigel, had sailed her westward via the Panama Canal and the Pacific; thus she had now completed her circumnavigation. Proud of our fine seaworthy ship we drank a toast to *Hope*, and one to us as well.

Food was important to us, and stocking up for long voyages and the cooking of tasty and nourishing meals was largely my domain. Tinned corned beef was a staple. Butter, cream and condensed milk came in tins, and the rest of the pantry was made up of rice, beans, rolled oats, flour, instant mashed potato, freeze-dried peas, powdered milk, sugar, chocolate, nuts and of course a large store of tea and coffee. Rubbing eggs in Vaseline to keep out the air seemed to make them last indefinitely and I never had one go bad. Special occasion dinners consisted of tinned ham, which in the absence of refrigeration had to be eaten in one day. Fresh vegetables, stocked up before leaving port, rarely lasted beyond a week but ham went well enough with applesauce, pineapple, beetroot, asparagus and the good old stand-by of mashed potatoes and fried onions.

Breakfast was porridge with powdered milk and honey. Morning and afternoon snacks were pikelets, pancakes, or packaged biscuits. For lunch we had fresh fruit or shared a tin of fruit topped with custard or cream. Dinner varied and might be bully beef, an omelette, or a tinned soup enriched with potato, onions and whatever fresh vegetables had survived. One failsafe meal when it stormed and the boat heaved in every direction became known as Tongan Stew (I have no idea why). I simply emptied one tin of corned beef, one tin of tomatoes with all their juices and one tin of drained green beans into a pot and warmed it up. Pepper on top, and pronto! A fancier version was to fry onions first, fiddle with the spices and add mashed potatoes.

An absolute favourite was fish steaks – tuna if we were lucky – made to a recipe that my international cookbook listed as Austrian (!). I don't generally bother with quantities and for this particular one my suggestion would be: start with a good quantity of sliced onions, gently fried in butter. When the onions begin to colour, add fish steaks on top. Mix cream with salt, pepper and a generous amount of sweet paprika and pour over the fish. There should be enough cream to almost cover the fish. The trick here is to use a pot that is just the right size to snugly hold the fish steaks so as not to overdo the cream. Cover and cook gently over a low heat. Noodles are lovely with it, but potatoes are okay too.

Keeping bread was the most difficult. The choice was to eat it soft and cut off the mould as it grew, or to dry it out and eat it hard. We opted for the latter and when that ran out, the galley was free for whoever felt like producing a substitute. I did a reasonable job at making damper, and Graeme had fair success at baking pre-packaged cake mixes in a covered frying pan, the heat from the stove diffused by an asbestos mat.

Meals were cooked on a double-burner kerosene stove, surrounded by a guardrail and set in gimbals, reasonably level even in the wildest sea. The galley was positioned aft on both sides of the companionway; a cutting board placed on the top step of the companionway provided the workspace. The spray dodger above kept things dry and allowed fresh air to circulate; a perfect place to cook and a good place to talk to Graeme sitting in the cockpit steering. Egg dishes invariably caused a squabble because I couldn't resist chucking the eggshells overboard, past Graeme's head, and no matter which way he ducked a bit of egg white would invariably end up on his face.

'Do you have to do that?' he'd shout. 'Stop it! Here, give it to me, I'll do it... give it to me!'

But I kept chucking and laughing, the secret revenge of the galley slave.

The bitter note in my South Atlantic cooking adventures was Jinky's absence. Food preparation had been his favourite time and I missed him. Drawn by delicious smells he would sit in the cockpit, his body stock-still, his head following my every move just in case there was a treat for him, a tasty bit of fish or a lick of cream. I thought of him every time I opened a tin of ham, of his impatience, the way he shivered and meowed softly until he had his share; he especially loved the jelly around the meat.

It took a month to cross the South Atlantic, a quick passage with only one stop along the way. Sailing-wise we had the usual succession of calm, too much wind, blown-out sails and magical picture-book sailing in between. Noteworthy were the persistent long swells, sometimes two swells coming from different directions and the wind coming from another. A navy officer in Cape Town had warned us about the phenomenon, suggesting that 'rolling down to Rio' might have been coined because of it. I called it *a boiling mess* in my log entry. Poor *Hope* didn't know which wave to ride and quite often we literally did roll down to Rio. What baffled us was an almost complete absence of wildlife – few birds and hardly any fish. No swarms of flying fish, no dolphins, although one morning we did find a small dead squid on deck. It had tentacles about four inches long and very big eyes. We wondered what Jinky would have made of it.

The self-steering arrangement Graeme had built in Durban worked brilliantly. The ingenious device was the sailing equivalent of a mechanical automatic pilot. Set correctly it would keep the boat on its designated course, as long as the wind didn't change direction.[19] Once we had cleared the shipping lanes we stopped taking watches, with both of us turning in for the night – not entirely agreeable for me. In the daytime the self-steering arrangement was great, but both of us asleep at night left me feeling uneasy. Night watches had been my solitary time on deck, my time for thinking and reflection, for keeping an eye on things. And when it was my turn to sleep, the knowledge that Graeme was in the cockpit keeping things safe had me drop off in minutes, so deeply asleep that no storm, no flapping sail and no amount of rushing water would disturb me. Now, with both of us turning in for the night, part of my consciousness stayed awake, attuned to sailing. The slightest change in *Hope*'s movement or a different pitch in the wind would have me up in the cockpit investigating, checking the course, making sure the wind vane was set correctly.

On top of that the marvellous new self-steering gear brought another unexpected worry. To adjust the wind vane one needed to lie flat on one's belly and lean way out over *Hope*'s stern, and Graeme refused to wear a safety harness, hated them. 'Stupid things get caught in everything,'

---

[19] A wind vane mounted on the stern of the boat connects to a small rudder hooked up behind the large ship's rudder. The vane responds to the wind, adjusts the small rudder, which – in turn – changes the flow of water past the big rudder. The boat responds to the big rudder and thus sails itself according to the wind. If the wind changes, the course changes, but miles from anywhere small course deviations are not a problem. Sailing a little off course for one night can easily be corrected in the next.

he argued. 'I lean out and the damn thing stops me 'cause it's tangled around the winch or some bloody thing.' He argued that without a rope around him he'd be more alert and therefore safer. It made sense and to be truthful, I didn't wear a harness either, but then I always considered myself to be more careful than him. We argued about it for a while but he remained adamant, *no harness*.

'Don't be silly, do you think I want to die?' was his last word on the subject.

A reasonable enough argument but occasionally, woken up by a strange noise, I'd find myself sitting upright in my bunk shouting, 'Are you there?' The answer was always 'I'm here, go back to sleep', either from the bunk across from me or from the cockpit, but the thought of waking up and finding him gone kept haunting me.

Two weeks out of Cape Town, at 0830, Graeme recorded that the faint outline of Saint Helena had appeared through the horizon haze.

> *Fine on the port bow, just where we wanted it – to take advantage of the way the wind backs during the day. Behind us the sky is grey and cloudy after a fine night – perhaps we'll get some rain before we get in. There was a good omen for me at 0600 this morning – four bosun birds at one time circling the yacht!*[20] *Jutta was asleep and is she jealous!*

---

20 Bosun bird is the colloquial term for tropicbird, a term that reaches far back into sailing history. The bosun on the old sailing ships was the person responsible for maintaining the rope work and would always carry his tool, the marlin spike, with him. And so does the bosun bird, his long thin tail feather the 'marlin spike'. Bosuns are true seabirds and can have more than a metre wingspan. Their large webbed

We reached Saint Helena around lunchtime and motored slowly towards what looked like a reasonable anchorage. Graeme was on the helm and I was below, calling out the water depth from the echo sounder: 'Twenty feet, fifteen... eight...' finally screaming, 'Stop, stop, we're aground!' We weren't, and soon the mystery resolved itself. The echo sounder dial registered up to 50 feet; the electronic signal had gone right around the dial once without me noticing it, and my reading of 20 feet was in fact 70. Although close to the land, we still had 50 feet below us. Graeme was rattled, I felt stupid, but we both got over it and dropped anchor soon after in 15 feet of clear water. Jamestown settlement, flanked on either side by steeply rising cliffs looked treeless and grey, spread outwards and upwards into a long gully. A deep scratch marked one of the dark cliff faces, straight, like a chalk line drawn onto a blackboard. *Would this be the Jacob's Ladder we had heard about?*

Getting ashore wasn't for the fainthearted. A short wharf extended from the shore towards a landing platform that ended in steps going down into deep water. A long, slow South Atlantic swell was running, nothing big, perhaps a couple of metres. Graeme rowed the dinghy alongside, shipped the oars, and it was up to me to gauge the exact moment when to jump ashore taking the dinghy painter (tie rope) with me. The idea was to pick the precise moment when the swell was at its highest, that short still moment before the water dropped again taking us and the dinghy with it, fast like an elevator. After a couple of up and down rides I got the hang of it and made it ashore, my sudden

---

feet – round black patches against their white tail plumage – are not proper legs, and on land the birds can only use them to push themselves along. Watching a bosun bird glide with easy grace makes it difficult to imagine such clumsiness.

lunge catapulting me onto all fours. An inelegant landing, but I was happy to have extended my record of never having fallen in the water accidentally. The record still stood when we left the island five days later.

Saint Helena, a British overseas territory, is famous as the place where Napoleon was exiled in 1815, and where he died six years later. What I know about Napoleon's time spent on the island has come from subsequent reading. In Jamestown itself, Napoleon was never mentioned and there was no obvious information about him. Saint Helena's amazing history was still locked away; the island's ancient buildings and grey fortification stood unlabelled, unexplained and uncared for. Canons with the crest of George III (which Graeme guessed to be around 1700s to 1800s) stood pointing seawards. There were no tourists and the island's rugged beauty was reserved for the locals.

Once ashore we were met by Rudi de Wet, the island's Baptist minister. He offered a prayer for our safe arrival and took us to his house to meet his wife Yvonne and their young daughter. Rudi was a young and lively man seemingly starved for new company, and we ended up staying for their evening meal. Rudi told us that he enjoyed skindiving and that he was the only person on the island to own a little sailing dinghy; most of the people in his flock were not interested in such things. Rudi didn't complain; he had a lovely wife, a beautiful daughter and a good collection of classical music to make him happy. But he did mention the inbreeding of the island's population and talked (in the third person) of the loneliness that comes with insularity.

News travels fast on isolated, far-flung islands, and most of the people we met seemed to know who we were. A group of keen young men, VSO volunteers (Volunteer Service Overseas, a British foreign aid group) 'doing their turn', came to meet us, but I never found out what they actually did. The were captivated by our adventure and wanted to chat, *how does one start such a venture, what would it cost* ... Then there was Mr George, a dear Old Salt, unshaven and jolly, who must have watched us sail in, because a couple of days later he turned up with *Hope* correctly rigged inside a flat liquor flask. Delighted with our ship in a bottle we happily paid him the twelve shillings and sixpence he asked for – 'to buy another bottle' as he put it, and judging by the smell on his breath and his ebullient manner, probably for its contents.

Rudi remained our faithful guide. Determined to show us 'the best view in the world', he picked us up one sunny morning to drive us up to the top of the island on roads that wound precariously around the cliffs. The island is steep, one half of a volcano. It looks stark and forbidding from the sea, but as we drove over the crest above the town the scene changed to thick layers of vegetation and lush fields, a contrast so complete and unexpected it shocked the senses. Suddenly we drove through a different world, the road lined with stately old homes – seemingly empty – and clusters of small houses where local people stepped outside to look and wave. Winding upwards the road got rougher and narrower, empty except for the occasional man walking beside a donkey. Halfway up we stopped for the picnic lunch Rudi's wife had packed for us, but Rudi hurried us along, determined to reach the top before the weather closed in on us. Thin mist had begun to swirl around us and for all of Rudi's wishing the swathes of mist gradually thickened into clouds and we had no choice but to turn back. We had missed our chance and the 'most beautiful view in the world' stayed firmly wrapped in clouds for the entire time of our stay.

Exploring the township, we tried to get inside one of the large stone buildings facing the town square but found the huge wooden doors locked. A few questions led us to the harbourmaster's office, where one of the employees fetched a key for us, handing it over with a casual 'bring it back when you've finished please'. What a key! Hand-forged in steel, it needed a tight fist around its shaft to carry it and two hands to fit it into the lock. Opening the massive timber portals was the most exciting part of the adventure because once inside, the stone-flagged rooms felt creepy and oppressive; damp, dark and empty. There were fireplaces, but it was hard to imagine that open fires would make these rooms any cheerier, especially on long winter nights. Napoleon must have played his interminable card games in rooms just like these. I read somewhere that the playing cards got so damp that they had to be periodically dried by the fire to stop them from sticking together.

It was a relief to get back into bright sunlight again. After carrying the key back – how I would have loved to keep it! – we decided to climb the steep stone stairway, the chalk line running up the cliff we had spotted when we first arrived. Known as Jacob's Ladder, it numbers 699 continuous stone steps and leads to a settlement above Jamestown. We'd been told that the record for climbing it was held by a local man who did it in seven minutes. It took us forty-five minutes, and the reason we made it at all is that halfway up we had an argument that kept us both in adrenaline. I have forgotten what it was about (how come we never fought at sea?) but whatever it was, by the time we got to the top we dropped it, shamed into silence by the spectacular view. Leaning on yet another stone wall, we surveyed the neat model town beneath us: a square of solid buildings, one good patch of trees and a rectangle of sea wedged in by steadily rising, bare cliffs. *Hope* looked tiny, we could only just make out her topsides, a bit of white on the edge of an endless blue sea.

Climbing Jacob's Ladder (before starting our stomping-up argument) we had wondered why the steel pipe handrails on either side were so smooth and shiny, unusual in such salty air. Who would polish the rails and why? Climbing down the 699 steps, we learned the answer to our question. A shouted 'Make way!' had us jump aside and seconds later a young man whizzed past us at an incredible speed, his bottom perched sideways on the handrail and his arms outstretched for balance. Once past us, he gathered even more speed by casually stretching out one leg and kicking himself along the steps as if he was riding a scooter. The ultimate slide down a banister and the most efficient, if dangerous, form of public transport I've ever witnessed. Was this normal? Did everybody 'fly' downtown like that or was the young man in training for the Jacob's Ladder downhill speed contest ... up in seven minutes and down in seven seconds? The clean handrails seemed to indicate the former; polished to a perfect sheen by the bottoms of uptown residents.

We had hoped to pick up fruit and fresh vegetables for the next leg of our journey but there were none. The little shop in the square could only offer us peaches at one shilling and sixpence each; a few cases of them had been brought in by ship a week previously. Whatever was produced in those lush fields up beyond the grey steep cliffs must be for family consumption only. Water wasn't the best either and we were discouraged from filling our tanks; apparently it had worms in it. Luckily we didn't have to, our tanks were reasonably full and rainwater was easy enough to collect, but having to do without fresh fruit and vegies was disappointing. Rio de Janeiro was a long way away.

On our last morning we called in at the hospital to get a supply of antibiotics, just in case we needed them. Skin-diving with Rudi, Graeme had stepped on a sea urchin and the wound was beginning to look red and nasty. A sturdy British nurse in Reception listened to Graeme's request but didn't produce the goods. Her swift response was to stick a thermometer in his mouth, take his pulse and direct him to the waiting room. The thermometer in his mouth kept him quiet and I giggled, both of us aware that protesting was useless; this was a woman of authority, regulations had to be followed and *no arguments please*. Following the slow and proper order of proceedings Graeme eventually got his antibiotics, and free of charge.

But free of charge stopped when we had to pay the princely sum of two guineas for our port clearance. It was the first time we had been asked to pay and Graeme was hurt, pointed out to the harbourmaster that Jamestown was a British port and *Hope* was a British-registered vessel. A predictable stance from an Australian used to objecting to British authority in his home country, but the harbourmaster proved as unbending as the hospital nurse. Deaf to all objections he produced his book of *Rules and Regulations*... no money, no stamp. Brazil was our next port, we clearly needed the stamp and Graeme eventually paid up, yet even authority-conscious me was tempted to tell the harbourmaster to 'stick it' and simply sail on. We had South African port and customs clearance, and who was to know where we had been?

Rudi, Yvonne and their daughter stood on the wharf to wave us goodbye. I was sad as usual, seemingly unable to leave port without shedding tears. Saint Helena in its ruggedness and beauty had charmed me. Sailing westwards, we talked of the people we were leaving behind and the isolated lives they lived. Our world of wind, sails and unbroken horizon was isolated too but for us it was temporary, merely a phase in a string of adventures. Soon another island, another chunk of land would appear over the bows to give us new impressions, have us taste different foods and meet new people. I looked forward to Brazil; for me cruising had become an even mix of longing to be at sea and wanting to make port, a perfect reason to keep moving, because one could not exist without the other.

We set course for the Trindade group of islands, about 800 miles off the Brazilian coast (not to be confused with the famous Trinidad in the West Indies). Despite the trade winds playing hide and seek with us we travelled fast, clocking up several daily runs above 150 miles, good going for a 9-metre gaff-rigged cutter. I grumbled about the wicked swell but also knew that complaining was ungrateful. The wind vane did the steering, and both of us were well. Graeme's foot had healed, and I was feeling better after shaking off a bug I had picked up in Saint Helena. It wasn't seasickness as I had at first assumed, because strange symptoms besides the vomiting definitely pointed in the direction of a gastric complaint. I had revelled in the fact that I had not been seasick since Cape Town, and for reasons I can't explain it stayed that way.

Life at sea soon fell into its uncomplicated rhythm of

day and night, wind and sea. Our only fixed duties were to get good sextant sights and to keep an eye on the compass. There was nothing to hit, no rocks or shallows, deep water for miles and miles and no shipping to watch out for. We were free to watch the waves play, look out for birds and fish, sunbathe, read, play patience, listen to music and talk. Europe had entered our thoughts, and we began sketching out rough timetables and money matters, idle chatter because we could as easily talk about Australia, Africa or what Brazil might be like.

On the ninth day out, we celebrated Graeme's twenty-eighth birthday and on the following day, late in the afternoon, we caught our first glimpse of Martin Vaz, a huge uninhabited rock and the first outcrop in the Trindade archipelago. We were happy to see it because it verified our position. Recent cloudy skies had made sextant sights less reliable, currents were unpredictable and as I wrote in the log, *piling up on that lump of rock would mean goodbye Charley*. Not wanting to sail though the archipelago at night, we pushed on for another couple of hours and hove to. Setting the alarm for an early start, we turned in.

By 4 a.m. we were on deck, sailing into blackness towards Martin Vaz. By first light the island lay abeam, looking grey and shrouded like a mythical castle, home only to the birds wheeling above it in moving patterns of black dots. Thin curtains of rain erased the apparition for minutes at a time only for it to appear again, medieval and mesmerising, afloat in sheets of mist. I wondered what the Portuguese would have made of it when they first sighted it back in the 16th century, not knowing what lay ahead, one man plumbing the depth with a lead weight and another stationed at the lookout on top of the mast.

Compared to the explorers of old we had it easy, knew

Martin Vaz to be the first outcrop of a submarine volcanic chain. Our chart told us that Trindade, the main island, lay 25 miles to the west and that no rocks or shallows lay in between. We had been told that the Brazilian Navy had a base on the island but it was not used year round. I didn't care; always the romantic I confided in the log how thrilling it would be *to step ashore on a large totally uninhabited island hundreds of miles from anywhere.*

The wind was brisk and we reached Trindade a few hours later. Sailing into the lee of the island, we slipped under the shelter of Pico Monumento, a giant thumb sticking straight up above rugged terrain. Neither wind nor waves reached us; we needed no anchor, simply dropped all sail and sat there taking in the amazing scenery, our first bit of land in ten days. Thousands of birds – red-footed boobies, sooty terns and masses of frigate birds – noisily milled around the tall cliffs streaked with red, yellow and white, and in the shadows below *Hope*'s hull we could make out the slowly moving shapes of large turtles, their patterned humps and long necks squiggly in the deep greeny-blue ocean.

The cliffs bordering our resting place plummeted almost vertically into the sea, leaving only a couple of thin strips of beach at the bottom. Launching the dinghy seemed pointless; once we landed there would be nowhere to go. We would be patient; *there must be beaches on the other side of the island, that teensy bit of sand wouldn't be enough for all those turtles to lay their eggs. We'll check it out later.*

For now we would make the best of the calm water and do a few repairs. The stitching on *Hope*'s mainsail had rubbed through in a couple of places and I took heed of the adage that 'a stitch in time saves nine' and got busy. I'd learned the hard way that wind will find the tiniest gap in a seam, worry it, flap it around and next thing it'll rip metres of seam open like a zipper. Graeme checked through the rigging, tied on a couple of staysail hanks that had come adrift and took yet another photograph of me stitching up sails, my labour of love. A quiet cup of coffee, a goodbye to the turtles and we made sail for the windward side of the island.

The wind caught us as we rounded the point, sailing close to shore and keeping a lookout for the navy post. In sharp contrast to the tall cliffs on the windward side, we found sweeping bays and good deep stretches of beach, beautiful and inviting but very much open to the wind. Anchoring would give us a worrying and uncomfortable night. We eventually spotted the settlement, nothing more than a couple of low buildings, but a careful search through binoculars showed no signs of life, no person waving, no boats, only the wreck of a frigate washed up on a beach.

'I hate wrecks,' I said, 'let's sail on,' and so we freed the sheets and headed west once more. Pico Desejado, a rounded cupola tall above the rugged terrain (big brother to the Pico Monumento 'thumb' on the other side of the island) was the last bit of grey to slip below the horizon. I had missed out on exploring my deserted island but found balm for my disappointment in the fact that we had disturbed nothing. All those green turtles must have been pleased that we didn't walk all over their lovely beaches. But disappointment must have lingered. A day later I wrote to Mutti:

Mid-Atlantic 27th January
To find our journey suddenly extended by over a week is not the best for morale, but in spite of it we don't regret that we stopped to look. The island was very impressive, almost a moonscape, craggy and torn ... there would have been millions of birds – there were millions I am sure, I have never seen so many. One kind, called fairy terns, I like particularly well. They are snowy white like doves but much slimmer

with a long black beak and black eyes. They usually fly in pairs and to see them against the blue sky looks fantastic.

South America was 800 miles away, and the sea cast her spell once more. Graeme returned to his marine charts and the joy of putting crosses on the map marking our daily runs. Foolishly perhaps, I had never bothered to learn the intricacies of sextant navigation, and happily that worked out for me. My positioning strategy was more poetic than charts and triangles, I simply imagined *Hope* on a world map, my bird's-eye vision giving me the pleasure of seeing her distinct shape, bowsprit and gaff-sails finely sketched at intervals above a thin unbroken line, the way square-riggers (or Baltic Cogs for that matter) were drawn onto maps of parchment. My imagery put me into the company of explorers, placed me neatly into a specific part of the world. Steering into a dark night I sailed along my map, south was down, north was up and islands and continents fitted around the globe in exactly the way I had learned in geography classes.

I knew where I was. In the last month one arched line beginning in Cape Town had landed us smack on the dot marked Saint Helena. The next arch took us to Trindade. Here the line did a few half-moons, not touching anything, and then ran west again in a straight line aimed directly at Rio, tiny sketches of fully rigged *Hope* positioned into the ocean above it. In a few days she would reach the huge bulk of South America. All was well.

Winds were fair and we knew how lucky we were when the BBC newsreader told us of gale force winds in England, of a volcanic eruption in Sicily and of the damage caused by cyclones that had swept across Cocos Island and Mauritius.

We were on the other side of the world, blessed with warm sunshine. Graeme returned to a bathing routine he had invented on earlier trips. Soaping himself all over with shampoo, he would climb over the rail and lie on the bobstay (the wire that runs from the bowsprit down to the waterline of the boat) to be dunked and water-blasted as the boat rushed along. *Hope*'s bowsprit was nearly 2 metres long, giving plenty of room for his antics. Back on board, exhilarated and super clean, he would pity modern boats without bowsprits. My 'dunking baths' were limited to *Hope* travelling no faster than 3 knots; any more than that made it too difficult for me to pull myself out of the clinging water and get back aboard.

Graeme took up wood carving again, a model of our beloved *Hope*, and I began stitching up a small Brazilian flag to fly at *Hope*'s crosstrees, a courtesy gesture towards the country we were about to enter. Not an easy project: a blue circle within a yellow rhombus on a flag of green. I had planned to embroider *Ordem e progresso* written onto the band curved across the blue circle, but time ran out and I ended up printing it with marker pen.

At night, in clear weather, a large city can be seen from a long way off, its location revealed by the glow of lights reflecting from the clouds above. We had begun looking for it and suddenly, one night, there it was, a tiny umbrella of light stuck on the horizon. *Rio! Almost there!* But, as if to teach us patience, soon after sighting the tell-tale glow, the wind dropped to almost nothing. It took two very long nights of coaxing *Hope* along in the lightest of breezes before Rio harbour finally opened before us – a stunningly beautiful, almost otherworldly sight for two tired sailors. Gliding into the smooth expanse of silvery water, edged by rounded hills barely visible in pre-dawn light, we couldn't keep our eyes off the brightly lit statue of Christ, hovering above the still dark coastline, more distinct than any lighthouse could ever hope to be.

Rio de Janeiro

Rio held two drawcards for us. The first and most obvious was to experience Carnival, which would not happen for another month. The second reason was more immediate: Rio was said to be the only harbour in the world that could rival Sydney's in beauty.

Approaching the softly peaked hills at dawn, finding entrance into the safe harbour and coming to rest in the deeply sheltered bay off the yacht club was spectacular. The top of Sugarloaf Mountain peeked over the green hills bordering the bay and Christ up on the Corcovado blessed us with outstretched hands. On that first day I would easily have given Rio top marks over Sydney, but I modified this in weeks to come. Taking friends out on *Hope*, we found the harbour devilish to sail on. Fiendish winds changed direction in unexpected ways as they funnelled through the surrounding hills. Flattened one minute and flapping around in a calm patch the next simply couldn't compare to the joy of broad-reaching down Sydney harbour in a steady southerly. In a straight beauty contest Rio would have to win over Sydney, but talking as a sailor I will call it a draw.

The yacht club was huge, a suburb in itself with bars, dining rooms, tree-shaded verandas, a beautifully landscaped swimming pool, open-air coffee bars (serving free coffee day and night) and even a hairdresser. The lights never dimmed in the various clubhouses, with hundreds of people drinking and talking at leisure. Exquisitely dressed women flirted and laughed with tanned, casually dressed men, all of them infinitely sure of themselves. The club was an alien shore for rough adventurers. Yachting seemed a mere sideline, the boats stored in huge halls on acres of ground.

Our arrival drew a small crowd looking on in quiet amazement. *Why would people do such things, from Australia in that boat ... really?* One man winked at me, touched his biceps and said, 'You very strong.' Heavens, all I had done was tie up the boat! After a long shower and doing the best I could with my hair, I searched for make-up in the bottom of my bag. I found the small purse but looking at its contents, could not use it. I simply couldn't – being one with wind and waves for the past month had completely removed lipstick from my horizon. Staring at myself in a wall of mirrors I saw a red-cheeked, scrubbed girl in a rumpled shirt, exposed in a brilliantly lit room. Women on tall shoes moved around me swaying like willows ... was I the alien here, or was it that slim silver-clad creature next to me, huge black-ringed eyes and glossy black hair rolling all the way down her back – *Look, she is putting on lipstick ...*

I got over my culture shock and lipstick qualms. A couple of days later I looked at myself in that same mirror, grinned and said *Okay kid, you have entered lipstick land ... put on the red stuff and join the fun.* The man who had admired my biceps turned out to be Fernando, a very attractive 50-something charmer who never stopped flirting with me, especially in front of his 25-year-old mistress. He promised to teach me to samba – and other things – and I was never sure if he was joking or not. One day a group of us were standing at the bottom of Sugarloaf waiting for the cable car when

Fernando took me aside to show me the thick steel cables running over massive, greased wheels. 'You must not worry,' he said. 'It's very safe. This cable comes from a German coalmine ... very safe.' Did he really want to reassure me, or was he taking the Mickey out of me? It was the former; he did want to reassure me, the steel cable did in fact come from a German coalmine.

I made friends with Christine, a Brazilian girl who spoke fluent English, French, Spanish, and was now studying German. Her easy grace, her self-assurance, and her total air of *belonging* amazed and surprised me. Brazil was *hers*; she was Brazilian, she moved Brazilian, she laughed Brazilian. Her grounded-ness exposed my barely conscious desire to find a place where I could belong, made me question my roving ways.

Christine interpreted for us when necessary, she helped me get a haircut and took me shopping, dipping in and out of endless boutiques along Copacabana with much laughter and running commentary; *look at that man, whew he's gorgeous ... look at those beautiful kites ... do you like kites, do you like swimming* ... I bought shoes, not wicked high heels but gorgeous golden sandals, and a soft orange swimsuit because I couldn't resist it.

'For someone who doesn't walk much, you seem to need a lot of shoes,' quipped Graeme.

True, I had bought a lovely pair of pink suede sandals in Cape Town, but they didn't go with the new outfit Mutti had sent to Rio. Mutti liked to answer my long letters with parcels, and the one to Rio contained bikinis, shorts and a couple of skirts. She knew better than Graeme that a girl needs new clothes even though the company she keeps is constantly changing.

The Rio Yacht Club was an enclave for the elite, the club

members separated from most of Brazil's population by wealth, social standing and (more blatantly) by a high iron fence and armed guards at the gate. Perhaps Christine had whispered into the Commodore's ears that we were not rich (how unthinkable, poor people with a yacht!) or a short segment on Brazilian TV showing Graeme coiling ropes had made us visible, but suddenly we were handed invitations for club events with complementary tickets attached – tickets so expensive that the cost of one would have stocked up our pantry for a year.

Gerhardt, a Lufthansa pilot stationed in Rio, had seen us on TV and came to introduce himself. He was a keen sailor and, unlike most club members, actually sailed his boat out on the harbour. His wife was holidaying in Germany, and with time on his hands, he shepherded us around. He loved Rio and his travelling life, his only bugbear was the 'slipshod Latin ways'. When we first met he was still full of adrenaline, outraged at the audacity of one 'hick pilot' who had squeezed ahead of him just as Gerhardt was about to bring his 707 onto the runway. Flying a small two-engine plane *this guy just pipped ahead of him – like someone trying to be first off at the traffic lights*. Gerhardt had to abort his landing and launched an official complaint, but of course nothing came of it.

Gerhardt told us another, much more frightening story. One South American airline (which he refused to name) had a contract to use the Lufthansa maintenance facilities. One day the German mechanic assigned to service the foreign plane had stormed into the office red-faced angry, refusing to work on *that* plane. Inspecting the hydraulic system, he'd found jam tins hanging on wire loops under the line connections to catch the leaking hydraulic fluid. Whenever the plane landed somebody would hop up and pour the fluid back into the system. *Nothing wrong with that*, was the argument. *It works.*

That selfsame Lufthansa mechanic came down to fix our engine, which, once again, was on strike. The good man stepped aboard, sniffed briefly and said, 'What are you running this thing on?' It turned out that we had picked up contaminated fuel somewhere back in the Indian Ocean, a mix not quite petrol that made the engine cough and run intermittently. Washing the tank and cleaning the fuel lines finally fixed the problem.

We met a lot of Germans in Rio. Perhaps because I was German, or else the population had an above-average percentage of Germans. Often, when our fledgling Portuguese failed us, we would find someone speaking German – once a young woman who spoke a broad Bavarian dialect, difficult even for me to understand. We learned that her parents were German, that she had married a German man, and that her children were going to a German school, yet she had never been to Bavaria and was not in the least interested in going there.

Then there was George, a fierce German nationalist who declared that he would not put foot on German soil as long as occupying forces were still stationed there. He had been on the *Graf Spee* – a German WWII warship much hunted after sinking nine Allied merchant ships in the Atlantic. Badly damaged in one battle, the *Graf Spee* only just made the neutral port of Montevideo. Defying international law, repairs for the disabled vessel were refused and the *Graf Spee* was ordered to leave port. Faced with taking a sinking ship out to sea, the captain chose to scuttle the *Graf Spee* in port to save her crew. Did George mourn the loss of his ship, or the loss of the war? I never found out because back then I didn't know how to ask such questions.

Gerhardt introduced us to another German couple, friends of his, the husband a foreign correspondent for the Deutsche Presse-Agentur. Before coming to Rio, the couple had been stationed in Rome for ten years. I envied them for what I imagined to be a sophisticated gypsy life, staying in exotic places and being paid to get to know the people. Yet, an evening at their place was not as cosmopolitan as I had thought. It was more like a trip home; we had pumpernickel with quark and chives, small squares of bread with *Leberwurst*, dill cucumbers and *Braunschweiger*, a type of sausage I had not tasted in years. Drinks were *Schwarzwälder Kirsch*, German wine and spirits – the only exception was the ubiquitous whisky, for which there seems to be no national equivalent anywhere.

The view from their apartment high up into the hills, however, was uniquely Brazilian, a vast carpet of twinkling lights tracing random patterns around the dark waters of the famous harbour, the dark shape of the Sugarloaf dimly visible. Late at night, as we sat on low couches in near-darkness to enjoy the view, our host put on his favourite music and the slow and aching words from Verdi's *Nabucco* 'Chorus of the Hebrew Slaves' filled the room. *Schöne Heimat wann seh ich dich wieder*, rich and moving music that I have come to love since, but at the time it felt strange to be faced with so much homesickness, so much nostalgia. The million-dollar view and not wanting for anything stood in stark contrast to music that stirred up deep sadness and heart-wrenching longing.

We met Julio and Doris at one of the club events and accepted their invitation to stay at their property in Resende, about a hundred miles inland. Julio and Doris were Hungarians, possibly refugees from the 1956 uprising, but that is only a guess. One does not talk of hardship surrounded by beauty, at least not in Brazil. Julio had a business dealing in precious stones and like all the 'foreigners' we met, he *loved Brazil*. The four of us, Julio at the wheel, drove inland through lush green mountainous country. Green undulating fields bordered the road, each turn offering something different – a clump of exotic flowers or a view of distant mountains. A fertile and thriving countryside wrapped in warm moist air, the epitome of fecundity and as far away from the dry and dusty Australian outback as one can imagine. I was charmed to see truck drivers sleeping in hammocks slung underneath their cars parked by the roadside. The midday heat was overpowering, and siesta time was sacred. Heat and high humidity makes one want to flop and rest, and doing little more than wait for the cool of the evening soon became our habit too.

Julio, an expert in precious stones, was proud to show us Brazil's famous jewels: sapphires, tourmalines, emeralds and rubies. I should not have looked because I fell in love with a beautifully cut large round aquamarine, refracting every shade of blue, ablaze and sparkling like the sea. I wanted that stone, *I really wanted it* but sneaking a look at the price quickly made me realise that blue sea and sky would have to be enough for me. As I reluctantly put the stone back, my mind teasingly replayed a folk song I used to sing as a child:

Gold und Silber lieb ich sehr, kann's auch gut gebrauchen,
hätt ich nur ein ganzes Meer mich hinein zu tauchen ...

Listening to the lyrics going around in my head, I had to agree with the words... yes, I did like gold and silver in coin, but if it can't be had I'll settle for the silver in the moonbeams and the gold in the stars. And on that score I was rich, very very rich.

The person that came closest to connecting us with ordinary everyday men and women living in Rio was the painter Silva Costa. Only a few years older than us, he had travelled, studied in America and spoke good English. He adored his country and his people. Bursting with energy, he swept us along on various excursions. He took us into dusty favelas to listen to bands practising the samba for the coming carnival; scary places with tumbledown dwellings and no street names, where garbage removal did not exist and electricity was illegally tapped from overhead wires. We drank beer and shared pizza in a newly opened place in Copacabana, stacking up beer mats for each bottle consumed. Silva made it his treat to drive us up the winding roads to the Corcovado and stood beside us looking at Rio spread below, dwarfed by the 38-metre-tall statue of Christ behind us. We sat in his studio drinking, chatting and keeping him from his work; he was happy, tomorrow was another day. I loved his work, a style called encaustic painting; using a hot iron tool he set colour and gold pigments into a smooth thin waxy-looking emulsion with stunning results. Silva had the open heart and mind of an artist, childlike and sophisticated, as comfortable in the poorest parts of Rio as he was in the luxurious setting of the yacht club.

Suddenly, almost overnight, the languid yacht club scene changed as preparations got underway for the arrival of thirty-five international yachts, participants in the Buenos Aires to Rio yacht race. Wives and friends of the crews arrived and American voices added volume to the multicultural mix, loud with speculations as to who would win the race. The big day arrived and the first boat to cross the line was the 73-foot American *Ondine*, one of the new breed of super maxis. It was *Ondine's* first serious ocean race, and she came in a full twenty-seven hours ahead of the same-sized *Stormvogel*. The race had been tough, strong headwinds for the entire way, and the usually elegant club bar noises changed to a raucous show-off contest with rival boats bantering and mocking each other, reliving the moments, still running high on adrenaline. It was a man's world, one sailing master openly admitting that if his wife had been along on *that* trip she would be divorcing him now.

Very rich men, their names synonymous with well-known corporations, had escaped their boardrooms in American skyscrapers to sail their boats. The race had been won or lost and it was time for fun. At one end of the bar it was a contest for the best toilet stories. A crewmember in one of the crack boats had been silly enough to use the head (toilet) in the very forepeak when a huge wave lifted the bow *sky high* taking the sailor with it. Second later he was slammed down onto the toilet bowl so hard that *it came away from its moorings ... and here I was on the floor, wet weather gear round my ankles, fighting a ricocheting toilet bowl, not to mention the contents.* That story was quickly topped by another crew who had *pumped three days' worth of shit into the shore locker ... would you believe it, the rubber pipe running through the damn locker busted and nobody noticed. We'll be wearing T-shirts for the prize giving – our blazers stink.*

One lot of sailors hugged the bar drinking an invention they called Port & Starboard; a red drink for port followed by a green drink for starboard, some adding a 'clear one' for the stern light. It looked like Campari, crème de menthe and vodka to me. A killer mix which only tough sailors, hyper-charged with the excitement of beating into a South Atlantic gale for a week, could survive. The prize-giving celebrations (one crew did attend in T-shirts) were lavish, a fitting warm-up for the carnival celebration just around the corner.

~

Ash Wednesday marks the beginning of Lent, the traditional period of fasting and abstaining from bodily pleasures, and the three days prior to it is Carnival, a last wild uprising before the rules kick in again. Around three-quarters of Brazil's population is Roman Catholic, and walking the streets of Rio there is no doubt that people are religious. At any time of the day churches are visited, prayers are offered and candles are lit. We visited one cathedral, where offerings took the form of gold leaf pressed onto holy statues; the size of gold leaf dictated by the person's wealth, or perhaps by the weight of a sin committed.

Visible from almost anywhere in Rio is the statue of Christ, beloved by all. Yet the way people relate to the Redeemer differs from other Catholic countries. The people of Rio, or Cariocas as they call themselves, laugh with their God. We were told that Christ up there on the hill is watching them closely and when *just one person* does a decent day's work, He will clap his hands and of course He has not clapped yet. In another country such jokes might be frowned upon, even punished.

In Brazil it's okay, God is not so stern, He is one of the people, a friend you can bargain and laugh with. Their God lets them have Carnival, when He temporarily suspends the rules that chafe a hot-blooded people. For a glorious and brief time such commandments as 'thou shall not covet they neighbour's wife' are pushed into the background by the samba and then it's back to normal, lighting candles in churches.

Rio Carnival is an outrageous, three-day, full-on celebration revolving entirely around music and dancing. *Blocos*, meaning 'blocks' of people from specific neighbourhoods, prepare for the event all the year round and in the weeks before the big parade, samba practice reaches fever pitch and the sound of countless drums and tambourines, guitars and trombones can be heard from all quarters of town. Members of each neighbourhood have their own samba band, compose their own songs and wear similar costumes on the day of the parade. The bands are judged, and winning the yearly competition is a huge honour.

⁓

We bought tickets to watch the parade from grandstands erected on either side of the streets, but it was a waste of money because I could not sit still. The relentless samba had my legs moving and before long we danced with the *blocos*, swept along by long-limbed bikini girls, women dressed in ball gowns made entirely of feathers, grotesque half-naked humans painted green, and undulating bodies in slinky creations, tight as skin. Elaborate headdresses swayed atop gorgeous unidentifiable creatures, cross-dressed to defy whatever gender might be written on their birth certificates. To be who you want to be is the rule of Carnival and it mattered little that it rained for almost the entire time, a mere nuisance because nothing could stop the samba.

In the yacht club the celebrations were held with a *Goldfinger* theme and over a thousand invited sit-down guests. Rows of tables and chairs and a dance floor had been set up outside; starting time 10:30 p.m. And gold there was aplenty; the trunks of palm trees had been wrapped in gold paper, the grass was sprayed gold and golden flower arrangements floated in the swimming pool among the jets of a floodlit fountain. Huge bowls of fruits decorated the tables, watermelons cut in half, bunches of bananas sprayed gold. Next to each plate, a glass was fitted into a holder made from half a pineapple – sprayed gold of course. Birds carved from melon flesh, pinned onto slender sticks, flew above mountains of crabmeat and chicken legs. Every imaginable delicacy was laid out and an army of servants stood by to fetch whatever else anyone might wish for. Alcohol was free, empty bottles discreetly replaced with full ones. There was enough gold jewellery to satisfy a band of robbers, and James Bond would have felt blessed had he been allowed to team up with any one of the beautiful gold-lamé-clad women. Two large bands, made up largely of drums and trombones, took turns to play non-stop samba, leaving no time for talking.

At some time during the night, armed guards opened the tall steel gates enclosing the yacht club, and last year's winning Samba School was allowed to make a brief procession around the yacht club grounds. Everyone stopped and clapped while the group were given a glimpse of how the very rich lived. The procession snaked through the grounds, around the pool, back out through the gates and then it was back to dancing. It struck me that despite the glamorous setting and the elegant dress of the yacht club patrons, the samba and the dancing was the same as that of the visiting Samba School, no different to what we had seen on the streets of Rio. Clearly at Carnival time there is only one way to dance: wild, uninhibited and non-stop.

～

Dawn was breaking. Happily tipsy and all danced out, I began to think of bed. I found Graeme in the noisy crowd, still wearing a large cardboard kangaroo sprayed gold on a string around his neck – his Australian ID. We had 'one for the road' and as we rowed across the dark water towards *Hope*, pink light tinged the rounded hills. The golden moon sat low and each oar-stroke left small pools of phosphorescence in our wake. A romantic and still moment, the night was over and it would be sweet to cuddle up, talk about the party, make love perhaps... None of that happened, because as soon as I had stepped aboard, Graeme decided to go back to the party, turned the dinghy around and rowed off, leaving me sitting on deck.

Alone under the golden moon I felt sad, then miserable, then seething and finally furiously angry. *It doesn't matter where you get your appetite as long as you eat at home* popped into my head; one of Graeme's favourite one-liners re fidelity. *Very funny, ha ha hah ... out getting your appetite are you?*

'Hell hath no fury like a woman scorned', a maxim handed down from the 17th century, still held true 300 years later. *Hope* had to be slipped and repainted and my first rebellion was to refuse to work on the boat. It had never bothered me to scrub weeds and stinking anti-fouling paint off her bottom, my hair a wet mess and wearing throwaway clothes. This time it did. 'It's too hot,' I said, 'you'll have to find someone else to help you,' and headed for the bar to socialise over gin and tonic. My second more serious rebellion was to have an affair, which happened as soon as I allowed myself to have that thought, and with a man I really liked. I am incapable of making love without affection, an ethical lining around the cloud of my wickedness. The man was Brazilian, the very same 50-something Fernando who had admired my biceps when we first arrived weeks earlier. I had seen a bit of him since, our attraction was mutual, and he ended up teaching me more than the samba.

Our clandestine meetings were in his furnished room in one of the club's storage buildings, 'a bedroom away from home' as he jokingly called it. Fernando was married, had a house, grown children and a lover, *of course*; a crazy, warm and affectionate man. 'Stay with me, don't leave,' he whispered half-seriously, both of us naked far deeper than our skins, the depth and the fierceness of our encounter surprising us both. 'You stay young and I'll come back for you,' I teased him, tracing a finger around his dark eyes, smoothing out his laugh lines.

Leaving Rio three weeks later was easy and welcome. We rounded Sugarloaf and set course towards Ilha Grande, a short stopover before the long haul up the Brazilian coast. I happily left behind ease and luxury; my brief affair little more than a fevered dream all wrapped up in the colours of carnival. We were sailing again; I loved our boat, our life, the blue sea and the most beautiful part of the Brazilian coast ahead of us. But sexy Brazil it remained. Graeme and I made love on a lonely beach somewhere in the deep reaches of Ilha Grande. A horse sidled over to watch us, making us feel self-conscious, but we need not have worried. After a while the little white horse danced over to his horse-wife and began nuzzling up to her. We couldn't help but laugh, but when I thought about it later, self-consciousness returned. On the beach I had assumed that the horses were wild but perhaps they weren't. I seemed to remember a fence near the horse and fences mean people. Thus the horse must have had an owner, and he could have been watching us too. Thinking that made me smile because knowing a bit about Brazil by then it wouldn't have mattered. If he did watch us, more than likely he would have hurried home to make love to *his* woman, who would have sighed and wondered what got into him. Sensuous and unrestrained Brazil – horses and all.

South American coast

Ilha Grande, a couple of days' sail southwest from Rio, is a perfect cruising ground with hundreds of islands, small fishing villages and beautiful scenery; the Polynesia of Brazil. We'd been advised to see the historic township of Parati *and not to miss the excitement of riding down long smooth waterfalls on banana leaves.* All our expectations were fulfilled, yet after a week of paradise my log entry records a shamefully blasé attitude:

20th March 1968
Every anchorage is like out of a picture book and one gets quite matter-of-fact and complains if there is not even a waterfall or coconuts easily to be gotten. Time we go to sea again, cold, wet and miserable ... so that we have fresh eyes and a hungry mind to discover Bahia.

It was high time we kicked ourselves out of heaven, for many good reasons. The start of the Caribbean hurricane season was only two months away. We'd hoped to be in Miami by then, and here we were riding down Brazilian waterfalls like happy children. Backtracking eastwards we sailed past Rio at night, an umbrella of soft light suspended over the city, and reached Cabo Frio by midmorning. Once around the hump of Cabo Frio we could begin to sail north towards Salvador, Bahia.

It took three days to get around Cabo Frio. All day long we'd tack endlessly into infuriatingly light headwinds. By sundown the breeze would drop altogether and by sunup the ocean current had carried us back to where we started. The morning breeze would spring up and we'd do the same again. For three days it was *Good morning Cabo-bloody-Frio, I'm sick of you*. Graeme took it so badly he accused *Hope* of 'searching out calm spots'. Spending time with millionaires and seeing the amazing gear on some of the racing yachts in Rio had stirred his discontent. He kept himself busy designing a new boat, a 45- to 50-footer with a rig that would drive her 8 knots to windward, and a diesel engine to push her through calms. Contrary to past convictions, he now wanted to be rich, not rich like Rockefeller, but wealthy.

My response to sailing over the same ground for days was more measured.

31st of March
We are concentrating on staying sane. A pleasant way of passing the time for us is making future plans. We have gone through our Europe trip, Graeme's future job and study in the States, our future kids, our future yacht, our future home.

Privately, I thought about my little Rio affair. My conscience did a few callisthenics but there were no regrets. It had been good to sink into a world of pure feelings, to find a complete emotional echo and be adored simply for being a woman. Graeme often forgot that I was a woman *and* a sailor, that this was a cruise *and* a marriage. Leaning towards the pragmatic, he steered clear of emotional deep waters, saw no need for love tokens. The thought of him rowing back to the party after the *Goldfinger* ball still roused my ire, was hard to let go of. *Latin people kill for love*, I fumed. *Even men in freezing countries, the Russians, my own people; the cool Prussians shot each other for the honour of a woman. Aussie blokes kill for a cold beer.* But looking at Graeme busily designing another yacht for us, it suddenly hit me that there wasn't another man anywhere in the world I'd rather be sailing with. *It's what you signed up for girl ... sailing over ocean, not drowning in emotion.*

But still the tide of my discontent wouldn't turn. 'The best way to go cruising is to find a crew and marry her' dropped unbidden into my head – Graeme's stock advice for would-be sailors, another one of his beloved one-liners. How I hated that line, so dismissive, as if I was the crew he picked up in a waterside bar and lured me aboard with a bottle of gin. *What's wrong with saying you need a wife who loves the sea, who wants to sail and knows how to do it ... oh no, might take the shine off his crown ...*

Graeme is still busily designing our new boat, oblivious of the quarrel raging inside my head.

'What do you think of a foam sandwich construction?' he says. 'Kurt wants to build their next yacht like that.'

'Not sure I like that,' I reply. 'I'd prefer timber, don't like Tupperware boats.'

Looking over his shoulder at the plans he's drawn I suggest changes ... 'Does it need to be that big? We'd need a crew.'

'No, not with a sloop rig, we'd manage that easy.'

'But we'd have to have a steering wheel, I'd rather have a tiller.'

And with that little conversation my wrath vanished. As so often before, salty air, far horizons and sailing boats pared me down to my barest bones, where we were nothing more than a man and a woman hungry for life. I was hungry and *it felt good to be hungry together, greedy and adventurous; we'll have a baby in Germany and keep moving, we'll get another boat, travel Europe's waterways ... down the Danube looks good ... the Mediterranean perhaps.*

Prophetic words.

I was back on an even keel. After five years of in-love-ness and one crazy little Carnival affair a different feeling emerged, a stronger, safer base. We'd be okay; we were right for each other.

Both of us wanted a child, had talked about it for some time, and I decided to stop taking the Pill.

～

Cabo Frio finally slipped astern, and we headed up the Brazilian coast. Light winds prevailed and we had to claw every bit of northing away from the mean current. And if that wasn't enough trouble, on one bright and sunny afternoon a coastal freighter headed straight for us with alarming speed. We assumed that he was coming over to look at us – freighters often did – and would soon change course. Not this one, he kept going straight for us, and fast. Graeme grabbed the Very pistol and shot a flare directly at his bridge but there was no response – nobody on deck and nobody on the bridge. Siesta time. Luckily our engine started first go and we got out of his way by a slim margin. 'Bastard!' Graeme yelled after him as the ship's wake rocked *Hope*. Everything happened so fast that we registered neither name nor nationality, just a big rusty hull hurtling past. I stood shaking, weak with fear and relief. *Rust-bucket! Careless, murderous crew!*

Less dangerous, but also noteworthy on that journey, is

the fact that we overdosed on bananas. As we left one of the villages in Ilha Grande a casual bystander had heaved a large eight-hand stock of green bananas onto our deck, simply lifted it off the stack piled onto the wharf for pickup. I wouldn't have dared, *surely this was stealing*, but pleased with our farewell gift we strapped the bunch up against the boom crutch. It took a week before the vivid green fruit turned to a softer yellow, but our idea that they would ripen one hand at a time proved wrong. They all ripened together.

'Do you want your bananas sliced lengthwise or crosswise before I put them into the custard?' – or the fruit salad, the ham sandwiches or the bully-beef curry.

Maybe crabs eat banana – I tried feeding it to the little beasties packed tightly around the boat on yet another day of calm. There were thousands of them, cute miniatures only a centimetre across their red furry backs.

Maybe the manta wants banana – a huge ray, which we estimated to be 8 feet across and weighing around 300 pounds, had jumped clear of the water and plopped down again with a massive noise.

Monkey jokes abounded, I performed a poor copy of a Josephine Baker dance, and finally the lusty rendition of 'Yes! We Have No Bananas' in two languages.

Nicht Erbsen, nicht Bohne auch keine Melonen,
Bananen verlangt sie von mir ...

... and with that the stripped stock, with a few hands of overripe bananas still attached to it, was consigned to the deep blue.

Monday 8 April 1968 – Graeme's log entry shows the relief of finally making port:

Salvador Da Bahia at last! Yesterday at midnight we dropped our anchor at the yacht club, 15 days 6 hours out of Ilha Grande. Looking back it was a pleasant if slow trip. Under the circumstances we couldn't have done better and we have learned a lot about taking Hope *to windward ... Bahia is a perfect mix of old and new, rich and poor, pretty and ugly. It's a million-inhabitants city with a small-town atmosphere. A big overgrown place, added onto from all possible angles.*

Fifteen days at sea, standing watches all the way and the excitement of a new port took their toll on me. Returning from our first shore excursion I wrote to Mutti:

I was totally exhausted when we got home. I stretched out on the carpet to relax and woke up four hours later. It's now 9 p.m. and I'm happy as can be, but it's beyond me how I could sleep for four hours, lying on three square-metres of carpet without a pillow and my legs curled around the table. Graeme tried to wake me several times but couldn't.

Almost the first person we met in Salvador was the harbourmaster; he was delighted to learn that Graeme was an engineer ... it would please him if Graeme could give a site inspection for a building. In heavily accented English he explained that he belonged to a group that channelled spirit beings. The group had begun building a two-storey community centre, the calculations for it transmitted by one of their mediums from 'a German engineer' who had passed away. The woman transcribing the information had no technical knowledge and it would be good to have Graeme's professional assessment ... *the group is meeting tomorrow, can you come please?*

Bemused at the unusual request for his professional services, Graeme agreed and the harbourmaster picked us up the next day. The building, a small unassuming concrete structure, was still very much in the beginning stages. The foundation, columns and first-floor slabs had been poured, and people were working at different parts of the building in a seemingly random way. 'What's it like?' I whispered. 'Not brilliant,' he whispered back. 'Won't fall down, if that's what you mean?' It was what I meant, and that was what the harbourmaster wanted to know too. He was pleased and invited us to stay; the group was due to meet in the building next door.

We were curious. Had we been invited to a Macumba meeting? We'd heard that Macumba, based on African beliefs and practised by Afro Brazilians during the 19th century, was still prevalent in the Bahia region. Speaking with the harbourmaster this seemed unlikely. He was educated, had a good job and a family – not the kind of person I imagined would practise Macumba, a secretly performed black magic condemned as superstitious witchcraft by Brazilians we'd asked about it back in Rio. *But was it?*

A group of about twenty people had assembled, young and old, most of the women dressed in white. We were introduced; there were smiles all around and the harbourmaster translated their gratitude and compliments. Graeme was the hero; he had looked at the new building, it was sound, and everybody was excited about it. The formal meeting began when a group of men and women took up chairs placed in a circle facing inwards. Everybody else, including us, stood outside the circle. The whitewashed room had an electric light bulb hanging off the ceiling, almost too bright, no secrets here. A bit of shuffling, an air of expectancy and then a motherly looking black woman read a passage from what we recognised as a Christian Bible.

Then total silence, soon broken by a slight young woman sitting in the circle beginning to moan and twitch. Everybody's attention quickly centred on her, but nobody moved. The twitching increased, her eyes rolled to the ceiling and suddenly she crashed to the floor, thrashing about wildly. Two men from the inner circle jumped up to hold her down. The girl, her eyes shut and her face distorted, kept kicking, trying to break free, the room noisy with moaning, heavy breathing and chairs kicked and falling over. A third man jumped up to help but suddenly, as quickly as it had started it was all over and the girl lay still and exhausted on the floor. I sat stunned, frightened by the spectacle of seeing a small girl, still a teenager, show the physical strength to break the grip of two big men. Had it not been for the happy faces around me, obviously pleased with the visit from the spirits, I would have fled. I have no idea what the girl was shouting, what kind of spirit had entered her, or what the significance of the visitation was.

Chairs were straightened, the girl got up and smoothed down her dress, and everybody sat down again. People could now ask the mediums for messages from the spirits, and that included us. The way to get this information was to stand behind a medium sitting in the circle and touch her shoulder from behind. Graeme chose one woman and she began muttering something about sailing and him being strong, which freaked him out because she spoke in English. I didn't fare much better; when I put my hands on the shoulders of another woman, she began uttering German words and made distressed machinegun noises. What was I to do with that information? I knew that machinegun noises were part of my history along with other scary things, but her making those noises could as easily mean that I was threatened now, or in the near future. I tried to find out from the harbourmaster, but he couldn't tell me either. He simply accepted what had happened, no need for reasons, no extrapolations.

I must have hidden my doubts well, because after the meeting the harbourmaster invited us to his home for dinner and let us sit in on a healing session he'd planned for his young daughter – after the spirits had come was a good time, his daughter had not been well.

The little girl was about 7 or 8 years old, pretty with dark eyes and long black hair, clearly very much loved by her parents. She was resting on the couch in their lounge room, fussed over by her mother and greeted with much affection by her father. After the meal – which the girl didn't share – her father began the healing session. He sat very still for a time, concentrating while the almost dark room grew eerily quiet. After a time he got up and bent over his daughter, speaking words I didn't understand. The girl closed her eyes and became tense, almost rigid, seemed to stop breathing. I wanted to jump up and hold her but didn't ... *it must be okay*. The mother sat silent and serene in a chair beside her daughter. After a minute, perhaps longer, the girl's features began to relax and she started to smile. Her mum and dad were smiling, too, and laughing after that; the bad spirits had left their daughter and she was in good hands again.[21]

---

[21] Later reading has convinced me that we had met Spiritists, slightly different from Spiritualists. Spiritists hold reincarnation as a fundamental belief and followers engage with, rather than interpret spirit entities. Spiritualists (as a whole) may or may not believe in reincarnation, but both groups believe in God. Their practice is known as white magic and thought to be good since God is invoked first, hence the Bible reading.

Freedom of religion is enshrined in Brazilian law and many faiths flourish, often unique to specific regions. African slaves brought their ancient cultures with them, western beliefs have added to them and religions such Candomble or Umbanda are now widely accepted. Many Christians, Catholics and Protestants alike, openly believe in the Orishas[22] and may attend both orthodox churches and spiritualist meetings. Putting a bet each way, Brazilians have God as well as the ancient spirits looking after them.

Walking the streets of Salvador had me question the strong religious bent. I found it distressing to see young people lying silent and unmoving on the streets, clearly very poor *but were they still breathing?* The harbourmaster, our guide and companion, dismissed my concerns. 'It is normal, it is their fate, it could be me in my next life,' he said, and if a person's legs were in his way he simply stepped over them. Where was the compassion, I wondered; Mother Theresa would have given them a good talking to.

For all the distressing aspects of poverty and injustice, ease and lightness seemed to rule the days. The churches were busy, the streets were busy, the crowds happy and noisy. Little boys tried to sell us combs, and round women wanted us to try food cooked on open roadside stalls. In the huge waterfront markets crammed with every necessity and luxury one might desire, I bargained for a colourful double hammock, my own piece of Brazil, *mañana* woven into it. The attitude of mañana attracted me and enticed me. If swinging in a hammock could make me forget my

---

22   Orishas – revered in many parts of the world – are spirit manifestations of Olodumare, the supreme Being worshipped by the ancient African Yoruba people long before Christianity, Islam and other religions were established.

father's dictum that *I must not leave for tomorrow what I can do today*, Brazil had transformed me.

We checked for letters before we sailed, but nothing had arrived.[23] I wasn't concerned; sometimes mail got lost or took longer than it took a yacht to sail there. We rarely stayed in port long enough for a proper exchange of letters anyway, and Mutti and I had got used to our one-way conversations. The questions I had asked of her in my letter from Rio might now be answered in Trinidad, the next address I had given her. Telephoning was out of the question; even if a connection could be made via umpteen exchanges, the cost would have been horrific. Besides, I liked being unreachable, it was half the charm of cruising – to be at sea, away from it all. Mutti knew where I was, and I faithfully sent bulging envelopes from every port. They always seemed to get there.

~

Hope's pretty silhouette was once again sketched above my imaginary line on the globe, curving gently in a half-circle around the broad shoulder of the South American continent, past the huge triangle of the Amazon Delta and on towards the Guyanas. We had skipped Recife, unwilling to stop because fair winds had us sailing like devils. We were back in the trade wind belt, the winds blowing at their perfect best. The current was with us for a change and *Hope*'s stern wake was a streak of bubbles; glorious 'blow the man down' sea shanty weather. This is what we had longed for inching our way up the Brazilian coast, barely ghosting through the numerous calm patches. Stopping was unthinkable, a refusal

---

23 The cruising community shared a list of addresses: c/o Embassies, Trade Commission, or simply poste restante for a smaller town. In Bahia it was c/o the British Consul.

of a heavenly gift. Graeme's crosses marking our position on the chart every noon made huge jumps towards the chain of the West Indian Islands... *not far now.*

Europe and going home had began to feel like reality, could be as little as three months away. I listened to a tape my brother had recorded for us, playing it again and again. To release the sound of Frank's voice in the vastness of the Atlantic drew him close. I had last seen him in Sydney over four years before. He was a married man and father now, his son nearly 2 years old. I looked forward to meeting the little family, and Frank's ears must have been burning with the love I sent him.

The Southern Cross sank a little lower each night and I began to recognise star constellations I had grown up with. In shipping lanes once more, we set night watches, but sitting in our snug cockpit, illuminated by the soft glow of the compass, was easy and enjoyable. *Hope* steered herself, her slow dipping and rolling and the sound of the waves pushing her along deeply familiar. Occasionally I would put my head above the spray dodger to look around and watch the sails create kaleidoscopes of shapes against the night sky. Sometimes, high up in the rigging I could hear a woman's voice calling words into the wind or intoning melodic mantras. If I felt strong and well I added my own voice, harmonising softly with her tunes. At other times I felt it better not to and I simply listened.

The choice to call in at Georgetown in Guyana was arbitrary; we might as easily have picked its immediate neighbours Dutch Guyana (now Suriname) or French Guyana next to that. Georgetown apparently had a yacht club; it would be good to speak English again and from there it would be a quick jump to Trinidad, the starting point for the last leg of our journey. Formerly British Guyana, it had gained independence two years earlier, and we expected a similar environment to Kenya.

We were wrong about the yacht club. There was none, and we ended up anchored off the docks, in the strong tidal flow of the yellow-brown Demerara River. The wharfs looked dilapidated, and flat, muddy-looking land stretched into the distance. The official language was English and the population a complex mix of descendants of European immigrants, indentured labourers, African slaves, East Indians and Chinese as well as indigenous Aboriginal Indians. Guyana had gold and mineral resources, but it didn't look a rich country.

Georgetown's harbourmaster was Australian; his wife and children were with him, their oldest son at boarding school in Sydney. What we heard over dinner wasn't encouraging. Crime was high and we were warned not to go out at night and keep to the main road in the daytime. One of the local specialties was called 'choke and rob'. The thief would ride up behind the victim on a bicycle, put an arm around their throat to choke any cries for help, extract purse or wallet with the other hand and ride off again at great speed. A similar system operated in the movie theatres, and solo patrons would not sit alone, but would join a cluster of viewers already seated. We assumed it to be small-time crime and took care not to be caught out, but vigilance was not enough.

Georgetown in April was unbelievably hot and sticky and coming home late from a party in the rowing club one night, we made up separate bunks to get some air; Graeme opted for the main cabin under the skylight, and I took my sheets to the forward bunk under the open hatch. Almost asleep,

I heard steps on deck. Instantly alert, I sat up to check but was quickly pushed back onto the bunk with the point of a machete. *You scream and I kill you*, was all I heard before I sank into a slow-motion dream state, the world spinning into shapes. Focussing hard on the arm reaching through the hatch and the gleaming black face above me I willed myself not to move, to stay conscious and not disappear into tempting blackness. I could hear people moving around in the main cabin, soft voices. *Where was Graeme?*

I don't know how long this man stood over me, only that it ended. Shaking and weak I lay still for a long time, too terrified to leave my bunk in case one of them was still aboard. When all was quiet I crept on all fours into the main cabin. Graeme was lying in his bunk, unmoving, and for a frantic second I thought they'd killed him. But then I heard his breath, a little snore, and shaking him hard I whispered, 'Wake up, please wake up, we've been robbed.' He murmured drowsily 'Go to sleep, you're dreaming.' He'd had a lot to drink at the party and it was hard to rouse him, but when he did and saw it was true, he was on deck in a flash ready to fight.

The thieves took money, our entire camera equipment, binoculars, radio, pots and pans, food stores bought that day and not yet stored away, clothing and shoes. Looking at the mess in the cabin showed that they had taken their time to check through everything carefully. They'd even gone through Graeme's trouser pockets, discarded the trousers but decided to take the belt. The brazenness was upsetting. The thieves knew we were aboard, it was obvious; *Hope* was anchored in the river and our dinghy was tied up behind.

The police came but it was mere formality, *nothing can be done about it, sorry*. The local papers ran an article about it and people stopped us on the streets afterwards to apologise, begging us not to judge their country by a few 'undesirable elements.' I was unnerved by the incident, and the harbourmaster's family took me in until we could sail again. Graeme stayed aboard, setting traps, sleeping with a gun beside him. My peace-loving husband (known to happily share his car with spiders) turned would-be killer. It took a couple of days for us to restock and replace what we had lost. To pay for it we broke into our emergency fund, a parcel of (luckily) well-hidden Australian opals, which we sold to an Indian jeweller at a reasonable profit. Electronic banking did not exist, and I sent an express letter to Mutti asking her to transfer money from our German account to a bank in Trinidad, our next port.

We left on the afternoon tide with a lively breeze behind us. Gradually the broad yellow river dispersed into blue water and it felt fantastic to be away. But when the wind eased and the turning tide threatened to pull us back into the river, deep anxiety swamped me. How vulnerable we were, barely clear of the land; any little motorboat could come alongside throw us overboard and nobody would ever know. Not a good thought for watching a ruby sun sink into yellow-streaked water. I was exuberant when the breeze sprang up again and the low land dropped behind, leaving only a dirty smudge topped by a string of lights.

Sailing free, I counted our blessings. It was fortunate that Graeme had slept through the robbery – sober and awake he would have fought the intruders, got hurt and possibly killed. Equally fortunate, and a little surprising, is that the robbery left no traumatic memories for me, no dreams or flashbacks, no fear of going to new or strange places. It happened in Guyana and I seem to have left it there. At some level of my consciousness I must have known that the men were simple thieves and had no intention of killing us. They played with us, *rich people on white yacht* ... a machete at my throat an effective way to keep me quiet. I imagine that an *intention to kill* would convey a much more terrifying energy, and happily I was spared that.

Calypso country

Edged by the Atlantic swell rolling in from the east, the West Indian Islands, Virgin Islands and the Bahamas run like stepping stones from above the South American continent to the southern tip of Florida. Taking good daily runs and anchoring most nights, a couple of months should be plenty of time to cover the distance of about 1,500 miles, weather permitting of course. The hurricane season had already started, but nobody seemed to care. Locals and yachtsmen agreed that should it happen, there would be plenty of warning. But crosses and inscriptions, flattened trees, damaged wharfs and smashed boats high above the tidemark, their ribs protruding from the sand like skeletons, spoke their own warnings. Listening to the weather forecast became a not-to-be-missed morning ritual.

Port-of-Spain in Trinidad was our first West Indian port and has remained the most memorable for me. Still flush with money from our opal sale, we treated ourselves to a night out with dinner and floorshow at the Hilton nightclub, a huge party in a riot of noise and colour. Rum was the favoured drink and did much to heighten the overall exuberance. I can't swear to this, but I'm *almost* certain that the bottle of rum on the table was free and only the mixers had to be paid for. A steel band produced glorious calypso sounds with the dozen or so band members laughing and shouting at least as much, if not more than their adoring audience. Dressed in white suits, tall and handsome with huge smiles and glittering eyes, it would have been a sin not to adore them.

The lead-up to the floorshow was a group of crazy performers dancing on broken glass (no blood). Next came a limbo dancer, a snake of a man with rubber limbs. Seeing is supposedly believing but watching him limbo-dance his way under a burning rod resting on two small Coca-Cola bottles had me sceptical... *surely not ... this had to be a trick of the light.* But the star of the night was the Calypsonian, a traditional composer-singer improvising funny songs drawing on political or social events, often spiked with sexual innuendo. Ours was a clever performer with an outrageous laugh, jumping all over the stage picking up words and phrases shouted at him from the audience. Seconds later, backed by the steel drum band behind him, he'd composed a cheeky song around them; never lost for words or a song. On this night he made Graeme his target and amid much laughter managed to end every ditty with the refrain that *de man with de beard has de big bamboo* – his body movements leaving no doubt what *de big bamboo* meant. Port-of-Spain was still an out-of-the-way place, and a yacht from Sydney Australia tied up at the wharf didn't go unnoticed in the cricket-crazed island.

But Trinidad wasn't all smiles for us; there was no mail for me at the Post Office and the bank draft we had hoped for hadn't arrived either. Did Mutti not get my Georgetown letter? *Maybe I should place a person-to-person call to Mutti ...* But telephoning her from distant place had never worked before, and it would be expensive and money was scarce. The bank clerk had no way of checking if a deposit had been made; all he could do was to give us a list of islands where the bank had branches and the solemn promise that he would forward the money if it arrived. It was tempting to stay in Trinidad, we couldn't think of a better place to get stuck, but in the end we decided to sail. At a pinch we had enough in the kitty to get us to Miami, provided we stayed clear of nightclubs.

With the trade winds strong on our beam, *Hope*'s best point of sailing, we headed northwards along the leeward side of the West Indian chain of islands, sweet and gentle sailing with wild bits in between. For a time, *Hope* would graciously glide along in flat seas in the lee of an island but once past the tip of it, the strong trades funnelling between the islands would catch her full on the beam and she'd take off like a wild thing, her lee rail under and flinging rainbow-tinted spray all around her. For a time, we'd race across bright choppy seas, and just when it was beginning to get too wet and uncomfortable we'd slide into the lee of the next island, back to gentle sailing, dawdling along in search of a good anchorage.

Some islands were independent; others were British, French, Dutch or American, each with its own distinct character. Grenada and the Grenadines showed off with the prettiest scenery (and, happily, delivered our anticipated bank draft). Martinique was laid back and relaxed, with French street cafes; St Martin looked positively Dutch, with squeaky-clean, red-roofed houses; and Antigua boasted the best, 100 per cent hurricane-proof harbour. We made brief stops at most of the well-known islands but favoured less-known places and deserted bays. Marking an untouched beach with our footprints was still the essence of cruising for us. The pleasure of travelling with the wind and charting our own course had not paled.

One of the most memorable anchorages we found was marked *Deadman's Chest* on Peter Island, one of the Virgin Islands group. Always keen to climb the highest peak for exercise and a good view, we found that Peter Island rewarded us amply on both counts. First with a hefty climb through dense scrub, which left us scratched, hot and winded, and secondly with a heavenly view, which gave us the feeling that we had reached not just the top of an island but the top of the world. Far below us *Hope* rested prettily, snug and safe in the lee of the land, a palm-fringed beach curving around her. The wooded land sheltering her gradually eased down towards a long, low point, where fierce winds pushed the sea into fantails of long ripples, shaded in different blues. Across the stretch of wind-driven water stood another island – softly folded green peaks above white beaches, and beyond that only the faint shapes of distant undulating land. The only sign of life we could make out was another sailing boat, a white dot far out across the water, hours of sailing away, too far out to even guess what kind of boat it might be.

❦

Our first American port was Charlotte Amelia, the capital of St Thomas in the Virgin Islands, and there was no doubt that we had reached America. Taxis were air-conditioned and the local radio station beamed out almost non-stop, noisy, over-the-top commercials; one memorable one promoting laxative chewing gum. *So convenient ... and nobody will knoaw your proablem.* Graeme liked to pun and soon he was off ... '*The more you chew the more you go,* what if you swallowed it, would it *gum you up?* ... What would it do to the bedpost overnight ... does the mint flavour—'

'Okay, okay Graeme, enough.'

But miserable feelings crept in soon enough when we sought out yacht brokers to list *Hope* for sale. With Miami still a thousand miles away it felt sneaky to do this to her, rude, like telling a guardian angel to get lost. *Should we do this at all ... maybe we should keep sailing? The Panama Canal isn't far, then Galapagos ... Tahiti would be amazing, but then what? What about Europe?* I had not seen my family in years, we wanted to have a baby ... *Maybe I'm pregnant already ... what if Hope doesn't sell?*

Feeling the pressure, Graeme and I ended up fighting about nothing in particular and ruining our supposedly peaceful onshore domesticity once again. I stormed off, walked the town for hours, drank too much coffee, hated St Thomas and ended up buying a dress; a very pretty white linen dress printed with yellow daisies, which unfortunately did nothing to cheer me up. It took another couple of days of feeling gloomy before I was back on course. *Hope will sell, and it's the right thing to do. No more ifs and buts!*

Ready for the last leg of the voyage, we set sail for the 600-mile leg to San Salvador, a small island at the edge of the Bahamas and the place where Christopher Columbus is said to have made his first landfall. San Salvador means 'Holy Saviour' and paradise must have been on Columbus's mind when he first sighted the lush green hills. His journal notes that *the beauty of these islands surpasses that of any other, and as much as the day surpasses the night in splendour.* We totally agreed with him, but that is where the Columbus comparison ended.

The most obvious difference was that we had detailed charts to help us navigate through the 2,000 cays and 700 islands that make up the archipelago. And on a more personal side, Columbus was a God-fearing man and we were fast turning into sun-baked hedonists. Sometimes alone, but often in the company of other yachties, we did little more than swim, snorkel and party. Rum was cheap and excellent, and we kept an earthenware jug of punch cooling in the shade of the spray dodger for afternoon drinks, generally assumed to be legitimate *after the sun has dipped below the yardarm*. Mixing the punch was simple, the recipe easily memorised: one part of sour (limes) two parts of sweet (sugar) three parts of strong (rum) and four parts of weak (water).

And if our rough-and-ready punch wasn't sophisticated enough for us, we were always welcome to join super-friendly, super-rich American yachting folk, travelling on huge yachts and luxurious motor cruisers. It was their fashion to raise a cocktail flag at sundown to let everybody know that drinks (with ice cubes!) were on. For many of our hosts Australia had not yet been put on the globe. *Australia, you come from Australia, oh really, that's nice, what's it like ... must go there one day.* Graeme swears that one man asked him if they spoke English in Australia.

Graeme's guitar, stored away for samba-mad Brazil, made a comeback. If the company was receptive, we'd sing Australian folk songs, but Calypso tunes seemed a better fit by far. Just about every island was featured in a song and before long we sent 'Bail down to Bimini' with the Kingston Trio and sang Harry Belafonte's 'Jamaican Farewell'. My personal favourite was the Beach Boys' 'Sloop John B', the refrain about wanting to go home now holding new meaning for me.

For a time we shared anchorages with a young couple sailing a yellow catamaran and the singing switched to 'Yellow Bird Up High in Banana Tree'. The *Yellow Bird* couple were sailing their last season. The wife had inherited a modest sum of money and felt it needed to be put to good use, to buy a house or something. 'Money is a bloody curse,' Graeme muttered. 'They're crazy ... just think how long you could cruise on forty thousand smackeroos.' 'Forty years,' I replied dryly; we lived on about a thousand dollars a year.

If we were lucky, we might squeeze another year out of our dwindling finances but never mind, we had a song for that too; our all-time favourite 'Side by Side' – almost a theme song with its theme of travelling into the unknown, sharing whatever might come.

∽

The Virgin Islands behind us, we slipped into the clear waters of the Bahamas. To glide through invisible liquid over very-much-visible sandbanks dotted with rocks and coral was scary at first. We had reasons to be careful – *Hope* drew 6 feet – but I soon learned that there was no need to panic; every time I dashed to the depth sounder there were still metres of water beneath the keel. Crossing the Great Bahama Bank on our way to Nassau was especially eerie. For an entire day we sailed over evenly shallow sandbanks, dark shapes and shadows whizzing past beneath the keel. By then I had learned to trust the charts, and sitting on the crosstrees high up on the mast, the camera slung around my neck, I took pictures of *Hope*, pushed along by three white sails through a watercolour world tinted entirely in aqua and blue.

Anchoring in the many cays and islands became easy teamwork. I'd climb aloft to shout directions and point the way while Graeme handled the boat. From up high the map was laid out in brilliant colour: blue was deep, turquoise deep enough, whitish turquoise still okay, turquoise-green meant patches of seaweed, brown showed rocks to be avoided, and deep purple indicated coral heads and a definite no-no. We would search out a good patch of sand and once the anchor was down, look over the side to see if it had 'bitten', *does it look okay or should we put down a little more chain perhaps?* In one place, unhappy with where the anchor had dropped, Graeme jumped overboard, pulled himself down along the chain, picked up the anchor and carried it to a better spot. Foreshortened by the clear water he looked like a dwarf in a Grimm Brothers fairy tale, clumping along, weighed down by a mighty plough.

The long chain of the Exuma Cays, our last bit of flawless tropical splendour, dropped behind, and civilisation closed in on us. Nassau proved frustrating, with an unexpected battle over our American visas and with the heartache of making the rounds of yacht brokers once more. Again we were told that it wouldn't be easy to sell *Hope*; she was a classic wooden boat, immaculately kept and maintained, but she was 36 years old and, as one agent told us, Americans liked new things. If the identical boat, gaff-rigged and all, had been built yesterday we would have no trouble and she would fetch a good price. 'Is he telling us he wants a replica when he can have the real thing?' I fumed. 'He can't be serious, does he want a fibreglass *Hope* with aluminium spars and a stainless-steel galley?' I felt cross and refused to believe him. *There should be more respect for our grand old lady, everybody loves her, she is sound through and through and will still be sailing when she's a hundred years old.*

·~·

I kept my faith even after we arrived in Fort Lauderdale, Florida's major yachting centre and boating supermarket.

Never mind the thousands of other boats for sale, somebody would fall in love with *Hope* the way we had; somebody who knew and loved boats would really want her. I was sure of that.

We found a berth at the Marina del Americano and went to collect our mail at the British Consulate in Miami. I hadn't heard from home since Rio de Janeiro, over four months past, and there was a stack of letters from friends and family, forwarded from places as far back as South Africa. But the news from home was unsettling. Mutti had not been well; high blood pressure had caused blood vessels in her eye to burst and she was recovering from a difficult eye operation. My brother's letter was uncharacteristically sharp; he was clearly annoyed that we had not been reachable and, as I had to admit with a guilty stab, he was right. *Perhaps I should have made that call from Trinidad ...*

Feeling shocked, selfish and guilty in turns, all I could think was how lucky it was that nothing more serious had happened. Mutti seemed to be okay now, but what if she hadn't been? *Too bad, Mutti, sorry, I'm busy sailing, having a good time ...*

Graeme and I sat on the embassy steps to talk things through, and the solution was relatively simple. I would fly ahead to be with Mutti, and Graeme would stay behind to sell the boat. We tracked down a cheap flight on the same day; a small inter-island plane would take me to Nassau, another to New York and yet another across the Atlantic.

And so, five days after our arrival, we had a miserable farewell at Miami airport. The little island hopper plane took off into bright sunshine and, in what seemed like a special favour to me, banked very low over Fort Lauderdale. I saw rows of boats tied up at the Marina Del Americano, knew that one of them was our beautiful *Hope*. My heart ached, and closing my eyes tightly to stop the tears I sent a silent, fervent message down to her. *Goodbye little ship, you are the best little boat in all the world.*

A homecoming

My emotions still ran wild hours later, stuck in the transatlantic plane rushing me eastwards. Leaving *Hope* and Graeme behind hurt like crazy, but slowly a potent mix of homesickness, anticipation and anxiety began to seep in. I had put off going home for so long that having it happen so suddenly was overwhelming. It was hard to believe I was actually on my way, would be home tomorrow.

I arrived nine hours late, not at eight in the morning as scheduled but at five in the afternoon. The non-stop New York to Düsseldorf flight was re-diverted to London and then re-diverted once more to Cologne. By the time we crossed the Channel and headed for Germany I was manic and overwrought, infecting everybody on the plane with my wild excitement. Word got around that I had been away for eight years, had sailed the world on a yacht. People changed seats so I could sit near the window to look down on Germany, and the woman next to me kept handing me tissues. I can't explain my emotional upheaval (it's happened many times since) but I can understand when people get on hands and knees to kiss their home soil. An invisible thread seems to tie me to home and family, and when the thread is finally reeled in it just about pulls me to the ground too.

The airline paid for a taxi from Cologne to Düsseldorf

(where I should have landed) and I found Mutti and Frank in the airport lounge looking tired and dejected. I shouted and Mutti ran towards me so fast she almost knocked me over, couldn't stop hugging me, relieved to see me safe. My long delay had rattled her and driving back to Dortmund, Frank joked how she had almost hauled an airline hostess across the counter to make her own up that my plane had crashed. 'Nine hours! For heaven's sake woman tell us what's wrong!' Even in the car Mutti couldn't settle down, incredulous at the mess-up. 'Why didn't they tell us the plane had been diverted to Cologne, we could have driven there to get you... all we did was sit around in Düsseldorf and worry.'

A two-hour drive home, a climb up three flights of stairs to Mutti's apartment, and my eyes could no longer stay open. 'We'll sort out the sleeping arrangements later,' Mutti said, and almost undressing me, pushed me into her bed. To be in Mutti's bed was one of my childhood treats and nothing had changed. Hugged by one eiderdown underneath, another on top with my head resting on a huge European pillow I might as well have been 6, not 26 years old.

Sound sleep and several cups of Mutti's strong coffee helped me to settle in. So much had changed. Mutti had moved to a small flat after Pappi died and I kept walking around her place looking for familiar things.

'Where is the pale blue and carmine Venetian bowl?'

'It got a chip in it and I've put it away.'

'Where is the Elbing shield?'

'Here, I'll show you, it's in the bedroom.'

'Mutti, where is the painting we had in the lounge room?'

'Which painting, Kindchen?'

'The one of the boy lying on his back in the meadow.' Pappi had bought that painting.

'Oh, it was too big for this flat,' she said, 'I couldn't keep it.'

A homecoming

It was unreasonable of me to feel cross about it, I knew, but *it was Pappi's favourite painting, how could she get rid of it?* At least the watercolour of the boats sailing in the Baltic was still there. And underneath it, on the back of the lounge, sat three little koalas for the Australian travellers, one for Frank, one for me and an extra fuzzy one for Graeme – because he had a beard.

~

Mutti was still convalescing, the swelling around her eyes still prominent. She would have to get used to poor vision in one eye but felt well and was thinking of going back to work. We did the rounds of my aunts, uncles and cousins and I was welcomed with hugs, sometimes tears. Spoilt with food and drink we stayed for hours, talking and talking. I was loved and welcomed as a returning daughter, the wild adventurer who had sailed the world in a yacht; most of my family had had their share of bravery and survival, they knew what it meant. *Well done girl ... you're your mother's daughter.* I no longer minded playing second fiddle to my mother; it was as it should be. My resentment towards her, so overwhelmingly strong in some of my night watches, seemed to have evaporated. It had finally sunk in that I wasn't her keeper, that she never intended me to be that; she could no longer 'swallow me up'. It was good to be home, good to be with her, and we spent many evenings talking over glasses of wine.

With amusement I recognised myself in some of her ways but in the months to come I also had to admit, reluctantly at first and only to myself, that I was indeed a lot more like Pappi; reflective and introspective, born with a persistent streak of his sombre Slavic disposition. Mutti had always complained that I was too serious – she still did – but I didn't care. It no longer felt like disloyalty to be unlike her. It was okay to be different, have my own shortcomings, my own ways of living, laughing and dealing with the world. It felt safe to love Mutti as the person she was, an amazing woman with mountains of courage, fierce, hot-headed and hugely generous with those she loved.

Yet for all my budding self-assurance I couldn't stop myself from bringing up childhood events again, had to talk about the bad times, needed her to confirm and verify the pain of the child I once was. A little-girl part in me still carried a grudge for felt injustices, wanted to hurt her, make her say that she was sorry. And in a way she did. She listened, disbelieving at times, sad and shocked at others *but that was all so long ago ... did I really say that, do that? Yes you did*, and I filled in the details; a particular day, things she said and did, the colour of her dress, beatings, fights she had with Pappi...

'You poor child,' Mutti said. 'You remember more than I do.'

But my irrepressibly optimistic mother took my accusations in her stride too. 'Komm Kindchen,' she would laugh, 'I'm taking you out – got to make up for being a Rabenmutter!'[24] and she would shout me a visit to the hairdresser, a blouse I liked, a second piece of cake in the *Konditorei* or a cognac with my coffee.

Visiting my father's grave for the first time was hard; a plain headstone engraved with only his surname in a large beautifully kept cemetery, almost a park, interspaced with long avenues of tall trees. Mutti walked away to give me time alone and there I stood, lost, not knowing what was happening inside me. Pappi's authority seemed to leap from

---

24 Literally 'raven mother' – the raven considered a bird of ill omen. Used colloquially as a term for an uncaring, unnatural mother.

his grave at me, making me shrink to half my age. I so much wanted to reach out, love him and touch him, but it didn't happen. Something within me stubbornly refused, still wanted to argue, still wanted to slam doors. I kept looking at his name on the gravestone, mesmerised, dumbstruck, saw us standing at the front door the last time I left, neither of us knowing how to say goodbye.

I couldn't speak then, couldn't speak now – wished I could cry, shout, anything to shift the heaviness in my chest stuck solid between head and heart. *I can't do this, not now*, I thought, *Pappi will have to wait*, and I quickly walked away to look for Mutti. I found her walking among the trees, smiling at me. I smiled back pretending cheerfulness. 'It was good, Mutti, good to see him. I talked with him,' and linking arms, we wandered off in the direction of the tram stop.

Seeing Frank again was as if we hadn't been apart, instant rapport, our friendship intact and no complicated emotional baggage. I visited often, getting to know his wife and their little boy, my godchild, chatting non-stop to his *Tante von Australien*. The family lived in Unna, a small town not far from Mutti's place, in the upstairs part of Helga's parents' house. In the evening we'd sit around talking about travel, and it became our joke that whenever Australia was mentioned Frank's eyes would go distant and his arms grow into wings. He would have liked to go back to Australia and his wife was happy to try living in another country, but it wasn't to be. Helga was an only child and her parents clung fiercely to her and their grandson.

It became another joke that whenever I visited, I had to dress lightly. Helga's father was in charge of the basement boiler and regulated the heating for the entire house. Herbert was a frugal man, mindful of precious fuel, but when I came to visit, the upstairs flat was almost tropical. 'That girl from

Australia must be feeling the cold,' he'd say and stoke the furnace until it roared. One night it got so hot that Frank sat on the lounge stripped down to his singlet.

※

Four months went by, and everybody kept asking me *where's your man, hasn't he sold that boat of yours yet ... tell him to hurry up*. Mutti had returned to work and I passed the time with reading and sewing. I thought of Graeme and *Hope* and grew impatient; had I been too hasty, should I have stayed on? My flight home had emptied our bank account and until we sold *Hope* we'd be broke. Graeme was keeping afloat with money he earned from delivering boats, and judging by his letters he was having a great old bachelor time with no end of parties. Not overly optimistic, I began reading boating magazines to get a feel for what was available for river travel. Travelling down the Danube had been our favoured plan: the Black Sea, Istanbul and the Turkish coast perhaps ... the options for European travel were countless but boats, as always, were irresistible. I desperately wished for something to happen.

Then something did happen and suddenly I had all the time in the world. I had missed one period but thought nothing of it; being off the Pill had made me irregular. A month later I had a mini period, but when nothing happened after that the possibility that I might be pregnant suddenly hit me. It was a slim chance, but wouldn't it be wonderful? If it were true, I'd be four-and-a-half months pregnant, *how could I have missed it?* Mutti made a doctor's appointment for me.

An examination proved that I was indeed pregnant and when the doctor began asking questions to establish the

A homecoming

likely birth date I started laughing, told him I could give him the exact date of conception: the last night on *Hope*. We would have a *Hope* baby and I had a sudden image of a new spark of life, one tiny bit of Graeme flying across the Atlantic with me, clinging tightly, not minding altitude, long delays, tears, upheavals or changes of season. Graeme and I were going to have a strong baby, a tough little traveller. *Good on you kid*, I thought.

Knowing how excited Mutti would be, I rushed back to her place to ring her at work, but she had left for the day. Pacing her apartment, I watched the clock; it would take her about half an hour to get home. When I heard the click of the key in the front door I rushed to meet her in the hallway.

'Well,' she said, 'quickly, tell me the news, are you pregnant?'

'Yes, Mum, yes, I am, I am!' and we hugged and danced around and around each other like children.

Part Three

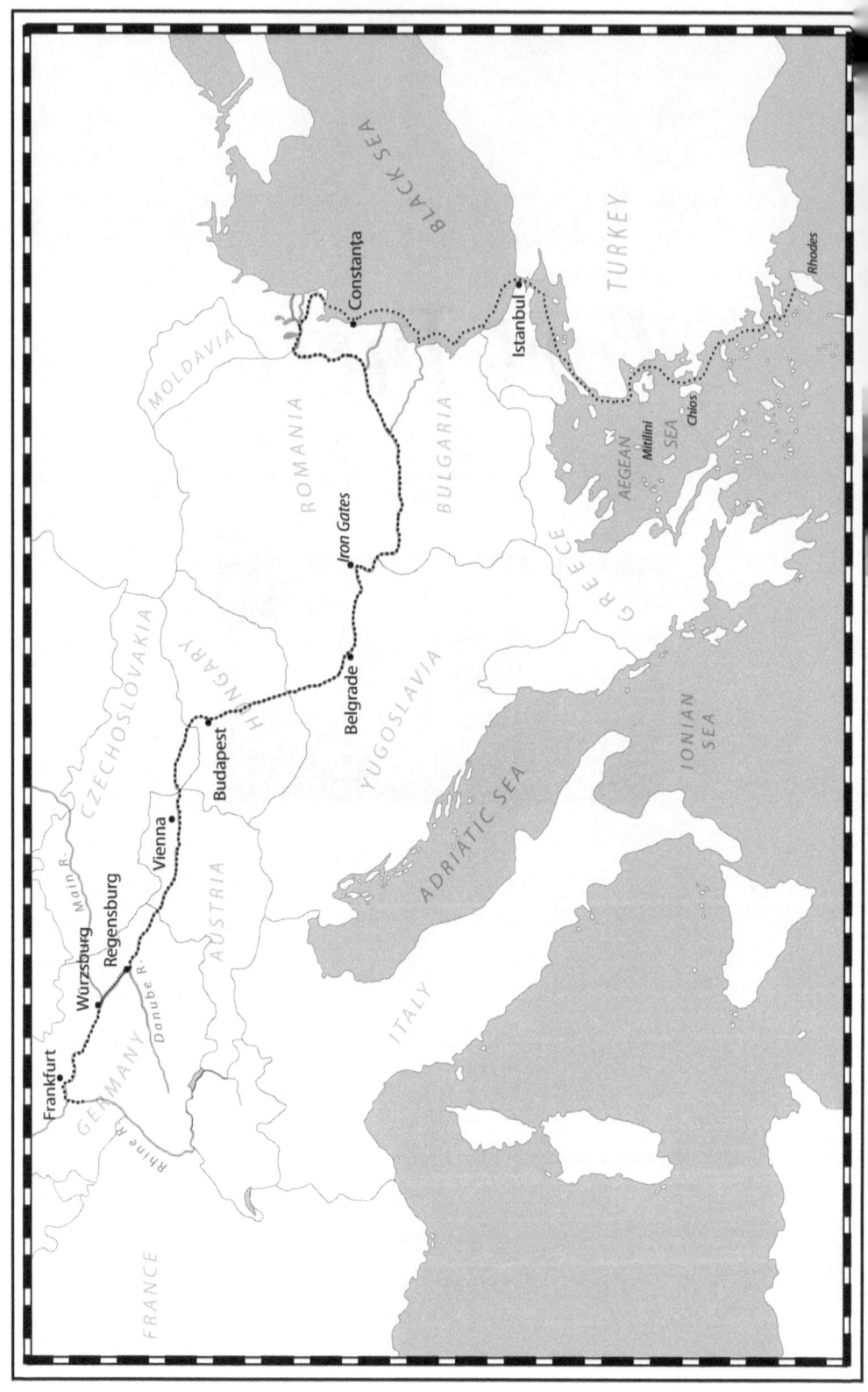

Home... and away again

November came to an end, and I began to worry that Graeme might miss Christmas, and perhaps even the birth of our child. It became harder for me to dismiss the yacht broker's negative forecasts, but in the end my optimism proved right; a woman with the lovely name of Marina fell in love with our boat. On Friday 13 December 1968 she, and her German partner, took possession of *Hope*, and two days later Graeme was on an aeroplane to Luxembourg. Why Luxembourg I can't remember, but it suited me. I wanted us to have time alone after so many months apart; especially with me being pregnant and all the rules changed.

An early train took me to Luxembourg and I booked us into a hotel, a two-storey slice of old stonework facing a broad tree-lined street, a doll's house squeezed into a row of similar-looking ones. The room was on the second floor. Dark beams spanned the low ceiling, and sunlight filtered through a small, white-curtained window onto a wooden bed made up with billowing feather quilts and large square pillows. To reach the little hideout, one had to climb up flights of narrow stairs, the landings between floors patterned with multi-coloured light spilling from stained-glass windows; a perfect setting, romantic and beautiful. The elderly woman showing me the room must have noticed my excitement (and my pregnancy) and I couldn't stop myself from telling her that my husband had been away in America for many months, that he was coming back today, this afternoon. I needed to tell somebody, and she seemed to understand the significance. Giving me a sweet smile, she touched my arm softly, reassuringly, before gently closing the door behind her.

Temperatures outside hovered around zero and I put on my most becoming maternity dress (milk-chocolate-brown crepe with a baby-blue collar), knee boots, a thick overcoat and my mother's fur hat to take a taxi to the airport. I must have looked positively round because on top of all I wore, I carried an overcoat for Graeme to put on as soon as he got off the plane. Would he recognise me? We had known each other for seven years but he'd never seen me in heavy winter gear. Too excited to contain myself, I cried long before the plane landed and a lot more after it did, but seeing Graeme walk out of Customs with about half a dozen pieces of odd-shaped luggage slung around him soon returned me to a more useful frame of mind. There were bundles, boxes and bags, and one 'shape' carefully wrapped in canvas and tied with rope turned out to be *Hope*'s compass; he had carried it in his arms, couldn't part with it.

The narrow staircase to reach our hotel room proved a challenge for his assorted luggage, but Graeme's wonder at finding the 'two of me' was as romantic as I could have wished. Afterwards we sat downstairs in the cosy wood-lined dining room eating rich onion soup with big chunks of warm bread. Life was good.

～

Since we were financial again, our travel plans quickly took shape; it was to be a trip down the Danube on a motor cruiser and if things worked out, we would travel on through the

Black Sea, the Bosporus and onwards into the Mediterranean. After the distances we had sailed, Europe seemed a very small place.

The baby was expected on 5 April and there was plenty of time yet. Graeme started work in the foreign division of a large German engineering firm in a neighbouring town and got to know the miserable side of winter: leaving and returning from work in total darkness and stamping his feet on windy railway platforms. But much to his delight – and mine – he also got to see the pretty face of winter, because we had more snow that year than even I could remember. It started snowing in late December and at Onkel Fritz's New Year's Eve party, the young and old of my family stood outside in the snow to let off end-of-the-year fireworks into a crystal sky, *Happy New Year and all the best for 1969*. My cousins, fuelled on champagne, grabbed sleds from the basement and began chasing each other down the slope at the back of the house. I was too pregnant to join in, but Graeme did and promptly fell off, sliding downhill feet first, his clothes rucked up under his arms. Shivering with cold, his bared chest scraped red, he shouted '*hat ein Glück, tut kein weh.*' Yes, mate, you were lucky you didn't get hurt – his fledgling German came out in strange ways, but we understood him and happily laughed along with him.

It kept snowing well into February, and sometimes our car parked by the side of the road was a billowy VW-shaped hump in a row of other rounded humps. Pushing the snow off and scaping the ice off the windshield became a necessary ritual, but once on the road the traffic flowed easily enough. Streets and highways were cleared of snow and de-iced daily, and nothing could stop us from driving into the surrounding countryside. A novel experience for me because my family had never owned a car, and slipping into my faraway bird's-eye view I saw our little car meandering along a network of long dark ribbons, edged in fairy-tale whiteness.

I wanted Graeme to see my country and picked out my favourite places for weekend drives; sometimes we would take off alone, but more often in the company of Frank, Helga and Mutti. One Sunday, on my request, we all headed for Burg Altena, a 12th-century castle in the Sauerland, a forested area south of the Ruhr Valley. Both Frank and I had stayed at the castle at different times, a stopover on weeklong bike tours during school holidays, when the castle still operated as a youth hostel and only people arriving on foot or on bicycles were allowed to stay. For me Altena was synonymous with balmy evenings, singing around a fire in the courtyard, and sleeping soundly under tightly tucked-in grey blankets provided by the hostel, one end thoughtfully stamped with a large black FOOT END.

None of my remembered images held true, and I barely recognised the solid stone castle I had known so well. High up on a hill, backlit by a thin afternoon sun, Burg Altena had transformed itself into a delicately painted stage backdrop, its steeply sloping roofs dark and shiny like polished pewter, and every horizontal surface covered with glittering snow. Slowly climbing the track upwards through wintery forest soon had us enchanted, especially after spotting a deer bounding away in a flurry of snow. Better still was finding the entire castle courtyard deserted, blanketed in thick powdery snow, clean, white and totally unblemished. Pregnant or not, I just couldn't stop myself from running around madly throwing handfuls of the stuff at everybody, as energetic and childlike as I had been in the hot summers a decade and a half previously.

Graeme may remember the castle for a different reason.

He needed to pee, and with everything shut, Frank suggested an area directly below one of the courtyard walls. Graeme disappeared and Frank motioned us a silent *come and look* gesture, pointing over the wall. Throwing snow at someone having a pee is a little boy's game and barely able to suppress our giggles, we watched as Graeme carefully picked his way down the slope until he found a likely spot, extricating himself from layers of clothing as he went: gloves off, undo overcoat, pull up jumper, find the pants zip and finally a frantic search for the opening in the new long johns. And just as he was about to wet the ancient walls, the four of us watching him pushed ten centimetres of snow off the ledge directly above him. The shock on his face was priceless but as he claimed later, the shock to another part of his anatomy might well render him impotent forever (unfounded I might add).

My tummy was growing well rounded by then but true to my family's dictum that expectant women need plenty of exercise,[25] I thought nothing of taking hour-long walks through acres of snow. One Sunday, Graeme and I even climbed the tower of the Stadtkirche, a beautiful old church in Unna, my brother's hometown. Finding a *No Public Access* sign at the door of the tower posed a bit of a problem, but drawing on some of my Mutti-inherited charm ('my husband is from Australia, he's never seen a church this old'), I managed to wangle the key off the church warden, leaving us free to explore the tower at our leisure.

Pleading that my husband had never been in a church tower this old was certainly true, but it is likely that I hadn't either. Growing up in a country with seemingly endless history had not sparked my enthusiasm for remembering

---

25 There is a picture of my heavily pregnant mother riding an ancient bicycle along a tree-lined country road.

historical dates, or for wanting to know when, how, or why castles, churches, bridges or universities came to be built. For me it had always been enough to simply immerse myself in the atmosphere such places convey, to feel and smell them and let my imagination wander. To run a finger over an ancient block of stone gives me a sense of touching the hand that carried it, carved it; perhaps even died for it.

Climbing the well-worn stone steps of the church tower as they steadily curved upwards in a tight spiral, I thought of the hardship the workmen endured, of their wives packing their lunches and their children already working at a young age. Stepping carefully along dim pools of light cast by bare bulbs dangling into the stairway, I imagined what it would have been like to climb the steps lit by a flame torch or a flickering candle. Walking carefully onto wooden platforms built over the void I thought of the men putting down the first planks. How were they secured, how many workmen had tumbled into the dark void? The thought that my forebears, related to me in some distant way, carried out the work made the climb more intimate, almost eerie. It made me shiver to think of them; clad in rough homespun garments, toiling away, cold, possibly hungry.

It was a relief to finally push open a heavy steel door and step out onto the open-air walkway surrounding the base of the spire; we had climbed as high as it was possible to go. Hushed by the steep climb and the sudden rush of cold air, we peeked over the top of the carved stone wall into the town spread out beneath us, pretty and well laid out, remnants of the ancient wall that once enclosed it still clearly visible. Gazing outwards over snowy roofs and misty fields stretching far into the distance, I tried following the line of streets to find the way to Frank's house, past the railway line, past the sprawling Kur Park with its snow-dusted trees, but I soon stopped. Standing atop an ancient stone tower, suspended between a glittering sky and the muted world below, demanded stillness and reverence, nothing else but breathing in and out. Gazing down into the toy town below, I was surprised to see two dark-clad figures step from a doorway and hurry across the market square.

~

By the end of February the snow began to melt, and with it my languid time of 'expecting' came to a sudden end. Our baby decided to slice over a month off his expected date of arrival, but as Mutti reassured me, that too ran in our family. On a cold March dawn Graeme and Mutti took me to the hospital where I disappeared behind grey doors into the stainless-steel cleanliness of a German labour ward. Birthing was nurses' and doctors' business and company was not allowed. I was received by a female dragon who felt it necessary to spell out to me that women have had babies since time immemorial and that I had better not make a fuss. Frightened and left alone in a neon-lit room, I tensed up and the pain got worse. But I was lucky; the next shift brought me a darling old nurse with soft hands and a kind smile. She took one look at me, pulled a chair over to my bed, held my hand and simply said, 'It hurts doesn't it.' 'It does,' I sobbed. 'I didn't know it hurt this much.' 'I know,' she said, stroking my face. And with that the floodgates opened and Danny was born within the hour.

He was tiny, just under 5 pounds, but healthy and well. Mum and Graeme celebrated at home and by the time they arrived at the hospital at proper visiting hours, bringing flowers and their happy tears, Danny was safely tucked away in the nursery. They were given a look at him, held up to a pane of glass by a smiling nurse. I had to stay in bed, but they told me he was beautiful. When I see such scenes in old black-and-white movies I find it hard to believe that I actually played one of those parts.

Apart from being underweight there was nothing wrong with Danny, but German rules decreed that he could not leave hospital until he weighed 2½ kilograms. I was discharged (no choice there either) and for the next two weeks I could no longer touch him, only deliver my milk and bawl my eyes out looking at him through a glass window. Nowhere else in the world would I have allowed anyone to do this to me, but German authority, so much part of my childhood and personified by white-coated doctors and nurses in starched uniforms, rendered me obedient. All I could do was silently beg my baby to grow. *Come on Danny please just a few more grams.*

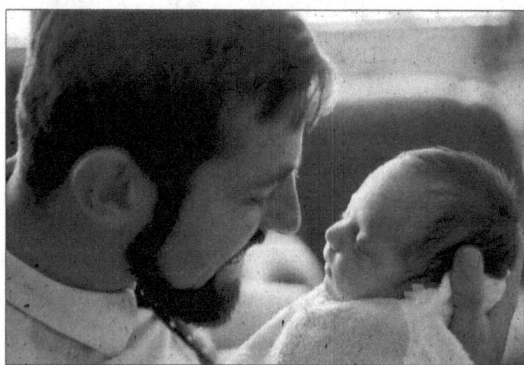

Graeme and Danny.

The way I dealt with having my baby imprisoned was to dive headlong into activity. I cooked fancy meals for Graeme and Mutti to come home to from their respective jobs, and in between I scoured the ads in boating magazines to find 'our' boat. I bought things we would need, and Mutti's lounge-room floor began to look like a warehouse. Beside our bed (picked up every morning and leant against the wall) was the pram waiting for Danny, plus a mountain of nappies and baby clothes. Next to it stood a fold-up bicycle for us to have aboard, and Frank had added a beautiful hand-cranked sewing machine he had restored for me.

Finally, well into March, Danny had gained enough weight and we brought him home, a little bundle wrapped into a red plaid rug. Driving home through fields still patterned with snow I held him tightly and told him not to worry, that the three of us would soon be rolling down a big river, living by the sun *and good riddance to that awful hospital.*

My promise to Danny came good when he was ten weeks old and I found the boat we were looking for, in Gernsheim, a small town on the upper Rhine, just south of Frankfurt. She seemed to have the right credentials; solidly built of timber, an overall length of 8 metres, and a 36 horsepower Mercedes diesel engine promising a cruising speed of around 8 knots. We drove the 280 kilometres from Dortmund to Gernsheim to check her out.

The boat was on blocks, out of the water for the winter, and Graeme and I climbed all over her, thinking, measuring and dreaming. The German Navy had commissioned her as a pilot boat, but the project had been abandoned in 1944. Fifteen years later the present owner had bought the hull and fitted her out to suit his needs. Half the boat was cockpit, the steering position sheltered by an extended cabin roof. The galley was to port and had plenty of cupboard space, a sink and a two-burner stove. A table amidships could be lowered to fill the space between the two settees, thus creating a double bunk. A marine toilet and washbasin were housed in a closed-in compartment next to the companionway.

In the loveliest of all German traditions, the proud owner selling his treasure invited us to his home for cake and coffee.

We met his wife; chatted for a little while; and a couple of hours later the boat was ours.

Shopping and planning now moved into top gear and everybody helped. Mutti, good at sleuthing out bargains, found us a rubber dinghy, and there was a hilarious night when we decided to blow it up inside her lounge room. Fat, round and yellow, we christened it *Gummischwein*. A photo shows Mutti and me sitting inside our 'rubber pig', laughing and pretending to row this thing around the lounge room. I bought pots and pans, cups, plates and cutlery, spare fuel canisters, clothing for all weathers and finally a huge supply of disposable nappies. I knew we wouldn't be able to get disposables in the communist countries and calculated a six-month supply; the girl in the warehouse wasn't the only one agog at the quantity.

Transferring our gear to Gernsheim to start our journey deserved a gold star for faultless organisation. Graeme and I went ahead in our car, with the backseat removed and assorted gear stuffed right up to the roof. Once in Gernsheim, we worked like crazy to organise a crane, get the boat in the water, clean her up and make her liveable. A couple of days later Frank drove Mutti and Danny down in his car, bringing the rest of our gear. Karl, a friend of Frank's, had also managed to squeeze into the car. Mutti couldn't drive and Karl had offered to drive our VW back to Dortmund where Mutti would sell it for us.

The four of them arrived around lunchtime. Danny was welcomed aboard and I made cups of tea and sandwiches, but with goodbyes hanging in the air we couldn't get cheerful. Mutti kept holding Danny, sad to let him go. She had watched over him almost since conception and would miss him. She would miss all of us, she said. I was jittery and anxious, as always before a new venture, but before tears could flow, my brother (the family champion of very fast goodbyes) pushed Mutti into his car, Karl jumped into our VW, two car-horns bipped and they were gone.

∽

The rush was over and we settled in to become a family afloat, happily distracted by our little cabin boy, by playtime and four-hourly feeds. There was still plenty to do, to clean and paint, fit new carpets and make cushions and curtains. Against our better judgement we installed a small gas fridge. We had never bothered with refrigeration before, but Danny's vaccinations had to be kept cool, and gas refrigeration was the only option. Tucked into a corner, outside, under the roofed part of the cockpit seemed the safest place for it.

Visas for Czechoslovakia, Hungary, the then Yugoslavia, Romania, and Bulgaria had arrived on time. We had also applied for a visa into Russia, but that had been refused; the Cold War was at its height and it was not the time for a private boat to go nosing around Russian Black Sea ports. Another small hitch had been Danny's nationality. Although born in Germany to a German mother (me) some rule I didn't bother to fight decreed that he take the nationality of his father. We had registered his birth at the Australian Embassy in Cologne and he travelled on Graeme's passport, his birthday duly recorded and a photo of his sleepy head stamped with the official seal. I now had the pleasure of the company of two Australians.

May arrived and we were ready, right down to the boat's name painted on the stern. We had named her *Puck*, after the merry wanderer from Shakespeare's *Midsummer Night's Dream*. *Puck* had also been the name of a broad rowing shell my father had owned back in Prussia, a boat on which he had taken Mutti for jaunts on the Elbing River. Choosing the same name as Pappi did for his boat felt like a good omen; it aligned me with the man Mutti knew and talked about, a happier man, a romantic idealist whose genes I carried. Travelling on a boat called *Puck* promised good times.

Two rivers

Leaving the sheltered harbour of Gernsheim we slipped into the swift current of the Rhine, running downstream towards Frankfurt and the mouth of the Main River. After eleven months on dry land, it was good to be afloat again, good and different. *Puck* was a metre less in length than *Hope*, but comparing the two boats would be like looking for similarities between an eagle and a bumblebee. I missed the weight and solidity of *Hope* but soon made friends with our noisy bumblebee. *Puck* was the right boat for river travel; the thought of *Hope* in shallow water, hemmed in by riverbanks, was absurd, impossible to imagine.

The journey itself was different too, vastly different. Our push and enthusiasm for adventure hadn't waned; we had our boat again, had merely exchanged the glittering iridescence of ocean water with the darker water of inland rivers, less blue, less bright. Looking down from imaginary heights I had seen *Hope* storming along arched lines drawn onto a world map, sailing vast distances from one continent to another. Now I saw *Puck* meandering along a blue snaky line, through green valleys, past shady ridges and big and little dots denoting towns and cities. Having left home so early I hadn't actually seen that much of Germany, but my fascination for charts and atlases (right back to the large, cracked map hoisted onto a stand for our primary school geography lessons) made the setting deeply familiar. This was my country, and seeing myself travel along a meandering blue river gave me an odd sense of pride and strangely unfamiliar feelings of belonging.

River traffic to Frankfurt was hectic, but once we passed the metropolis with its factories and port facilities, the Main River became the sweetest river in the world. Flowing gently, it curved in generous loops, first one way and then the other, taking us through Germany's most beautiful countryside. Dark forests and chequerboards of tilled fields slid by. The hay season had begun and farmers were out on their tractors. A familiar sight for me, but not for my city-bred husband; whenever we saw a group of women in colourful head scarves turning hay, Graeme couldn't stop himself from doing a perfect Bing Crosby 'Galway Bay' impersonation, crooning about rippling trout streams and hay-making women.

The towns and villages along the Main are picture-book pretty. Sometimes it was possible for us to tie up right in the middle of town, do our shopping and take Danny for a walk in his pram. Lugging first the pram undercarriage ashore, then the hooded carrycase that fitted on top and finally Danny dressed for shore leave invariably drew an audience, and sometimes reporters. One newspaper article reported us as *'modern nomads, who do not rush through the countryside on four wheels but have opted to "chug" gemütlich along romantic waterways'*. A photograph in the *Schweinfurt Tageblatt* shows me about to ride off on my fold-up bicycle while Graeme, his pipe clamped into his mouth, sits in the cockpit minding the baby.

At night we tied up to whatever wharf we could find. Sometimes we simply tied up to a tree, as we did in a place called Gmünden, our most beautiful anchorage ever. Cautiously nosing up an uncharted sidearm, we slipped underneath three low stone bridges and finally came to rest under the overhanging branches of a large weeping willow tree. The evening sun shone through curtains of mint-green leaves and once the engine was shut down a flotilla of white swans came streaming over to check out the newcomers. Danny was still too little to appreciate the amazing scene but I showed him anyway. 'Look, Danny, swans!'

Almost every town offered something special, a castle to explore, a beautiful old church to rest in, or shops selling handmade crafts. In Miltenberg we had lunch at Zum Riesen, Germany's oldest tavern, its intricate façade unchanged for millennia. Sitting over a beer in the ancient rooms made it easy to imagine the rulers of old alighting from horse-drawn coaches, or stepping off their boats demanding the best that kitchen and cellar could offer. And naturally, no self-respecting German town would ever be without at least one *Konditorei*. Sending out divine smells of coffee and displaying sinful cakes, they instantly reignited my childhood cravings for lots and lots of cake. I could not have it then, but now I could; there was no need for frugality now, on any level.

Some locks were tiny.

To keep us on our toes, every so often we'd have to pass through a lock, each one taking us one step higher into more mountainous country. Sometimes it would be hand-operated locks, just big enough to accommodate *Puck*, but more often we'd have to fit in with commercial shipping. Locks meant paying attention, staying clear of loaded barges and waiting for directions from the lockkeeper. If the lock was occupied with bringing ships *down*, the wait could be considerable. Traffic would bank up and along with everyone else we'd have the engine kicking over just enough to remain stationary against the current. And once the lock had emptied and the gates were open, the lockkeeper would direct each waiting boat into the chamber via a loudspeaker, a bit like fitting different-sized fish into a sardine tin. In view of our size we were usually given separate instructions, carefully guided to an area away from where tons of water would rush in to fill the chamber.

Safely tied up to bollards within the lock and the lock gates shut, it was time to relax and chat with the barge families. And whatever qualms I might have had about travelling with our tiny baby simply evaporated. I'd seen nappies drying on clothes lines strung across the boats, knew that babies travelled on the river, but it was in the locks that I actually met the mothers. In comfortable sisterhood we leaned on the handrails admiring each other's babies. *Isn't he gorgeous ...*

your first? How old is he now ... we have two girls and wanted a boy, but maybe next time ... Then the lock gates would open, we'd give each other big smiles, a wave and everybody would be on their way again.

By the time we reached the city of Würzburg we realised that it had taken us six weeks to travel a mere 250 kilometres of river; we'd taken the modern 'gemütliche nomads' label rather too literally. The summer wasn't endless, the idea was to travel to the Black Sea and we weren't even on the Danube yet. The link connecting the Main River to the Danube (making it possible to travel across Europe entirely by water) had not yet been completed, and to get *Puck* into the Danube we had to organise overland rail transport.[26] Würzburg, known for its beautiful Baroque architecture, seemed the perfect place for us to stop and make the necessary arrangements. The Mozart Festival had just begun, Mutti had come to stay with us for a few days, and following time-honoured European tradition, we perambulated leisurely through carefully manicured parks listening to small ensembles and full orchestras playing Mozart in open-air concerts.

On 5 July *Puck* was hoisted onto a flatbed railway carriage and strapped down. To keep an eye on her, Graeme travelled inside *Puck* as she made her way to Regensburg, a stowaway

---

26 At the time of our travel (1969) the Rhein-Main-Donau Canal, sometimes referred to as the Europe Canal, had not been completed. Plans to connect the Rhine and Danube rivers (and thus the Atlantic to the Black Sea) were first envisaged by Charlemagne over eleven hundred years ago. But the emperor's dreams and ambitions did not become reality until 1992 when the last section of the canal was finally opened for shipping. Starting from the Main River (231 metres above sea level) eleven locks take ships up over a mountain range cresting at 406 metres. From there, five locks bring ships down to the level of Danube, 338 metres above sea level – in short: 175 metres up and 68 metres down, over a length of 171 kilometres.

on his own ship. Danny and I followed in a comfortable passenger train and had the job of finding him at the other end. It seemed that the stowaway had a dreadful time, *the rockiest ride of his life*, but there he was, shouting instructions and overseeing the return of *Puck* into her rightful element. The length of the Danube is marked in kilometres, beginning with zero at Sulina in Romania, where the river flows into the Black Sea. *Puck* was lowered into the water at Regensburg, 2,375 kilometres upriver, and we allowed ourselves roughly three months to reach the zero marker; plenty of time as it turned out. The Danube runs swiftly, and it didn't take us long to find out that our dawdling days were over. On the Main River we had travelled upriver against the current, slow and easy. Now we were motoring downstream, and adding *Puck*'s travelling speed to that of the river made everything happen so much faster.

The relentless current demanded care and unwavering attention. Shopping for necessities, fuel stops and finding shelter for the night needed planning. There were no weeping willows to tie up to, no swans to greet us, and even if the riverbank was shallow enough to allow us to anchor, it left us open to the danger of being pushed ashore by the powerful wash created by passing ships. On some nights we sleuthed out a small side arm clear of the current, but tying up to a proper wharf in a designated harbour proved the safest and most comfortable option.

Sometimes I felt that simply rolling down the river and never stepping off the boat was enough for me. Following the majestic Danube lay at the heart of the adventure, it was what we had come for. It was exciting to work in with the shipping, the cruise boats, ferries and the ever-present barges. There was the thrill of passing under modern and ancient bridges – dozens of them, every township had at least one. And quite apart from that, the passing scenery alone provided rich offerings. Fields and forests, castles and historic buildings slid by like an interesting documentary, rolled out in vibrant colour, the wind blowing around our noses giving it reality and substance.

Revelling in our freewheeling gypsy life we played with Danny, bathed him and fed him. Early nights became the norm rather than the exception. Shore excursions became unplanned spur of the moment events; we'd spot a wharf or a small harbour, take the pram ashore and walk around to see what offered itself. Sometimes we'd find a market of local produce or a bakery full of temptations. At other times it was simply a walk through narrow twisted alleys edged with Tudor-style houses, intricately decorated with scrolls of gold lettering.

In Passau we happened to be in the right place at the right time to attend an organ recital in the St Stephan's Dom, a huge Baroque cathedral famous for its frescos and the biggest church organ in the world, with some 17,000 pipes. I don't remember which pieces were being played, but I will not forget sitting in the vast cool space under soaring arches with tears rolling down my face, touched by the music like a blessing, a gift of love and grace freely given.

꩜

The Danube is lifeblood to the land and the people who have lived on her banks since ancient times. Fantastic tales of shipwrecks, back in time when the Danube was still wild and untamed, have been passed on over the centuries. The centre of one whirlpool near Grein in Austria was said to have measured 1½ metres below the surface of the river. It is said that the Romans threw coins into it to honour the river god Danubius, and if any hapless person was unlucky enough to fall into the river, no rescue attempts would be made; it was simply assumed that the gods had claimed them.

Today's modern locks have slowed the current, regulated water depth and reduced the danger. Having negotiated a good many locks on the Main River we knew the basic rules, but we were not prepared for the enormous differences in size. On the Main River each lock had taken us *up* by a few metres while chatting comfortably with the barge families. Now we were taken *a long way down*, carefully positioned among huge convoys of international ships and barges. In the Aschach lock we dropped an impressive 15 metres in a chamber 230 metres long, 28 times the length of Puck; a tadpole among the big fish, proudly flying our big Australian flag. For that we often got a friendly salute from the lockkeeper high up in his tower, or from the captain of one of the big ships. Australia was well known in Europe, and it was rare to meet a person who didn't know somebody who in turn knew somebody else whose friend, brother, uncle or neighbour had immigrated to Australia; *do we know this person, his name is X,Y,Z ... they went to Sydney ...or maybe it was Melbourne ...*

No, sorry, can't help you there... Australia is a big place.

❧

It took two weeks to travel from Regensburg to Vienna, averaging 300 kilometres a week. Not a great distance, but comparing it to our leisurely dawdle of 40 kilometres a week on the Main River we were practically racing, steadily pulled along by the mighty Danube. Vienna lay ahead, and to slow things down we put in a few rest days in a small town a day's run short of the city. We tended to bypass big cities, happy to skip the fuss, the noise and difficulty of finding a berth, but to bypass legendary Vienna would have felt like a crime. Besides, we needed an exit stamp in our passports before entering the neighbouring communist country of Czechoslovakia.

Arriving in Vienna, we innocently (deliberately) ignored the 'Water Police Only' sign and tied up at the wharf reserved for police boats. Seeing a couple of uniformed officers walk down the marina towards us, we fully expected to be told to move on and move on quickly, but the legendary Vienna charm was in full force on that particular day. Making an exception to the rule, the Water Police allowed us to remain at their wharf; a rough equivalent of a lottery win and the safest possible anchorage, right in the heart of Vienna. With *Puck* under constant police guard we could relax, roam the city at leisure and visit the famous landmarks. And if Danny was having an afternoon nap, we could leave him safely guarded with one of the police dads while we snuck off for a Vienna coffee. Making the most of our good fortune, we stretched our welcome as far as we dared. We knew that once we left, barely half a day's ride downriver we would be in Czechoslovakia, and we hadn't the slightest idea how we would be received there.

Danny in his cot – a room with an ever-changing view.

Travelling through communist countries

With our passports stamped, waved off by friendly police officers, we headed for the Czechoslovakia/Austrian border, 44 kilometres downriver from Vienna. River traffic gradually thinned and at river marker 1,708 kilometres we motored through the 'iron curtain', the physical and ideological boundary between East and West. The contrast was stunning. The Vienna Water Police had told us that within their area of surveillance there were about 10,000 private registered boats. After crossing the Czechoslovakian border, *Puck* was the only one. And almost immediately, we were spotted. An armed patrol boat cruised over, her uniformed crew gesturing for us to follow them.

We must have looked a strange convoy, *Puck* pert and shiny with her blue covers and red Aussie flag, and ahead of her a drab grey patrol boat with guns mounted fore and aft. Easy-going and lighthearted Vienna suddenly seemed worlds away. Watchtowers stood at intervals and, imagining myself magnified by powerful field glasses, I had the silly urge to strike funny poses, wave an arm (or a naked leg) but was too scared to do it. Someone might be offended and who knows what consequences that might have.

I knew enough people living in East Germany to know that Communist ideology did not tally with reality. Onkel Willi, Mutti's brother, his wife and their children lived in East Germany on the Baltic island of Rügen. Almost everybody I knew had friends or a relative somewhere in 'The East'. We knew what went on for them, stuck behind barbed wire, ruled by fear and repression. I recalled a time in 1952 when Mutti and I travelled by train to visit Onkel Willi. Mutti had coached me endlessly to *keep my mouth shut* long before we got to the border, telling me over and over *don't speak* no matter what the man with the gun was asking me, *just be quiet*. By the time the train stopped at the border into East Germany, I was so terrified that nobody would have got a word out of me, no matter what. Strangely enough I wasn't the only silent one, because everybody on the train seemed to abide by the same rule. Silence prevailed while armed guards slowly worked their way through the train compartments checking visas and luggage. One woman was ordered off the train and that set my heart racing even faster. *What if they took Mutti and left me on the train?*

When at long last the train took off again, the atmosphere in the carriage suddenly became buoyant. Sandwiches and Thermos flasks were brought out, food was shared around and everybody was chatting and laughing. One woman told Mutti how she had smuggled West German Deutschmarks across the border, rolled them into a tight wad she had pushed into a *Leberwurst*. 'Easy to do' – she laughed – 'I make my own sausages. Mutti only told me long afterwards that she too had smuggled money, one hundred German Westmarks notes, each one folded tightly into the cloth-covered buttons on my double-breasted overcoat. 'West German money fetched four times the official exchange rate on the black market, one was crazy not to smuggle.'

Motoring behind the Czechoslovakian gunboat past the sinister-looking green watchtowers brought back that train ride, along with shreds of the suffocating fear I had felt, but a quick reality check reassured me that we had nothing to worry about. We carried no contraband whatsoever, no undeclared money, no guns and no drugs... squeaky clean. And as it turned out my fleeting agonies proved unwarranted. Arriving in Bratislava half an hour later, we were directed to a wharf, customs and immigration officials appeared and all formalities were courteously and efficiently dealt with.

Bratislava felt buzzy; people talked a lot, still fired up over the Czech/Slovak uprising from the previous year. It was explained to us that under Dubček's leadership the Communist Party had initiated reforms to advance democratisation and free speech. But popular support for Dubček's policies had been deemed undesirable by Russia and tanks were sent in to crush 'counterrevolutionary' elements.

Political discussions, fuelled with beer or home-brewed wine, could be had anytime, day or night. Fights would flare up quickly, but could as easily dissolve into bantering and laughter. German was understood and spoken by many people, the Austrian border was not far, and illegal TV watching of Western channels had made people aware of the world beyond. Once again, Australia as the land for immigrants was well known and much to our surprise, when Graeme got out his guitar to play 'Waltzing Matilda' more than a few voices joined in the chorus.

We had arrived during the week, and on the following Sunday crowds of people came down to the river, a perfect place to picnic and talk. Blankets were spread, food unloaded, beer fetched in canisters from a nearby pub and the long, slow day began to unfold. As honoured guests we were offered food and drink by everyone, and Danny, now nearly six months old, had plenty of laps to sit on. Small children happily switched blankets, spoiled by whomever they visited, while their older siblings showed off a new trick they had invented.

Inspired by the fast flow of the river, they had hit onto an ingenious way of 'surfing'. It involved climbing onto a flat board tied to the shore by a long wire and manoeuvring it into mid-current. The skilled ones (which included Big Kid Graeme) managed to stand on the board 'surfing' the current and riding over the waves created by passing barges. Everybody stood up to watch, cheering both success and failure, and in a sudden deja vu I remembered the family parties from my childhood, after the war, when everybody was poor, homebrew was shared and being together and having fun was all that mattered.

∽

Also of the party were five Germans, who unbeknown to us had been rowing the Danube in a four double scull with cox. Like us they had been on the river since Regensburg, but Bratislava was the first time we met up. The rowers were two students on semester break and three professional men who'd 'escaped' (their word) from wife and work. The rowing boys, as we called them, were also headed for the Black Sea, and with 1,700 kilometres of river ahead of us more meetings were likely.

A few days later, as we planned the grand exit with everyone waving us off, whispered voices spread the news that Apollo 11 was about to land on the moon. *Would we like to come to Janek's place and watch it on television?* Watching Western TV was forbidden, but Janek had rigged an illegal antenna and was able to get a reasonable picture from an Austrian station. *Of course, we would love to watch it*, and carrying the inevitable bottles of beer we were welcomed into Janek's lounge room, already filled with neighbourhood men and women grouped around a tiny black-and-white TV set. The big moment arrived, the chatter stopped and we watched in silent awe as shadowy pictures of the actual landing filtered into the dark room. *Could this really be happening ... a man on the moon?* The feelings in the room were solemn, subdued. No one spoke; we knew that this was history in the making and that irrespective of nationality we were all part of it.

Held up by the Apollo 11 party, we had to rush madly to make the Hungarian border before our Czechoslovakian visa expired. We made it on time, but once there our haste turned into total standstill. The public servant authorised to stamp our papers was late and we were told to wait. We sat in a stifling hot waiting room as one hour turned into two, and finally into three. Every so often a slim, moustachioed 'prince', as we came to call him, strode in to inform us that his superior (his indication of him was playing the flute on his shoulder) was still not in. 'This is ridiculous, why can't the prince do it ... all we need is a bloody stamp!' Graeme was ready to rail against gross inefficiency, but having once again slipped into my obedient border-crossing mode I begged him to 'Please, please be quiet – just shush, if you annoy them they can keep us waiting for days, weeks if they want to.'

Three-and-a-half hours later the big boss finally turned up, and as so charmingly indicated by the 'prince', there were indeed plenty of gleaming stars on his epaulettes. Another hour passed while he had his lunch, and at long last our visa was sighted and we were given our stamps. Happy to leave the hot building and the long lines of barges behind us (all waiting for Mr Big Shot), we jumped aboard *Puck* and took off at great speed, only to stop ten minutes later for a wild, water-splashing, frustration-releasing swim.

To cut out the black market, tourists coming into Hungary were required to exchange a set amount of their home country's currency into Hungarian forint. The amount was calculated per person, per days of visa and ordinary car-driving, hotel-staying, eating-out tourists would have had no trouble spending their forced 'allowance'. We didn't have such costs and the five-day visa for the three of us (Danny counted as a fully-fledged consumer) left us with more forint than we knew what to do with.

Spending big in a poor country didn't feel good. I remember my acute embarrassment standing next to an old woman in a small village store, the rickety shelves half-empty. Dressed in a long black skirt and headscarf, she was buying three slices of salami while I, resorting to a great deal of sign language, tried to get the girl behind the counter to understand that I wanted to buy the whole sausage. The old woman next to me gave me a hateful look and I didn't have the language to explain to her that I wasn't rich, but that the rules of her country forced me to spend so much money. I wondered afterwards what she would have done if I had given her the sausage. Hungarians are a proud people, and she may well have thrown the gift at my feet.

Spending money in the big city of Budapest was easier, more anonymous. We bought stores of tinned food and a couple of cases of excellent red wine by the name of Bull's

Blood. We filled up our tanks and spare container with diesel fuel, and still we had money left over. And so in the company of the rowing boys caught in the same predicament, we ate out in expensive restaurants, serenaded by gypsy musicians. If the menu was in French we had a vague idea of what we were getting, but if the menu was in Hungarian we simply opted for 'pot luck', ordering the most expensive dishes from the top of the list.

In one restaurant the guests at a wedding party invited us to celebrate with them. *Come in, come in* they gestured, the more the merrier, it was good luck for the couple. The bride, smiling and radiant in her long lacy dress, even allowed Graeme to kiss her cheek. He was Australian and that would have to be extra lucky. Once again Australia was well known, because many of the thousands of Hungarians fleeing their country after the 1956 revolution had found a home there.

A five-day Hungarian visa had seemed ample, but Budapest was seductive and another night out with the rowing boys made us late once again. It made the rowing boys *very* late. We had thirty-six horsepower, they had four manpower, and making a *once only* exception they allowed us to tow them for the last stretch.

Approaching the border we dreaded the possibility of another long wait, another 'prince' and another 'big boss', but nothing like it happened. Leaving Hungary was done in minutes. A hand-painted poster in the customs office declared FRIENDSHIP FOR THE COUNTRIES BORDERING THE DANUBE, we were wished bon voyage and everybody had a smile for Danny. Giving a *see you later* wave to the rowing boys, we quickly slipped into Yugoslavia.

By now we had travelled more than a thousand kilometres of river and our trusty diesel engine had never complained, never faltered, but suddenly it developed intermittent hiccups. It slowly got worse, but blessed by the river gods we didn't have the final breakdown until we arrived in Belgrade, a big city with an Australian Embassy. Procuring a spare part for our Mercedes marine engine through ordinary channels would have been time-consuming if not impossible, but the men and women of the Australian Embassy knew the shortcuts; an agent was found, orders were placed and within three days the necessary part arrived from Germany via embassy mailbag. Spoiling us even more, we were treated to a real Aussie dinner at the home of the embassy's medical doctor and his wife: roast leg of lamb, mint sauce and all the trimmings. Lamb was not yet my favourite food, but Graeme was in mini heaven. My special treat was to have a long phone chat with Mutti. 'We're okay Mutti, Danny is fine, the doctor at the embassy gave him his immunisations… you should see him Mutti, he's grown, trying to sit up now… We're off again tomorrow… the Iron Gate is next… you mustn't worry. Graeme sends his love …' Telephoning Mutti from the Eastern Bloc countries had been difficult, but the embassy phone lines were faultless and it was hard to stop talking.

The most demanding stretch of the Danube, collectively known as the Iron Gates, lay ahead. Here the southern tip of Romania's Carpathian Mountains and the upper reaches of the Balkan Mountains begin to converge, forcing the Danube into an ever-narrowing valley. Over a distance of around 130 kilometres, the Danube has to squeeze through a number of gorges, of which the third, the Kazan Gorge, is the most famous. Kazan means 'boiler', a no-nonsense hint of what to expect when huge volumes of water push into an opening of the cliffs a mere 150 metres wide.

To make the river more navigable, construction of the Iron Gate Dam, incorporating a huge lock, was jointly undertaken by (then) Yugoslavia and Romania and had been underway for five years. Communication was poor, and we were unable to find out how far the work had progressed. Yet, the instructions for how we were to proceed were precise. Queuing up for our obligatory stamp at the border post we were told to go straight to the pilot station in Orsova, where a pilot would come aboard to guide us. Our river map showed Orsova as a small Romanian township, a little way past the great Kazan Gorge and just before the dam construction site; about a day's run away, we should make it by afternoon.

༄

For some reason downriver traffic had almost completely stopped: no ferry boats, no barges, nothing. Some shipping still came the other way, but going downriver the river was ours. *Ah well ... I guess we will find out what that means soon enough.* For now, less traffic simply meant less to worry about. Negotiating a narrowing river, a number of lively gorges and finally the big Kazan Gorge would be enough excitement. We were ready and *Puck* settled into her stride.

Flat lands gave way to densely wooded headlands, one folded behind the other, seemingly blocking the way and giving no clue which way the river would turn next. At times, and especially in the broader reaches between gorges, it felt as if we were travelling on a beautiful mountain lake, the surrounding hills prettily decorated with castles and red-roofed houses. But soon the current would push us along again, and taking careful note of the kilometre markers flashing past we figured we'd reach Orsova by early afternoon. All being well we might even get through the construction site of the dam.

At first gradually, and then quite suddenly, the gentle hills steepened ever higher into bare, almost sheer cliffs, the current got strong, and we knew that the Kazan Gorge (nicknamed the 'great boiler') could not be far. And then, inexplicably, *Puck*'s engine began to falter. Impossible... *this can't be happening*. With the 'boiler' just around the bend and no engine we'd be in major trouble. Graeme reacted quickly and used the last of *Puck*'s momentum to steer the boat straight into a patch of reeds on a muddy shore. Throwing a grapnel anchor, we sat stunned. *Please, sweetest* Puck, *please, please don't do this to us ...*

Graeme had barely undone the engine casing to check for causes when two very young armed soldiers appeared at the shore, their guns at the ready, furiously gesturing us to move on. At any other time, it would have amused us to see two kid soldiers in full uniform standing knee deep in the reeds, gesticulating wildly. Not this time. Feeling closer to tears than to laughter I gestured a helpless 'broken down'... 'kaputt', while Graeme let fly in unchecked fury. 'What the hell do you think we're doing ... sneaking into your bloody country, stealing bloody state secrets... bloody hell, get lost... bastards.'

We never found out what troubled *Puck*'s engine, but after a short rest and a bit of fiddling she innocently started again. Waved on by the gun-carrying kid soldiers we crossed our fingers and moved back into the fierce current. *Not far now* as first the hills, and then ever steepening cliffs began to squeeze the Danube into the narrow opening of the Kazan Gorge, its 150-metre width only allowing shipping to pass in one direction at a time. Watching the signal station we assumed a clear run, but were told to wait. Keeping up my mantra of *please, please engine don't stop* we waited, *Puck's* engine in reverse to hold her against the current, quivering like a racehorse at the starting line. Finally a barge emerged from between the cliffs; the signal station gave us the all clear and with full power ahead to keep maximum steerage, we shot into the gorge. The milky sun disappeared behind the cliffs, leaving us in cool shade and dark rushing water. We caught a glimpse of the ancient path cut into vertical cliffs, the famous Tabula Traiana simply flashed past and minutes later we slipped into calmer waters.

For all our relief and elation there was a touch of disappointment when we realised that we had just experienced the fastest historical tour ever. We had looked forward to seeing the Gorge, the path and the Tabula Traiana, but the fierce current had made it impossible to slow down for a good look, let alone stop.

The path we had glimpsed had been part of a military road, commissioned by the Roman Emperor Trajan so as to supply his troops fighting to conquer Dacia, a region covering most of present-day Romania. Roman engineers were famous for their road- and bridge-building skills, but even in ancient times the path along the Kazan Gorge was recognised as an outstanding feat. Completed in the year 103 CE, the Tabula Traiana hewn into rock at the end of it commemorates the achievement, documents the lineage of the emperor and assigns him the credit for 'excavating mountain rocks and using wood beams to make this road'.[27]

---

27 Since completion of the Iron Gate Dam, water levels have risen by around 40 metres. The road is now underwater but the Tabula Traiana (approx. 3.6 metres

Cutting a road into vertical rock beside a body of fast-flowing water running a good 50 metres deep would be a challenge today. The Romans completed the task with manpower only, and having seen (however briefly) the vertical cliff face and felt the powerful rush of water, we could only marvel.

~

With the 'great boiler' behind us, and back in the sun, we made a quick run to Orsova to pick up a pilot, as instructed. We didn't know why we needed a pilot ... had we underestimated the difficulty of the next stage? A question left hanging, because at the Orsova pilot station we were told that all river traffic had been suspended for the next five days while the first of the lock gates was being installed. *So much for hoping to get through by nightfall.* Suddenly it made sense why we had seen so few boats on the river. Everyone else must have heard the news over two-way radio and found more hospitable places to wait.

Orsova was one of the towns to be flooded when the Iron Gate Dam was finally completed; right now it was a ghost town, little more than a heap of rubble. A few people still lived there, but most of the administrative structures had gone – including the banks. One small shop still operated, but having entered the country only that morning we had no Romanian money. As it turned out we didn't need money: we had a baby, passport to many hearts. Danny's ready smile was all it took to supply us with milk and fresh crusty bread,

---

by 1.6 metres in size) was cut from the rock in one piece and fixed 50 metres above its original position.

the shopkeeper dismissing our apologies, and our thanks, with a wave of the hand and toss of his head.

Taking our daily walk ashore had to be authorised by uniformed guards patrolling the town. Looking back, I see myself pushing Danny's pram along a deserted street, lined with broken-down houses and piles of bricks. There is not another person in sight, but I am smartly dressed in my sleeveless white shore outfit, the hills around me steepening into gently rounded peaks.

Most of the town was cordoned off, and the eerie stillness was punctuated by the sound of tanks crashing into houses, horrendous explosions and bursts of machine gun fire. A man we met on one of our walks explained that the dying town was being used for training manoeuvres by the army. Another man didn't think that was the case; he'd heard that a movie was being made. We asked our friendly shopkeeper, but he simply shrugged his shoulders, *it doesn't matter, the town is finished anyway.* Our one privilege in this unhappy town was that we were allowed to swim in the Danube. It seems that the remaining Orsovians were not permitted to do this because they might defect and swim across the river to Yugoslavia.

Five long days later, boats and barges began banking up along the shoreline, and early the next day, without notice or further explanation, a pilot stepped aboard. *Puck*, being the baby of them all, had been assigned a place in the first convoy to go through the newly installed lock.

Past Orsova the Danube broadens, and soon we caught our first glimpse of the dam construction site, a concrete wall more than a kilometre long across the valley, spiked at intervals with red construction cranes. The long-awaited dam would make river traffic infinitely easier, because at this point, even though the river is wide, the riverbed is rocky and the water too shallow to allow passage even for the flat-bottomed barges. To facilitate river traffic was a slow and tedious business. Two solid stone walls, roughly a ship's width apart, had been built close to the edge of the river. The artificial channel thus formed was dredged, and a locomotive chugging along atop one of the walls pulled ships going upriver through one at a time: a towpath with a difference. A time-consuming exercise, because long convoys of barges needed to be uncoupled, pulled though the channel one at the time and reassembled at the other end.

We also needed to go through the channel, but travelling downriver the current was with us and no locomotive was needed to pull us. Instead we had the excitement of whooshing through the dredged channel at a cool 18 knots; 8 knots of *Puck*'s cruising speed added to 10 knots of current made it a wild ride. Pleased and relieved that all went well, we slipped into calmer waters. It was hard to tell what our pilot felt. He left steering the boat entirely to Graeme, didn't speak a word, and the best we could get out of him was a brief smile as we dropped him off at the pilot station.

Now for the last obstacle, the actual dam. Heading midriver once again, we steered for the lock opening, a huge gaping chamber with massive steel doors wide open. Five years of work had progressed to the point where the first convoy of boats could traverse. The significance of the occasion only struck us when we entered the lock and rows of workmen and women standing high above us started cheering and waving. It was a surprise to be greeted with so much exuberance, but like a diva stepping into the limelight we accepted the honour happily, bowing and cheering back at the crowds. Directed to the front of the lock we secured *Puck* onto vertically sliding bollards and waited for the boats behind us to enter and take up their places. The entire process was a dress rehearsal of sorts, the lock not yet ready for full-fledged operation, and happily everything worked perfectly. The upper gate, still painted in red undercoat, shut obediently and enclosed us in the huge chamber. The water level fell by a few metres, the lower gates opened and our way to the Black Sea was cleared. No hitches, no fuss, a perfect day. [28]

Iron Gate lock entrance.

With no more mountains in her way the Danube began to slow down and spread out, and traffic increased. We saw occasional paddle wheelers, popular because of the river's shallowness, cruise ships (the nationality of the tourists ever changing) and modern and efficient hydrofoil ferries. The hydrofoils, about 30 metres long, ran between towns and villages carrying a mix of passengers ranging from well-dressed tourists to farm women, wearing long skirts and head scarves, transporting a live goose or an armful of complaining chickens. Tugs of different nationalities pulled

---

28 It would take another three years to complete the dam, and water levels in the locks now drop (or rise) by a massive 30 metres.

as many as twelve barges behind them, and for the first time we saw powerful Russian tugs that didn't pull but *pushed* linked-up barges ahead of them, huge and unbending like skyscrapers placed flat on the water. The push-tug convoys travelled steadily throughout the night, feeling their way along the shore with powerful searchlights. Super-efficient, they must have operated with a minimum of manpower; we never caught sight of anyone aboard and made sure to keep out of their way.

Romanian authorities had issued us with a list of towns we were allowed to stop at, but pleading ignorance we would occasionally break the rule. Sometimes we got away with it, at other times we would put some unfortunate soldier into such a sweat that he insisted on 'guarding' us until his superior could be notified.

In one (forbidden) town I got talking to a German-speaking woman in one of the shops. Erika liked what I wore – which had started the conversation – and I told her that I made my own clothes. 'Oh, so do I,' she said, and I told her I'd be happy to give her some of my magazines and pattern books. She was delighted and came down to the boat later that afternoon. We chatted a bit more, I handed her the magazines, but she had barely taken a couple of steps away from the boat when an armed soldier stopped her and confiscated them. I was furious, *the stupid, stupid fool ... do I look like a spy?* There was nothing I could do, other than hope that Erika wouldn't get into trouble.

For a time Romania remained on the left, but not long after the Iron Gate, Bulgaria took the place of Yugoslavia (now Serbia) on the right. For kilometre after kilometre, both the Romanian and the Bulgarian banks were dotted with watchtowers in sight of each other. Propaganda placards placed on both banks faced the river screaming their messages. It seemed bizarre. Was the propaganda aimed at river travellers, or was one communist country trying to tell the other how much better they were?

We couldn't read the posters but had no problem deciding that Bulgaria was a better place for us, a little friendlier and less regimented. We were allowed to stop wherever we wanted and move around as we pleased. The food supply was better. Restaurants in the bigger towns were good and plentiful, and market shopping in smaller towns and villages along the way was unbelievably cheap. It was the peach season and for literally cents we could buy a whole bag full, soft and ripe and smelling of summer.

In Bulgaria we also ran into the rowing boys again; a welcome reunion, because apart from an occasional guarded chat with a person speaking German or a little English, our social interactions had been minimal. It was good to lift the sombre atmosphere with our silly jokes and join up for nights on the town. Seven like-minded adults and a baby (now happily sitting up and joining in) made for some lively parties. Again we reverted to ordering our meals according to price and ended up with some very strange banquets, although, from memory, cabbage cooked in countless ways was invariably part of it.

For a few days we travelled in convoy, meeting up in the evenings for meals aboard *Puck* or for riverside barbeques. We cooked mainly fish, but thanks to Graeme's insistence on buying local produce, one night we had roasted chicken on the menu. Graeme had spotted live chickens at a local market, cooped up in a cage and watched over by an old woman. But his assumption that the birds would be killed for him after he handed over the money proved wrong. Two beautiful rust-coloured birds were separated from their companions and handed to him very much alive and squawking. Seeing Graeme cautiously holding the birds, their feet stretched out in panic, set me off into helpless giggles. Amazingly enough I managed to take photos of both him and the chicken seller; a sweet old woman, her lined face framed by a neatly knotted scarf, her closed-mouth smile suggesting that she didn't have a lot of teeth left. I don't know who eventually killed the unfortunate birds, but I do know that two of the rowing boys were quarantined in the rowing boat towed behind *Puck*, yelling and shouting and throwing handfuls of plucked feathers about them like confetti.

By now the river had widened considerably and at times it felt as if we were travelling through a huge lake, its shores edged with forests and sweeping plains. One night, anchored in a side arm, we sat in the cockpit after dinner marvelling at the peace and stillness, when unexpectedly we heard wolves howling in the distance. I had never heard wolves howling and sat quietly, mesmerised, waiting for the next volley of low howls to carry across the water. Even Danny stopped jumping around on my lap and snuggled up against me. 'Danny... listen, listen, wolves... whoooo...' I whispered in his ear. But for all its charm and fascination, the persistent howling spooked me enough to make sure that our cabin doors were tightly closed before turning in for the night. I didn't think a wolf would jump aboard, but one never knew. I had read my fairy tales, knew that wolves ate children and was taking no chances.

For Love and the Sea

From the town of Silistra onwards, 375 kilometres from the Black Sea, Bulgaria slipped behind and we now had Romania on both banks. The watchtowers stopped and the atmosphere felt a little more relaxed; a welcome relief from regulations, mistrust and propaganda posters propped onto the riverbanks.

The Danube Delta spread out ahead of us and the prescribed route was for us to travel along the official shipping channel straight to the Black Sea. We had hoped to see a little more of the delta and its amazing birdlife, perhaps even visit one of the fishing villages nestled within. A visit to the Delta Museum in Tulcea made us more determined. Part of the delta reaches into the Ukraine, but the larger area is Romanian territory. Hours of waiting in dreary government buildings, a little arguing and some pleading eventually paid off and we were given permission to leave the prescribed route and explore the delta as we pleased. We soon realised that 'exploring' was a rather ambitious term. The delta covers an area of over 5,000 square kilometres, honeycombed with countless canals and dotted with swamps and vast lakes. Pushed by the unstoppable flow of the Danube, the best we could hope for would be a tiny taste of a unique watery world.

Our delta map wasn't much more than a sketch, but since all rivers flow to the sea we didn't expect to get lost. Going with the flow – in the truest sense of the word – we sometimes travelled along broad rivers, at other times along channels barely wide enough for *Puck* to turn around in. We slid past groups of men and women harvesting reeds, stacking the neatly tied bundles along the water's edge to be picked up later. A monochrome scene of grey water and yellowy reed, devoid of any distinguishing landmarks, had me wondering how the locals found their way about. Boats were the only mode of transport. Some of them had motors – little tug boats pulling others behind – but most of them were heavily built rowing boats shaped like double-ended canoes, propelled along with massive oars. We saw one such boat carrying a good-sized donkey amidships, a woman sitting in the stern and a man standing in the bows propelling the boat along with one oar. Later, in the big lakes, we saw more of these boats, ingeniously fitted with multiple lateen-rigged sails, crudely tied to short stumpy masts barely taller than the men crouched inside the boat.

Besides reed harvesting, fishing was a big industry. About twenty villages, their houses built on wooden piles and roofed with reeds, were dotted among the flat greenery. We stopped in one of them, tying *Puck* up to a sturdy wooden dock. Wandering through the village square and adjoining streets gave the feel of being on a floating island, suspended in a watery web. Nobody spoke to us. Adults simply watched, at best giving us nod without a smile. A young couple with a baby travelling on a foreign boat didn't fit any known concept. Only the children behaved like children everywhere. Unashamedly excited, they followed our every step, jumping and running ahead and behind us. I regretted not speaking their language.

Seeing large boxes of fish stacked by the dock, we tried to buy some before we left, holding up a couple of fingers of one hand and proffering money in the other. But the man we approached crossed his hands at the wrist and shook his head: *his hands were tied, he was not allowed to.* The catch belonged to the State. It was only after we left that we found two good-sized fish in the cockpit, thrown in while we weren't looking. Behind the Iron Curtain a lot happened in secret, including human warmth and generosity.

Deeper into the complex waterways we saw huge colonies of pelicans, swans, arctic geese, cormorants, flamingos and, with more careful watching, fish egrets, cranes and white-tailed eagles. The delta is a perfect breeding ground for water birds and a recognised stopover for migratory birds escaping the northern winters. Over 300 bird species have been recorded. But as in the other Garden of Eden, the delta also sheltered snakes. One morning, swimming in a shallow lagoon, we saw dozens of them swimming along with us. I have no idea if they were poisonous, but seeing them was enough for me to get out of the water very fast. We also learned to end our days early. By sundown at the very latest it was wise to be inside the boat with netting tightly in place. Swarms of mosquitoes would move over the water like clouds of smoke; I have never seen so many.

Our rough plan was to travel to the Black Sea port of Sulina in the northern reaches of the delta. We had wanted to pass the zero mark from which the length of the Danube is measured, but as we got closer to the Black Sea, it suddenly became important to get there quickly. The smell of salt water began to pull at our hearts and minds, passing the Danube's zero marker no longer justified the extra mileage and we decided on a more southern route instead. The new route would take us through the Razelm Lagoon, a huge expanse of water measuring close to 400 square kilometres. The lagoon is largely landlocked, but according to our map a small opening marked as Periboina, roughly 70 kilometres south of Sulina, would allow us passage into the Black Sea.

Our map had been correct. Arriving at Periboina a couple of days later we found a thin band of land separating the lagoon from the Black Sea, a bit of horizon clearly visible through the hoped-for opening. Rowing the dinghy ashore we rushed across the strip of land and stood, admiring the huge expanse of the water. We had arrived. Two-and-a-half thousand kilometres of river, winding its way through five countries, lay behind us.

Standing on pristine sand and seeing an unbroken horizon for the first time in a long while mixed with a sense of achievement and made us feel exuberant and light-headed. Breathing rich sea air felt like a reunion for us. For Danny, six months old to the day, it was a first, and in a baptism of sorts we solemnly dipped his feet into the salty water.

Tomorrow we would check out the channel for depth and tidal flow to give *Puck* safe passage, but for now we were content to row back to the boat, cook a celebratory dinner, have a glass of wine and enjoy our last night in the mirror-calm water of the lagoon. It was 1 September, the first day of autumn and, as if conscious of the big moment, the sun set with unusual splendour, casting golden light into the sky long after she had slipped below the horizon.

The Black Sea

Morning came, a brief reconnaissance by dinghy reassured us that the sandy passage was deep enough, and half an hour later *Puck* slipped gently and easily into the Black Sea. Heading south into a freshening wind, she jumped and bounced about a bit, but knowing that she was built by the German Navy to take pilots out to sea in all weathers reassured us. It might be uncomfortable at times because, unlike sailing boats, motor cruisers don't have a keel to steady them. Travelling the Black Sea in a sailing boat would have been preferable, but *Puck* was what we had, and apart from the one heart-stopping moment near the Kazan Gorge, the engine had never let us down.

Approximately 450 kilometres of coastline stretched between us and Istanbul; the first 120 kilometres Romanian territory, followed by Bulgaria and finally Turkey. Constanţa in Romania was our first stop, and finding it a modern well-developed resort after weeks in the wilderness was a shock. Tourism had taken off, and the limits enforced on the rest of the country seemed to have evaporated. Clusters of self-contained resort hotels had been built away from the

Romania we had seen. Propaganda placards, loudspeakers blaring in the streets and queues in front of shops had disappeared. Western tourists had come for the sea and the sun but that was all they got. The nearest village was a once-a-day bus ride away, making it virtually out of bounds.

In Constanța we met up with the rowing boys again. Their journey was over, their boat packed up and ready to be transported back to Germany. Two of the crew had bought bus fares home and two had wrangled a lift with German tourists travelling back by car. Hans, the university student, had a little more time and decided to come with us as far as Istanbul. To celebrate our meeting and ease our parting we shouted ourselves to drinks and a farewell meal in one of the big tourist hotels. After months of roughing it we felt we deserved a treat, not knowing what an unexpectedly bizarre experience lay ahead.

The hotel we had picked, a modern, many-storied glass and concrete structure curving in a U-shape around a swimming pool, turned out to be catering exclusively for German tourists. We dined in the outside courtyard near the pool, but even in the open air the walls towering around us made it an almost claustrophobic space. People sat on tiny balconies attached at every level like so many pigeonholes, laughing and chatting in German. The food was German, the waiters were German, the band was German and at one point the music stopped for an urgent announcement. A male voice speaking in German alerted all patrons that two young children had been seen on a balcony on the twelfth floor, *would the parents please go and check on their safety.* All eyes travelled to the twelfth floor; families knew each other, looked out for each other, happily holidaying on a make-believe 'island of luxury', shielded from all that was unpleasant about communism.

We knew differently, had seen the watchtowers, the soldiers and the food queues outside the shops. We had been governed by the same rules and regulations as the people on farms, in towns and villages, had smelled the fear and the secrecy. We had lived the stark reality of loudspeakers blasting propaganda into the streets, seen the absurdity of posters covering entire house fronts, had put up with the unending need to have bits of paper stamped. Like everyone else we had deemed it wise to keep our mouths shut, not because of intimidating guns but because we knew we could leave it behind.

The experience of travelling through communist countries had affected each of us in different ways. For Graeme it had raised disbelief and anger but for the rowing boys, and especially for me, there was deep gratitude that we had grown up in the democratic half of a still-divided Germany; we knew how lucky we were. But, drinking my wine and eating my grilled fish, I couldn't stop thinking of the fishermen back in the Delta, forbidden to sell us even a single fish. I was probably eating their catch right now, and more than likely with a thousand per cent mark-up.

Having Hans, one of the rowing boys, travel with us as far as Istanbul was great. He helped with the steering, and we continued to have lots of laughs. Crossing the border into Bulgaria happened without fuss and, choosing good weather for our daily runs, we drew steadily closer to Istanbul. We were keen to leave the communist countries behind, only stopping for the night and to stock up on food and fill up our diesel tanks. September was nearing its halfway mark and autumn was beginning to show its stormy face. We had a couple of exciting runs but, mindful of *Puck*'s size, we made straight for the nearest port at the first sign of bad weather.

Harbours became lucky dips. Varna presented itself as a sizeable town with a magnificent cathedral. Nessebar gave us safe shelter from a three-day storm. Mitchurin (now Tsarevo), a few kilometres north of the Turkish border and our last Bulgarian port, turned out to be the strangest mix of beautiful old stone houses and rows of tin sheds decorated with tiresome placards. Mitchurin became another three-day stop, not because we were stormbound but because we wanted to make sure of calm weather for our last 120-kilometre hop to Istanbul. Growing impatient, we eventually left, trusting our own assessment of wind and sky rather than the sign language advice given by local fishermen.

We should have listened. Barely out of port the wind piped up again, but having obtained our Bulgarian port clearance and keen to get to Istanbul, we decided to risk it. Two hours later we changed our minds. By then the wind was blowing very hard, the sea began to rise, and we ran for shelter. We had left Bulgaria behind us and had entered Turkish waters. A dot on our map marked Igneada seemed to indicate a township sheltered within a generous bay. It would be our first Turkish town, and rounding the headland we happily slipped into what looked like a newly built harbour. Rejoicing in our good fortune we motored in and tied up, the only boat on an empty wharf.

The drama began before we had a chance to step ashore. Two army vehicles raced down the hill and pulled up sharply, and quick as lightning a group of machinegun-toting soldiers jumped out and ran towards us. It looked comical, like a badly acted movie. Watching in total amazement we weren't in the least worried; perhaps this was some kind of practical joke and soon everybody would dissolve into laughter.

It wasn't a joke. Unbeknown to us, the dot marked Igneada was a Turkish army post and we had entered high-security territory. Against our will the four of us, including Danny, were ordered into cars at gunpoint and taken up the hill to an army camp, shut into a room and left to wait. Some time later interpreters arrived and interrogation began – in German and in English: Name; date of birth; where were you born; what is your work; what were you doing in the communist countries; have you served national service in your country; what is your father's Christian name, what is your maiden name; do you speak Bulgarian… It made no sense to us, but all our answers were translated back into Turkish and laboriously typed out.

Hours later we were given a plate of risotto – baby food and nappies had been fetched up from *Puck* – but soon after lunch the round of questions began again. This time from a plain-clothed official fetched up from Istanbul. Now we were getting worried and demanded that our respective embassies be notified, a request that was simply ignored. Six o'clock came, eight hours after our arrest, and we were finally told what was going on: the Turkish border patrol had reported that a Bulgarian gunboat had followed us and shots had been fired. Shocked, we could only declare our innocence: we had checked out from Bulgaria (with a stamp to prove it); we hadn't seen any boat following us. We carried no guns and had heard no shots.

But a small knot of fear remained: we had met three German men in Nessebar (also travelling to Istanbul on a small motorboat cruiser) who intended to smuggle a Romanian national into Turkey. We knew of their plan to unscrew the bulkhead of their boat, remove the water tank fitted into the forepeak, squeeze the man into the tank cavity and screw the bulkhead back again. We knew of the plan because we had agreed to carry their water tank on our boat, which they would retrieve once we got to Istanbul. Not only did we carry the odd-shaped tank strapped to our deck, but more incriminating still, we also carried the escapee's papers to make identification of him impossible should the venture go wrong. *Had the authorities discovered the refugee? Was that why we were being interrogated? Puck* had been searched in our absence and nothing incriminating had been found. But suspicion remained, and without an apology we were driven back to the boat with orders to leave at first light. An armed guard was posted alongside *Puck* to make sure we did.

Five in the morning and the wind blew strong from the south, not a good sign, but Istanbul lay roughly south and we felt that heading into wind and sea would be a safe enough course to steer. We had two helmsmen to take turns, *Puck* was a good boat, we had loads of experience and with care all should be well. We didn't know that the wind would strengthen to gale force, didn't know that the waves would reach towering heights and that we would come close to losing our boat and our lives. It still tastes bitter to think that the men who ordered us to leave must have known. They knew the Black Sea, knew how treacherous she gets in a storm, could see the size of our boat.

❦

The Black Sea is landlocked, the seabed shaped like a bowl with gently rising slopes. Waves created by strong wind have nowhere to run to, there are no islands to stem their fury and no openings for the mounting water to escape into. Waves whipped up in a storm do not roll along but rise upwards in peaks and columns. Russian folklore talks of 'killer waves', freak monsters that have claimed huge tankers and countless lives. We had seen plenty of big waves before, but never in such shape and formation. Two hours out from Igneada they came towards us so steeply that we feared being tipped over backwards. Like charging horses suddenly stopped, they'd rear up sharply, collapse onto themselves and even fall backwards. Each wave was unlike the next, each one a different assault. We briefly considered turning back, but riding such a sea with the wind pushing from behind would be more dangerous still. There were no harbours on the way and we had no choice but to keep going.

By lunchtime we faced walls of water with barely a trough between them. Graeme and Hans wrestled with the wheel, constantly adjusting speed and direction of the boat, easing her over each wave, taking care to avoid the big dumpers. Every so often *Puck* would be flung off the top of a wave, her propeller out of the water, the engine screaming, and then crash down again, shuddering violently before obeying the steering wheel once again. We all knew that one bad mistake at the helm, one faltering of the engine, one especially rogue dumper could slew us sideways and simply roll us into the sea.

Held rigid by the ordeal I stood in the cockpit for much of the time, only racing below when fear for our baby overwhelmed me. I had put Danny onto the cabin floor, wedged in with towels and cushions to stop him from being tossed around. Half-covered by a tangle of wet things he was happy enough, playing with whatever landed next to him, a shoe, a magazine or the contents of the vegetable basket – carrots, potatoes and onions tossed out of the lockers below the sink, the doors thrown open by the violent slewing of the boat. He only asked to be fed, and spooning jars of baby food into his open mouth I was the one crying.

The afternoon wore on, unending hours of struggle and awful noises. *Where the hell is the Bosporus; it can't be far now ...* Spume and green water thrown at us made it hard to get a bearing. I glanced at Graeme looking grey and exhausted in the failing light, mute and concentrating, his beard salt encrusted. Hans too was silent. There was no point in speaking. We were joined in a nightmare, no running away from the enemy, no screaming to hold it at bay, no waking up. Even my escape route of slipping into upper altitudes, of floating above unbearable feelings the way I sometimes had on *Hope*, was firmly blocked. I couldn't leave Danny behind. This wasn't safe old *Hope*. I knew *Puck* was out of her depth. I *had* to be there, willing us to survive, willing *Puck* to make it, my silent mantra of *please, please* pulling us forward, begging and longing... *please let us live*.

Daylight was fading when almost imperceptibly a tiny crack opened up in the dark rocky shore; unreal, dreamlike, like huge stage backdrops sliding apart on massive rollers. I stared at it, *could it be?* If this was the Bosporus it wasn't far. *It had to be the Bosporus*. Peering anxiously through binoculars I dared not hope, but minutes later the gap had widened a little... yes, it was the Bosporus, unmistakably.

The release from terror came quickly. A powerful current began to pull us into the opening and soon after, the shoreline shielded us from the worst of the wind. The sea flattened a little and at last we were able to travel at full speed. The current strengthened, and as if drawn into a funnel we slipped inside the Bosporus. Heading for the first sheltered bay we could find, we dropped anchor at the precise moment when evening prayers from a nearby minaret floated eerily across the water. *We made it.* With tears rolling down my face I sat quietly, holding a very damp little boy close to my heart.

Life itself, breathing in and out, was all that mattered.

Istanbul

Puck had been the perfect boat for river travel, but taking her into open water was ambitious, even foolish. As powerboats go she was probably the safest, although clearly not designed for extreme challenges. She was too small, had no self-draining cockpit (just a big space open to the sea) and to our shame we carried no effective life-saving equipment. Our survival in the Black Sea came down to pure luck and being humoured by gods and angels. I feel sick when I think of the risks we took, doubly so since we had Danny in our care.

On *Hope* the trip to Istanbul would have been an uncomfortable ride but not life threatening. Theoretically, *Hope* could take a complete tumble in any direction and provided all hatches were closed she would eventually come up the right way, steadied by tons of lead on her keel. *Puck* had no keel. She was a round-bottomed floating nutshell; her only grip on the water a churning propeller. One bit of dirt, one air lock in the fuel line, could have stopped the engine and left us entirely at the mercy of the waves. We had been lucky indeed. Breathing a sigh of relief we put the ordeal behind us, convinced and determined that it would not happen again. From now on we would take day trips only and keep the keenest eye possible on the weather.

For me to understand the legacy of the Black Sea storm has only been possible in retrospect. I know that it affected me far beyond the practicalities and changes of plan we made at the time. I know that on Thursday September 11, 1969, a filter, a thin little membrane removed itself from my vision and permanently altered my perception of life, making it richer and more precious than I had ever known.

⁓

Remembering our arrest at Igneada we made sure to see to the formalities first, cautiously mentioning the incident to both Customs and Immigration. Neither had any knowledge of it, didn't want to know, *it was Army business* and we saw no point in pushing it.

Outside the customs office we met up with the German men and their Romanian stowaway. They had been lucky. Travelling a couple of days ahead of us they had missed the worst of the storm, and much to everyone's relief the refugee had not been discovered. He looked grey and shaken and was very relieved to get his papers back. He would make his way to the German Embassy immediately to apply for political asylum.

Hans needed to get back to Germany, and after seeing him off at the bus terminal we took stock. Not usually enamoured of big cities, we made plans to stay in Istanbul for a week, maybe two, and then take off southwards towards warmer climes. But all that changed when we became guests at the yacht club in Fenerbahçe, on the Asian side of the Bosporus. A safe berth, the company of like-minded people and the lure of a fascinating city stretched our stay from the intended two weeks into well over two months.

We fitted in quickly, and taking daily shopping trips

along the waterfront of Fenerbahçe became a pleasant ritual, relaxed and comfortable. If we were early enough we would get a friendly wave from the fishermen living in decrepit boats propped up on dry land, their bedding spread out in the morning sun. Braziers were lit, and stallholders sold food or the ever-present glasses of hot tea. Barrows of fish arrived, their red gills turned inside out making them look as if they wore coral necklaces. The shopkeepers soon got to know us and dropped their 'tourist' prices. Delighted with our attempts to ask for what we wanted in Turkish, they tried to teach us more words, laughing at our pronunciation. The baker was especially keen. Holding the bread high, he would point at it, raise his eyebrows and say *'ekmek, ekmek'*. And if on the next day I actually asked for ekmek instead of pointing at it, he would grin broadly and throw in a crisp bread roll for free.

꩜

Istanbul in the 1960s was a vibrant and totally unselfconscious city, a place of commerce, not overly interested in tourism or in promoting itself. The streets, the shops and the crowds of people were a functioning mix of rich and poor, of old and new, of East and West. The language was loud and quick, impossible for us to understand, but English and especially German got us by well enough. If we needed information, we could usually get it from a smart-looking European-dressed passer-by.

The Bosporus splits the city; construction of a bridge to span the wide stretch of water (1.5 kilometres) was in the planning stages, to be completed in three years' time. For now, as in ancient times, ferries travelled ceaselessly back and forth between Europe and Asia. Not wanting to miss out on the famous sights, we took the occasional ferry ride across to 'European' Istanbul. I had stitched up a baby backpack on my hand-cranked sewing machine, and having Danny strapped to Graeme's back made our excursions easy. Barrows along the way sold roasted chestnuts, toys, combs, lighter fluid and the obligatory Turkish delight, so sweet it made one's teeth ache. Fruit shops held mountains of grapes, spotted with bees claiming their share of the sweetness. When we bought a bunch of grapes the shopkeeper would wave it around first to shoo off the bees, but one or two would invariably end up trapped inside the paper bag, buzzing wildly. But what charmed us most was the sight of public letter-writers sitting in parks under sheltering trees, their typewriters placed on flimsy card tables, clacking away furiously while their customers dictated, their faces blank, looking far into the distance.

The actual ferry ride was an experience in itself, the boats solidly built, top-heavy and painted in brightest greens, reds and yellows. Dreadfully overcrowded with goods and people, each departure became a drama filled with excessive amounts of fuss and shouting. There was no timetable, and even latecomers were accommodated with good-natured gusto, crowds of dockside onlookers and on-board passengers alike shouting to hold off departure long enough for them to make it aboard.

Old Istanbul (like Rome) was built on seven hills, each rise crowned by a mosque. In whichever direction one walked, the skyline showed a group of tall minarets, their shape and outline famous and vaguely familiar; one had seen it before, in photographs or history books. *Wow, look, there is the Blue Mosque*, and walking around buildings and crossing busy roads to reach it becomes part of the experience of being there, of actually seeing it. *There it is* – huge, real, three-dimensional. Once inside, city noises become muffled, rays of light reach into cool spaces, layers of thick carpets soften footsteps and after a time of reverie and wonder we step back into the noise and confusion of a crowded city, stilled and satisfied.

Istanbul wasn't an easy city to explore. Street signs were confusing, unmarked medieval bazaars stood next to modern buildings, and splendid mosques rose at the end of unimposing alleyways. We often got lost, only to find our way again by catching glimpses of the water surrounding the city; the Bosporus the most telling landmark, bright and unmistakable with its colourful ferries. We walked a lot, but once we learned to catch dolmush taxies, sightseeing became a lot more fun. Dolmush taxies were small minibuses endlessly travelling the city along set routes, stopping only on demand. Seeing a dolmush approach, all one had to do was put a hand up, and if there was room inside, the driver would pull over. Getting off the dolmush was even easier. Seeing one's destiny approach, one had to shout 'Stop!' and the driver simply pulled over to the kerb.

Sometimes our friends Gloria and Kurt, whom we'd met at the yacht club, showed us the sights. They had been living and working in Istanbul for six years and adored the place, keen to share their love for it. Gloria was a nurse, known in many places, and roaming the markets with her was pure joy. No shopkeeper would have dared to cheat or inflate prices: in the big touristy markets in the city, prices dropped the minute she started speaking Turkish.

The Fenerbahçe yacht club offered us the use of their facilities and it seemed prudent to slip and repaint *Puck* while we had the opportunity. Wolfgang and Edelgard, club members and active sailors, invited us to stay in their home until the job was finished; a much-needed pick-me-up for us. With Danny growing up, the boat seemed to be getting smaller by the day and it felt good to spread out, luxuriate in a bath and sleep in normal beds.

A week of shore rest revived Graeme enough for him to get out his list of repair jobs, attacking each one with renewed gusto. He even ripped off the rubber sheeting glued onto the foredeck, a makeshift arrangement that had annoyed him from the day we first saw the boat. Finding laid deck underneath, he happily began varnishing. In our effort to get everything shipshape we briefly considered getting rid of the little gas fridge too. It had served its purpose of keeping the immunisation serum cool (Gloria had given Danny his last injection) but we foolishly kept it. Had we known the trouble it would cause later, we would happily have ditched it along with the ghastly rubber sheeting.

The Fenerbahçe yacht club was proud to have Sadun Boro and his German wife Oda, the first Turkish couple to sail around the world, as their members. Their yacht *Kismet*, moored in the bay, was unmistakably a seagoing vessel, fitted with a wind vane, spray covers and baggywrinkle wrapped around the stays. Finding Sadun aboard one weekend, we had rowed over to introduce ourselves and find out about their travels. It turned out that the Boros had only recently returned from their world cruise, stopping in Thursday Island, Australia in 1967, a year after we did. Not only had we sailed along similar routes, but like us, they now also had a child, a daughter about the same age as Danny. We had much in common and a lot to talk about, often in the local pub drinking raki, grouped around a table overloaded with food. Sometimes the proprietor respectfully offered free drinks; as the first Turkish round-the-world sailors Sadun and Oda were celebrated like national heroes.

Sitting aboard *Kismet* one sunny Sunday, we discussed the wisdom of us wintering aboard *Puck*, keen to draw on Sadun's experience and local knowledge. October had arrived, boats were being pulled out of the water for the winter, and most people felt it was foolish to spend the winter aboard. *Too cold and windy* they said but Sadun disagreed. He reassured that the southern Turkish coast would be okay, as long as we watched the weather and (casting a discreet glance at *Puck*) made sure we were in port for storms.

Although October was half gone, it was still warm. Only occasional chilly winds, blowing in from Russia, reminded us that perhaps we had better get a move on, and eventually we ran out of excuses to stay even for another day. *Puck* had been slipped and repainted and, as a last job, Danny's bunk on top of the cabin cupboard had been made more secure. He could stand up now, and to stop him from toppling over the edge, Graeme had threaded a zigzag of ropes from the top of the cot rail onto the deck head. We had considered fitting vertical timber slats but, as Graeme put it, the kid would look like a canary in a cage. As it was, he was still in a cage, albeit a soft ropey one. And my concern of how to get him out of his enclosure was solved by Danny himself. As soon as he heard the click of the catches that lowered the side of the cot, he would throw himself flat on his back for me to slide him out.

Sadun and Oda came to see us off, bringing an embarrassing amount of presents; there was even one for Danny from their daughter Denizi. A second goodbye, with Kurt and Gloria, awaited us on the other side of the Bosporus. We had planned to anchor off their house before heading down the Marmara Sea, but freshening wind had us retreat into a little breakwater harbour just down from the Blue Mosque. *Can't leave a boat in a storm*, and so our friends came aboard instead. We dined on my special 'please-can-I-have-some-more' deluxe fish soup, and reluctant to part, we talked late into the night.

Meeting two people who had lived in Istanbul for years and still adored the place had made me think – as I had in many other places – *how would I like to live here?* The fairy tale-reading child in me was enchanted with exotic Istanbul, but not being able to get simple things like tinned or powdered milk was less captivating. The water was risky, pasteurised milk was only just becoming available, and Danny had already suffered one gastro attack. Import duty was high; my mother had sent two baby bottles that had cost more in import duty than their original price. Boat fittings, brass screws, and ship's chandlery in general were difficult to get; my trader husband had already worked out how much profit could be made smuggling in boxes of boating hardware. On top of that, drugs were shaping up to be problem. At the German embassy, specially affixed notices gave severe warnings about any drug involvement, posting newspaper articles of men and women being jailed for possessing little more than a joint. Not that we had anything do with the stuff, but suspicion of foreigners, and especially foreigners with boats, was high. I loved Istanbul, but ultimately not well enough to want to live there.

༺

Yet Turkey, and its people, remained a huge favourite, especially as we moved south into remoter regions. The town of Gelibolu (Gallipoli) is one example, three days and three uneventful hops from Istanbul though a calm Marmara Sea. We berthed in the inner harbour, a beautiful anchorage right in the heart of town. Modernity had not yet reached Gelibolu and horse-drawn carts, beautifully decorated with colourful pictures, far outnumbered trucks and buses. Graeme's log entry describes the atmosphere:

Everything here is done with a great deal of shouting. Just as I write this – early on Monday morning a ferry has come in, everyone on the ferry, everyone on the shore shouting – we wonder if they are trying to be the first to tell the latest news or gossip, asking for lines to be taken, or is it just the fellows trying to get appointed to carry someone's luggage? As the bow of the ferry reaches jumping distance from the quay, they jump aboard and push and jostle to get at the sacks, cases, boxes, trussed chickens etc. which clutter the deck – then the passengers go ashore: old ladies with shawls which look like blankets wrapped tightly around their heads and throats are being helped ashore with no less alacrity than the younger girls dressed in fashionable leather coats and sunglasses. The ferry too is a joy to behold. The hull was once a fishing boat, but on deck stands the body of an old bus; driving seat, steering wheel, horn etc. all as original. The only change one can see in the bus is the absence of wheels, and a self-conscious looking mast stuck on the roof.

For me Gallipoli prompted a re-organisation of my wardrobe. Disapproving looks from the women and wolf whistles from a group of soldiers stationed at a nearby army camps made me realise that my skirt, while not exactly mini, was definitely too short for backwater Turkey. From now on it would be back to jeans and long-sleeved tops.

A short run across the Dardanelles took us to Çanakkale, where our arrival coincided with a public holiday. The town was decked out in bunting, a procession was promised for the next day, but I have no idea what was being celebrated. We wanted to join in with the excitement but engine trouble put a damper on things. The smell of burning rubber had given us warning that something was amiss, and Graeme spent most of the day taking the engine apart. The smell turned out to be a burned-through exhaust connector, fixable without hard-to-come-by spare parts. Relieved that all was well and fixed, we quickly changed into party gear and made it in time for the parade.

Two brass bands led groups of soldiers doing fancy rifle tricks. Next came a platoon of stony-faced marching marines, a unit of uniformed police and then, closely behind them, a line of trucks loaded with hutches of chickens and rabbits. An agricultural pump sprayed the crowd with scented water and the fire brigade came past with flashing lights, followed by tip trucks 'a-tipping' and graders and bulldozers slowly raising and lowering their blades. The cheering was long and loud and everybody loved it.

But despite the excitement on offer, Graeme carrying Danny in his rucksack stole the show. A man carrying a baby in that way was a sensation. The local men didn't know how to deal with the phenomenon and came to shake Graeme's hand; whether in pity or admiration I don't know. The next morning half the town folk came to stare at us, sitting close enough for peanut shells and even the odd cigarette butt to land on our deck. It was time to escape, and we hopped 10 miles across the Dardanelles to find a secluded bay at the very southern tip of the Gallipoli peninsula, calm and beautiful and not a person in sight.

Graeme had hoped to visit the sites of the Anzac landings but it proved too difficult. From where we were, it would have meant a 30-kilometre overland hike over rugged country, and for us to actually land in Anzac Cove we would have had to motor around the tip of the peninsula, up and back again – a detour which the lateness of the season would not allow.

And so, we hiked for a couple of hours over the scrubby hills above our secluded little bay while Graeme told me Anzac stories of bravery and courage. He talked of the dawn service he had been to as a boy with his dad in the rose garden in Willoughby Park near his home, where one rosebush was tended for each soldier lost from that municipality. He remembered the cool of the morning, the silence, and the softly lit cross glowing in the dark.

How different it is for the conquerors, I thought. In the very same war my father, 18 years old, had survived a burst of bullets, one of them piercing his lungs and another taking half his stomach away, yet his bravery and that of his fellow soldiers was not celebrated; least of all by himself. My father never spoke of the war, merely suggested for me to read Remarque's *All Quiet on the Western Front*. It would help me understand the futility of war, he said.

The Aegean

Next morning we were woken up at 5 a.m., hailed by two fishermen coming alongside, their fire torch fixed to the bow of their boat. We had exchanged greetings with them the previous evening and they thought we might like some freshly caught fish. A nice thought, no mention of money, and still half asleep we managed to shout a thank you after them as they rowed off into the darkness. Dawn was only just breaking but fully awake now, we cleared away the bedding, had a quick breakfast and made our grand entrance into the Aegean Sea lit up by a pink dawn and the promise of sunshine. It was hard to believe that winter was on its way.

Our plan was to winter on the Greek island of Rhodes, as far south as we wanted to go. Depending on how *Puck* behaved we might spend the following summer cruising the Mediterranean, but it was already clear in our minds that if we wanted to continue our roaming life we needed a bigger boat, and preferably a sailing boat. A raft of questions was attached to such dreams, all of them too difficult to answer.

Let time take care of it, we're sure to come up with something; for now the challenge of getting to Rhodes was more than enough.

Keeping to our Black Sea Storm resolve to watch the weather and make day trips only, we began threading our way south. As with our river travels we had no sightseeing agenda, but simply allowed wind and sea and our mood of the day to guide us. The ancient Turkish port of Assos, a tiny township nestled against a steep rocky shore, was an early stop. Parts of the breakwater surrounding the town had been washed away by the centuries, but enough was left to make it a safe anchorage. We arrived in streaming rain, and a Turkish fisherman rushed to take our lines and would not rest until *Puck* was snug, fenders and all. There was no stopping him, and by the time he was satisfied, his loose pants and woollen jumper were soaked through. Going ashore, we found narrow walkways between ancient stone houses, some empty and some occupied. Guided by our welcoming fisherman we bought eggs and ekmek (bread) in the local pub; a windy three-walled affair with a plastic sheet frontage.

Returning sunshine had us stay, happy to experience 'a day in the life of Assos'. It turned out to be more interesting than we could have imagined. Shortly after sunrise a team of eight men arrived on donkeys, with a goat in tow. Tethering the goat to a nearby tree they began building a wall of stones, which looked very much like the beginning of a house. Graeme was fascinated, nonplussed. 'Surely, if they want a house, they could repair one of the old ones?'

There were indeed plenty of unoccupied stone ruins about, but the men followed their own logic and kept building. At around ten o'clock two of them stopped work, slaughtered and skinned the goat they had brought with them, and divided the carcass into three large cooking pots placed over an open fire. A few hours later everyone stopped for goat stew and then it was back to work. Towards evening, the pots went on the fire again and now it was dinnertime for the entire population of Assos, eighteen people in all; the eight workmen, six local fishermen, the 'hotel' keeper and the three of us. Yet only sixteen people were present for the party; Danny was too little for goat stew and since I would have been the only woman in the male gathering, I opted to stay aboard. Thinking of the little bleating goat being killed had dampened my appetite anyway.

Next morning there was no sight of the workmen. We put Danny in his backpack and took off along a goat track towards the main settlement of Assos, roughly a thousand feet above sea level. Seeing neither goats nor people, we climbed the steep and winding path, fascinated by bits of carved marble column half buried among the bushes. There was no way of knowing which century they belonged to, how they came to topple down the hill or what kind of building they might have supported.

Finally, Assos proper appeared, a silent town clustered around the Athena Acropolis high up on a hill and almost as run-down as the Port of Assos. Mules were the only form of transport and walking through the streets, some of them paved, others simply compacted dirt, offered a tableau of ruins and ancient dwellings. In some areas, a more modern building had slipped in among the old ones, giving away the fact that this was the 20th century. The houses seemed occupied, but the only people we saw were sombre men in black and occasionally an older woman dressed in a thick long skirt, beautifully decorated with colourful stitching, matched by a shawl in deep earthy colours.

The Athena temple up on the hill, its crumbling walls clearly visible from the town, was built in 530 BCE, although settlement around Assos is thought to have begun as far back as 2000 BCE. History tells of kings and conquerors, of changing fortunes in and around the area, but Aristotle remains the most famous name tied to the region. He opened his School of Logical Thinking in Assos, stayed for three years and after marrying King Hermeias's niece Pythia, sailed away to the Greek Island of Lesvos. We only learned such snippets from subsequent reading. In 1969 Assos had no tourists, no guides, and as far as we could tell there were no archaeological digs.

༄

Following Aristotle to Lesvos was a tempting option. The island was close enough, a pale blue mound on the horizon barely 20 miles away, but Turkey held us up once again. Still diligently observing official rules, we made for Ayvalik to obtain Turkish customs clearance for Lesvos. Ayvalik lies a little way inland, at the end of a natural waterway, and motoring back out to sea again we caught sight of a beautiful little bay completely sheltered from the wind. It was too good to miss and next thing we had the anchor down. The water was smooth and shallow, and with *Puck*'s bottom almost touching the sand we could step ashore in gumboots without getting our feet wet. Lesvos would have to wait. Warm sunshine had us in T-shirts, and we stayed put for almost a week, feeling no guilt whatsoever at yet another delay and doing little more than enjoying perfect peace and solitude.

༄

The need for powdered milk for Danny, precious and hard to get, eventually forced us to head for Mitilini. It was our first Greek port, and finding little shops filled with cheeses and other delicacies made for exciting shopping; dinnertime that night felt almost like Christmas. The downside was that the harbour was slick with oil (a pet hate shared by Graeme and me) but getting away in the morning as planned didn't happen. It took until late afternoon to find somebody to stamp our customs clearance, leaving us just enough daylight to get back to the Turkish coast. We had yet to learn that the Greek islands slowed to a crawl in winter. Tourists came in summer. Winter was the time to take life easy – very easy.

The sun low, we steered for Turkey, to a little dot on the chart marked Ilica. We assumed this to mean a town or a village, but as we got closer to the shore neither houses nor people were to be seen. Perhaps the town was over the rise of the hill? Rowing ashore to investigate, we stumbled over the ruins of an ancient bath fed by a hot spring. *Of course! Ilica must mean hot spring in Turkish.*

Four walls, about the size of a small bedroom, enclosed a pool of knee-deep warm water, the pool floor and surrounded ledges smooth with ancient tiles. Delighted with our find, we fetched towels from the boat and the three of us settled in for a communal bath. Danny splashed around wildly in what was the biggest bath he had ever seen. I shared his pleasure: I hadn't seen a big warm bath for a while either, and lying back contently I looked up at the darkening sky. *Why would anyone put branches on top of an ancient bath?* I wondered dreamily, noticing a raft of green branches spanning the top of the walls. *Green branches, how strange ... oh I know ... must be so the angels can't see us thieving a piece of heaven.*

It only occurred to me later that local villagers put green branches up there to dry them for firewood and that we were lucky not to be caught in our nakedness. But my theory of making the angels jealous held true. Later that night the door to heaven was unceremoniously slammed shut. A freezing onshore wind sprung up and we had to set night watches. We cancelled our much-anticipated morning bath and ran for a safer anchorage at first light.

҈

The next time we needed to shop and fill up the water tanks we choose the Greek island of Chios. By then we had dispensed with immigration and customs clearances and simply hopped across. No one seemed to notice or care and why rouse officials from winter hibernation? Remembering sleepy Mitilini we didn't expect a bustling scene, but finding the town of Chios (named the same as the island itself) completely deserted was weird and upsetting. We might as well have landed on the moon. *How could a whole township be deserted?* Our marine chart had promised fuel and water dockside but we found both outlets padlocked. There was no sign of where to get a key and no one to ask. Baffled and mystified we left early the next morning, still low on water and having spoken to nobody.

҈

An hour's rough ride in a hefty beam swell took us back to Turkey, into the bustling centre of Çeşme. *Hey look, the world hasn't ended, there are people about* ... lots of them walking up and down the waterfront. There was someone to take our lines and soon afterwards a trio of young Turkish men came to talk to Graeme, keen to practise their English. Mustafa was the front man, the primary talker, his halting English tinged with an American twang. He told Graeme that he'd picked it up from English classes given by Diane, an American girl stationed in Çeşme.

Later that night we met Diane along with two Australian women, Bev and Paddy, in the local coffee shop, a good place for a meal and for swapping stories. Diane the Peace Corps woman had been in Çeşme for three months and had learned a lot about Turkish customs, especially those surrounding love, sex and marriage. We knew that marriages were arranged and that young girls were hidden away, but it was interesting to hear how the young men coped. Deprived of even the simplest conversation with eligible women it was clearly frustrating, if not downright shocking, for young men to see bikini-clad tourist girls flirting and bathing on their beaches. The hippy trail had moved eastwards, but despite the influx of more tourists, Diane thought that modernity in the sex department had a long way to go. She told us how an American couple, both husband and wife, had been killed sunbaking naked on what they imagined to be a deserted beach. A silent watcher had emerged from the shrubs to assault the wife, the husband tried to fight him off and in the ensuing melee both husband and wife were knifed. Thinking of our bath at the little dot called Ilica, I resolved to be more cautious. I wondered how Diane got on; it seemed crazy to send an attractive young American Peace Corps woman into the heartland of male dominance.

Graeme's young Turkish friend Mustafa turned up for

more chats, one day with his hair considerably shorter and minus the beard he had been sporting. 'Hey... Mustafa, what happened, where's the beard, you look ready to go to school!' Graeme lost no time teasing him. Smiling awkwardly, Mustafa explained that he had to shave his beard off; Ramadan had begun and only men that had been to Mecca were allowed to grow beards. 'Poor Mustafa,' said Graeme, grinning broadly and stroking his own full beard.

We knew about Ramadan from our visit to the Comoros Islands three years earlier, yet customs here seemed very different. Loud drumming with an almost African beat indicated sunrise, giving the signal that no more food or drink could be consumed. Sunset, when eating could resume, wasn't announced with drumbeats, but by a single cannon shot. Diane told us how families sat around tables laden with delicious food, poised and ready to tuck in as soon as the cannon went off. Apparently every night was a feast, and special breads and sweets were prepared ahead of time. How difficult it must have been for the women cooking up the feast throughout the day without the pleasure of slipping the odd morsel into their mouths.

We had no call to join in on the deeply religious Ramadan festivities, but soon found our own reasons to celebrate. Staging a little party aboard *Puck*, we toasted the arrival of Danny's tiny upper teeth. He now had two Bulgarian and two Turkish ones. The fresh air was obviously agreeing with him. He was growing fast and was beginning to climb up on things, not a good thing on a boat and a worrying development for his mother.

Our first brush with Turkey's fledgling tourism industry came in Kuşadasi. Two tiny cucumbers cost one-and-a-half lira, a custom agent offered to handle our business *for fifteen dollars only*, at every step taxi drivers offered lifts to nearby

Ephesus and all this in spite of the town – including the souvenir shops – being practically shut down for winter. It didn't bear thinking about what it might be like at the height of the season. Seeing Ephesus and the ruins of the Temple of Artemis (hailed as one of the Seven Wonders of the World) would no doubt have been educational, but we declined. Finding a lonely anchorage was more to our taste, like the little bay we found before heading for Kuşadasi. As so often before, we had climbed high up onto the rocky cliffs to look far into the distance, and to admire *Puck* anchored prettily beneath us, the only one in a vast sheet of blue water. Gazing down into water clear and deep enough to reach into nothingness was preferable to spending a day among dusty ruins, however ancient and important.

The decision to leave touristy Kuşadasi was quick and unanimous. With so much bustle about and custom agents watching us we thought it wise to obtain the necessary clearance for Greece, but, once again, the litany repeated itself. *The harbourmaster is not available, could we please come back. When would he be in please? We don't know, maybe not today.* And so, bravely and rebelliously, we left without a clearance and set our course for the Greek island of Samos.

~

Travelling fast through calm open water, we watched the blue hump on the horizon gradually shape itself into hills and valleys, and soon the houses of Tigani took on form, spreading white and beautiful up into the hills. Entering the breakwater surrounding the port we remembered the deserted township of Chios, fervently wishing and hoping that Tigani wouldn't be a repeat of that experience. It wasn't. Tigani turned out to be third time lucky, a charming village filled with lovely people, the Greece we had heard about and seen in pictures.

With *Puck* safely tied to a big steel ring set into the quay, we were free to have lunch in one of the small restaurants, join the locals sitting in soft winter sun drinking coffee, or simply walk around for daily exercise. Doing eight days of exactly that made us feel almost like locals. It was easy to imagine how expatriate writers could get stuck on Greek islands, sitting in small, whitewashed rooms tapping away at their typewriters, high above town, hidden away in a cascade of houses painted blue and white. Food was cheap, village life was simple and the peaceful atmosphere was sure to inspire reflection.

We met no writers, but walking the surrounding hills we came across a young German archaeologist digging away at a site that he claimed showed traces of a civilisation from 3000 BCE. He took us to his workroom full of carefully organised heaps of shards, ready to be pieced into clay pots, urns and vases. He came aboard *Puck* for an evening of food and drink, an encounter that left me in total awe of his patience and commitment. Archaeology was his life and I silently marvelled at how different we humans are; here was a man totally consumed with finding small bits of earth-coloured clay which I wouldn't notice even if I stepped on them.

We grew fond of our little haven, and Tigani fooled us into thinking that winter did not exist. The fishermen had warned us that winter storms could be fierce and could last for days, but we weren't overly worried, thinking that the breakwater would give us ample shelter. And when the inevitable storm finally hit we were indeed safe, but could not have imagined how hellishly uncomfortable it would get. In an incredibly short time the wind rose to force 8, straight from the south, bad for us because the breakwater was open to the south. It rained, it was cold, and soon the swell rolling into the harbour began bouncing back off the quay sending up explosions of water. We were tied to that quay and it became impossible for us to leave the boat; the water far too rough for us to step ashore.

Two days of storm and the situation got worse, our mooring ropes tightening to near breaking as each long slow surge threatened to suck us away from the wall. The fishermen tried to help and pointed to a mooring further into the harbour for us to pick up. Not an easy job in the fierce wind, but we managed to do it, adding our anchor just in case. We were now safe enough, but three days of living in a boat that behaved like a washing machine had us deplore Tigani harbour, the boat, and lastly our own stupidity at being caught out.

As soon as the chilly southerly was replaced by an even colder westerly, we made a beeline for Myndos in Turkey. We had learned our lesson; it was time for us to get to Rhodes where we could relax and wait for spring. After Myndos, we needed one more run to Bodrum and from there a final hop to Rhodes. All being well we could be there inside a week.

Six-and-a-half hours of motoring in chilly winds took us to back to the Turkish coast, to the tiny village of Myndos. Graeme's log entry describes our approach in (for him) unusually poetic terms:

A fine though cold day. The coast was, as usual, extremely pretty – mountains up to 3,500 feet high, and white housed villages nestling in their laps. It seems as if someone went out in a boat and said, 'yes, we'll have a town here, and one there, and yes that's a pretty spot for one too.'

Up close, Myndos was quaint rather than pretty, the most out-of-the-way Turkish village we had been to, different to all the others. Stone houses came right up to the water's edge, and a black-and-white photograph I took from *Puck*'s cockpit shows a man on a donkey pulling a heavily laden camel along a narrow strip of pebbly beach; a photograph that could easily have been taken in another century.

Onshore, men and women emerged from the houses to greet us. It was the first time that women, wearing headscarves, jackets and baggy trousers, came to see us. In other villages we rarely saw women, but here they came to smile at Danny and show me their children. I also got to see their cattle, and stroked the sweetest little calf. One woman took me by the hand to take me to the orchard at the back of her house, where she picked mandarins for me to take.

In a quirky touch two soldiers appeared later in the day, shouting instructions across the water which we could not understand. A complicated exchange of sign language began and eventually we twigged that we had failed to hoist a Turkish courtesy flag, which, of course, we did, immediately. The soldiers conveying the message were extremely apologetic, indicating with another volley of gestures that the superior who had ordered them to do this was giving them plenty of headaches. Luckily we were not asked to show customs papers, because once again we had left Greece doing away with such irksome formalities.

Bodrum was our last Turkish port. *Puck* found a safe berth tied to a broad quay alongside the ruins of a crusader castle, a space made available for her alongside the fishing boats. The town had teahouses, restaurants and plenty of food shops. There was a garage where we could fill up our gas bottles; water and diesel fuel was available dockside; yet for all the plusses I took a dislike to the place.

I'd had enough of the maleness of the country, every shop, teahouse or restaurant always full of men. On top of that I got a toothache, which the local dentist fixed with a foot pedal-powered(!) drill, a novel experience. Last and worst of all, I fell into the water while stepping ashore, the first time after nearly six years of boating. The strap of the boat cover I was holding broke and in I went, feet first into very cold water. Watched by a platoon of ogling Turks I clambered back aboard, furious with myself. I had hurt my hand and ruined a lovely pair of wide bottomed, pure wool jersey pants which I had only just finished sewing. My only consolation was that I wasn't carrying Danny when I fell in.

My log entries keep recording bits of misery: Danny's disposable nappies finished; powdered milk finished; and although I boiled the local milk for ten minutes it did not agree with Danny and he cried all night. But another storm and consistently bad weather forecast left no choice: like it or not, we were stuck there for the next three weeks.

Graeme loved the place and his log entries call me critical. He writes of the lovely Crusader castle above us, of sponges drying in the square, of interesting boats and friendly and helpful people, of old men sitting in the sun all day and fishermen mending their nets. He praised the trust of the shopkeepers who gave us credit (once again we were waiting for a money order), records meetings with a poet and painter couple and of dining out with Peace Corps people.

All that was no doubt true, but I was no longer receptive; I needed to tie up securely for the winter, stop watching the weather and buy a decent bottle of milk to feed Danny properly. My wish came true on 23 December. After a very long run, the last two hours by the light of the full moon, we tied up inside the old Mandraki Harbour in Rhodes. It was past nine o'clock and with the engine shut down and not a puff of wind, all was calm and peaceful. Danny had already turned in for the night and after a short hello to the people on a large Canadian motor yacht on one side and an equally large American yacht on the other, we did too. *Christmas Eve tomorrow*, I thought sleepily. *How lovely.*

Rhodes

Waking up in Rhodes was a fabulous Christmas present. I got up early, the sun not yet up, to look around to see where we had landed. Wreathed in the faintest mist, the harbour felt safe and looked beautiful. Across the water two stone seawalls, good and solid, attached at right angles to a circular fort. A row of ancient windmills stood atop one breakwater, while the second, shorter one ended in a column marking the harbour entrance. Two hundred years BCE a tall bronze statue, the Colossus of Rhodes, stood at the harbour entrance. What a sight it must have been. Old etchings even imagine him straddling the harbour entrance, tall and muscular with sailing ships passing beneath his legs.

On either side of us, a row of yachts and motor cruisers were tied stern to against the quay, but judging by the tangle of mooring lines and fenders showing tidemarks, these boats hadn't been outside the harbour for a while. There were still a few spaces left, but it looked very much as if we'd been the last boat to dash in before winter was official. It felt good to be here, a fine place to winter. We'd been travelling alone for a long time and I looked forward to becoming part of a boating community again.

A Swedish artist couple, Nils and Katrina, living on their boat *Nika* a few moorings along, soon became friends. The couple had been living in Rhodes for years, chartering their boat out in summer to top up their finances, and relaxing and pursuing their art in winter. Nils sculpted for his next exhibition and Katrina made intriguing, surreal pen-and-ink drawings. They had no children, but going by the easy acceptance Danny found in Katrina's arms, it seemed that she would have liked some.

Nils and Katrina introduced us to their friends, many of them part of the American community living on the island. Sent from 'back home' they were given contracts to work at the local radio station, but rumour had it that it was *more than that ... you know, military stuff, don't ask*. The Americans were lovely people, generous and a lot of fun. 'Big Jim' especially stayed in my mind; the life of the party, ready to laugh and always ready to chat.

Katrina was presently the butt of his good-hearted jokes. The poor woman had jumped ashore when a sudden wind gust shifted their boat. Momentarily losing her balance she landed awkwardly, twisting *both* her ankles. Luckily no bones were broken, but with bandages on both ankles she had to get around on crutches and be *carried* on and off the boat. Katrina, vivacious and attractive, graciously put up with Big Jim's silly comments, but I knew how she felt. In the sixties and seventies, women yachties (like women drivers) still had to live with the chauvinistic assumption that women had to be either feminine or competent; they couldn't possibly be both.

~

It took no time for us to fall into a languid, recuperative winter pace. An undercover market a few steps across from the quay, literally metres from where we were tied up, supplied our needs. And even if I didn't need anything I would often step across just to enjoy the shouting and the banter, and to admire the mountains of fresh food, cheeses and salads, *look Danny ... real milk!* The markets, especially in the morning, were frantically busy, in sharp contrast to the rest of the town. Here the streets were mostly empty, in winter hibernation, every souvenir shop firmly shut. Life had slowed down and shops serving the local community opened at hours known only to them.

Graeme got himself a job re-varnishing the American yacht next to us (40 drachmas an hour would add to the kitty) and early in January my mother came to stay for three weeks. Graeme found himself a berth on another boat and Mutti stayed on *Puck* with Danny and me. It was the first time she had seen her grandson since he was a tiny baby, and he charmed her with his openness and ready smile. Danny wasn't shy, with her or anyone. He'd been with us twenty-four hours a day, always part of the action, and seemed to have no need for the much-touted routine prescribed for babies at that time.

The four of us (Danny in the backpack) travelled Rhodes by bus, visiting the sites, talking and laughing at lot. Mutti had begun to study 'a little bit of English', as she put it, and to hear Graeme and her conversing was highly amusing. We also laughed when we discovered why Danny cried whenever we put him on a stretch of grass, one of us in front of him on hands and knees trying to teach him how to crawl. The boat was too small for him to crawl around in and how was he to learn? We eventually twigged that he didn't like touching damp green grass. He hadn't felt the stuff before and refused to move. Crawling on rock was fine, but making friends with a stretch of grass took a little longer.

Mutti had brought the last batch of cash from our German bank account, enough for us to live on for the next six months, and much of our talk circled around the topic of how to continue our journey. Graeme and I had not talked about it in detail but seemed to have arrived at a similar conclusion; *Puck* was getting too small for us and we would have to call it quits soon. Counting our money, we decided to stay around the Aegean for the summer and then put *Puck* on the market in Athens.

It never happened, and the decision to quit was made for us by a terrifying event. On 24 January Mutti got on the bus to the airport, and falling into my customary habit for dispelling sad feelings, I got busy cleaning and tidying the boat up. I really got stuck into it, washing every dish, brushing the carpet, cleaning the windows and putting everything away into its respective locker. When everything gleamed, I put a pot of water on the stove for some washing and retreated to the cockpit for a breather.

Still in tidying mode I swept the cockpit floor, first around the engine box and then right into the corners behind the fridge and the two gas bottles. As I moved the disconnected spare bottle a little closer under the roof, out of the sun, it suddenly gave a loud hiss, releasing a jet of gas. Not even thinking, purely on instinct, I took a mighty leap below to quickly turn off the gas stove. It was too late and seconds later a huge plume of flame shot into the air. I grabbed Danny, the mighty jet of fire practically pushing us off the boat. Hands stretched down from the quay and I was pulled ashore and ran off across the road, terrified that the whole boat would explode.

Huddled around Danny I sat in the gutter, felt people touching me, talking, but the sound of the flames had me running off again, down the quay towards *Nika*, yelling 'Katrina, Katrina our boat is burning.' Katrina emerged from the hatch, Nils closely behind her and suddenly Big Jim was there too... lots of people. Nils ran off to help Graeme, and Katrina took me aboard *Nika*. I wouldn't let go of Danny, and putting us on the cabin floor she wrapped blankets around us, whispering over and over *it's okay, everything is okay, Graeme is okay, it's okay, it's okay* ... I couldn't talk, couldn't stop shaking and then I heard the fire engine and soon after Graeme was there too, red and dirty. It was over, the fire was out. I watched Katrina spray ointment on Graeme's singed face and hands, feeling hollow, different... unreal. I knew things were bad, but my tears wouldn't come. Only Danny cried – he had two shocked parents and refused to lie down and sleep.

It was taken for granted that we would stay on *Nika*. Later in the day, after Danny had finally cried himself to sleep, we went to look at what was left of the boat, along with half the population of Rhodes. *Puck* was a terrible sight and Graeme felt that the best thing to do would be to take her out to sea and sink her. Apart from parts of the foredeck, the entire superstructure was either badly charred or had burned away entirely. She looked like a huge, neglected dinghy, filthy water and greasy firefighting foam sloshing around inside the blackened hull. Looking for things that might have survived the furnace I spotted my handbag floating in the mess, and Graeme went to retrieve it.

The bag was soaking wet, but the money Mutti had brought for us was dry, zipped away in a side pocket, a small comfort. We went across the street to have some coffee and try to decide what to do, but it was too soon for plans. With our feelings still running high, all we could talk about was the fire, how could it have happened, what had caused it? Half an hour later we left the cafe, and still feeling dazed and fuzzy I left my wet handbag behind. Minutes later a man came running after us to hand me the bag – *here, you must have left this, there's money in it.*

There was, a small fortune, and I can't even remember if I thanked the stranger. The next day Big Jim turned up with more money; he'd put the hat around in the American community and a fair amount of dollars had dropped into it. The people of Rhodes added more money and brought bags of second-hand clothes.

We still had no plans. I was standing miserably in Nils and Katrina's guest cabin, trying to find something among the donated clothes that fitted me, when Katrina came in holding up one of her dresses. 'Here,' she said, 'have this. I think it'll fit you.' It was a blue and white check mini, one of her favourites, brought back from Sweden on one of her trips home. I had admired it on her before. 'Katrina, no, I couldn't... this is your favourite.'

'I know,' she said. 'That's why I am giving it to you.'

Katrina's words and her favourite dress were my turning point. A wall inside me collapsed and my tears started to flow at last. I cried, softly, ready to accept our loss and grateful for the kindness, love and compassion coming our way. The news of the fire had spread and we became known around Rhodes, smiled at and greeted wherever we went. Danny was given sweets at every shop and the thought of leaving felt awful. It felt wrong to take the donated money and leave. Yet we could not give it back, and when the shipyard offered us free slipping and a place in their yard for however long we needed it, we jumped at it. Yes, we would stay. Graeme would rebuild the boat; we would manage somehow.

It felt like the right decision. I was happy not to have to think of *Puck* ditched and abandoned, her blackened hull greasy with firefighting foam, Danny's toys, our books and clothes sloshing around in filthy water. I discovered that scrubbing filthy timber was a brilliant way to come to terms with our loss. I got to understand why communities go back to rebuild charred houses destroyed by bushfire, learned that the process is as much about rebuilding lives at it is about saving property. Accepting the inevitable and working hard gradually brings back the trust, *the gods might have been cross once, but surely they wouldn't do it again ...*

A boat isn't a house or a piece of land, yet it carried comparable memories for us. Danny grew up on *Puck*, we ate countless dinners around the little table, had visitors from many nationalities, discussions and arguments over this and that, cosy nights with the heater pumping, and sunny anchorages made in heaven. We had asked a lot of *Puck*, had pushed her to the very edge of what she was designed to do, and often more than that. She wasn't a perfect boat like *Hope*, but she was a *good* boat and it was only right to restore her, we owed it to her.

Outside help kept coming and soon our living arrangements were sorted out too. Katrina was known and liked around Rhodes; she spoke Greek and began asking people if they knew of somebody willing to let us have their spare room. One family living in the Old Town came forward – *yes they did have a room, would we like to look at it.* Katrina came with us to translate as Alexandros and his wife Evangelia showed us the room. It was a freestanding stone cube, as long as it was deep as it was high. A water tap and separate toilet room was attached to the main house, a few steps across an open passage. The 'cube' itself had wooden flooring and a small window opening onto a narrow laneway. Thick dust lay over an assortment of fishing gear stacked in the corners. It didn't smell good but I figured that once I cleaned it up and stacked the fishing gear into one corner, it would be okay. Katrina translated my thanks and gratitude and *yes, I would very much like to have the room.*

Could we come soon please, tomorrow perhaps?

Yes, we could, and nods were exchanged all around.

The 'cube', with doorway and window on the right, toilet opposite.

When I arrived early the next day, Danny sitting up in his pram and me loaded up with bags of stuff, Evangelia had been waiting for me. Rushing across the courtyard she came to open the door of the room. I walked in and just stood there, stunned. The fishing gear was gone and the walls had been whitewashed. There was a double bed with mattress and bedspread and a playpen for Danny next to it. Against the wall stood a kitchen table with a kerosene cooker, basin and water jug. There were curtains at the window, religious pictures on the walls and hand-woven rag rugs on the floor.

Everything had been aired and cleaned, and suddenly realising that the whole neighbourhood must have pitched in to get the room ready for us, I burst into tears – again. Not sharing a language all I could do was to hug Evangelia and she held me, gently patting my back.

⁓

We lived in our 'cube' for three months, the time it took for *Puck* to be back in the water. We both had our work cut out, but the actual task of rebuilding fell squarely on Graeme's shoulders. The damage was considerable, but not as bad as we had first assumed. The hull, apart from being filthy, had been untouched by the fire and only the structures above deck had burned away. The fact that I had tidied up and stored everything away minutes before the fire had saved some of our gear. The forward locker doors were charred but had not burned through, leaving our cameras, colour slides and all but one of the logbooks stored inside it intact. Our bedding, pushed hard into the forepeak, was mendable. Nearer the cockpit the heat had been so intense that Danny's clothes, put away in the locker under his cot, had kept their shape but crumbled into powder as soon as I touched them. Similarly, our much-travelled conch shell had kept its lovely shape but disintegrated as soon as Graeme tried to pick it up.

In need of some answers, we tried to reconstruct how the fire had started and came up with this as the most likely scenario: the bottle I had heard hissing was our spare bottle, disconnected and last filled up in Turkey. Gas bottles at that time were not exchanged but refilled at garages, and that particular bottle must have been overfilled, or perhaps the valve had been damaged in the process. The warm weather in Rhodes possibly expanded the gas, broke the valve and allowed gas to escape. The tiny pilot light of the gas fridge (stored in the cockpit next to the hissing bottle) was the only open flame that could have ignited the spurting gas into the roaring column of flame. Eyewitnesses told us later that shortly after Danny and I had got off the boat a second column of burning gas had shot metres into the sky. We could only guess that once started, the fire had burned through the flexible lead connecting our second bottle to the stove below, thus unleashing a second inferno.

It was little comfort to know that had it not been for the refrigerator pilot light, the gas from the faulty bottle might simply have evaporated. We never did like gas, refused to have it aboard *Hope*, and scolded ourselves for not throwing the fridge overboard in Istanbul after it had done its job of keeping Danny's vaccinations cool. Anger ran through me for the *cursed thing* but was replaced quick enough by deep gratitude; the thought that the fire could as easily have happened at sea was too painful to even contemplate.

For all the damage done we had been blessed. Danny and I had got off the boat unharmed and Graeme got a little singed, painful but not serious. Working on the boat next to us, he had jumped aboard *Puck* and tried to throw the burning bottle overboard, but the heat was too intense. The boats on either side of us tried to motor away from the quay but were held fast by the complicated network of mooring lines; nobody had a knife or an axe ready to cut the ropes. Fire extinguishers carried on neighbouring boats were aimed at the blaze but apparently had little more effect than spitting on it. What saved our boat, and to our immense relief the boats alongside of us, was the quick arrival of the Greek fire engine. The men moved like lightning and the fire was smothered with foam.

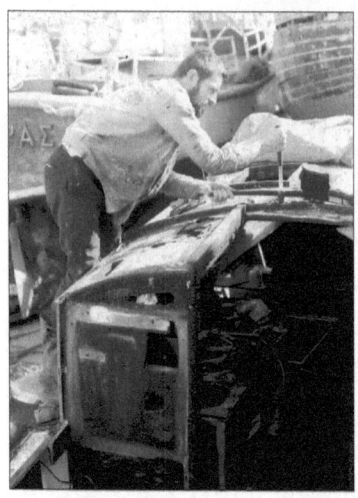

Rebuilding *Puck* meant stripping away the charred timber down to the hull and working upwards. Marine ply and epoxy glue were ordered from Athens, and Mutti sent screws and fittings, engine spare parts and countless other bits and pieces. Every Saturday morning she was ready at her phone, pencil poised, waiting for me to ring from the Rhodes post office with a list of things we needed. Graeme worked hard and after six weeks he had the cabin beams laminated, the bulkhead and the cockpit floor in, the steering mechanism fixed, pumps fixed, the engine stripped and cleaned, a new cooling system installed and the doghouse started.

I had the job of separating the spoilt from the usable, taking anything that could be carried – fittings and switches, dials and wires, handles, cups, pots and cutlery – back to the room to clean off soot, salt-hardened dirt, melted plastic and dried firefighting foam. I took my sewing machine apart, washed down the parts with kerosene and managed to get it working again, ready for making seat covers, curtains and a new cockpit awning.

Above: Graeme working on *Puck*'s charred superstructure
Right: Me with my sewing machine set up at Rhodes shipyard

Putting Danny into the stroller someone had donated to us, I would take lunch down to the boat every day, where we'd sit in the lee of the boat, watch Danny play in the sand and discuss progress. Graeme's to-do list, roughly six weeks into the work, is written up in the logbook:

Build toilet and hanging locker, bulkheads and doors, fit new glass to all windows, finish cockpit floor and engine case, fill and sand decks, cabin sides and inside cabin, make a couple of steering seats and a new steering wheel, rewire the engine and light switches, fuses etc., make a mast and flagpole, main door, instrument panel and cockpit lockers etc.

And then he added:

However, I seem to be making progress and I'm very happy. Each morning as I walk to the shipyard, I walk along the beach and watch the sea in all her shapes, gaze at Turkey in the distance ... Then at the end of the day, pleasantly tired, I wander back along the beach into a sun setting behind the turreted walls of the Old Town.

It was a simple life, no plans, just doing what had to be done while languid Greek life slowly wrapped itself around us. Rhodes Old Town, surrounded by a medieval wall, has around two hundred unnamed cobbled streets and laneways, and I had begun to find my way around. The ruins of the Temple of Venus near the centre of town were famous, dating back to the 3rd century BCE – as I found out later. At the time the ruins were little more than a landmark for me, a place I needed to turn right or left on my way to a bakery or a grocery shop. To get kerosene meant walking down 'our' lane, crossing three others and turning left until I got to a big barn-like gate with a donkey tethered beside it. Inside the cave-like structure a very old man would get off his rickety chair and fill up my container from an open 45-gallon drum.

❦

The town, although medieval, was very much lived in. Every house was occupied, and few things went unnoticed. As the foreigners with the chubby blond baby, we were watched over and spoiled by our neighbours. Walking to my kerosene man one morning I found the donkey gone and the gate shut, but I needn't have worried. I had been seen walking off with my empty canister, the neighbour knew that the man with the donkey was away, and someone had put a container full of kerosene on my doorstep.

When Danny was unwell, the whole neighbourhood knew it and women would come to give him 'baby pills' and raspberry liquid, and smoke him healthy again with clouds of incense. Georgia, our landlady's daughter, adored him and played with him for hours. On his first birthday he was gone half the morning and came back like a celebrated prince, cleaned up, his hair brushed and wearing a little bracelet around his wrist. Even our landlord Alexandros, unable to walk without fingering his fat yellow worry beads, allowed Danny the use of them occasionally. I knew how distressed Alexandros would be without them, and I would knock on their door across the courtyard and return the beads as soon as Danny could be parted with them.

Evangelia had shown me her house, small and cosy like a doll's house, spotlessly clean, the aluminium pans hanging in the kitchen shining like mirrors. The house was a bigger version of our 'cube', and I realised why the ceilings of the ancient houses were so high. At Alexandros's and Evangelia's place a mezzanine reached halfway into the room, an open platform made safe with a sturdy handrail and accessible by a broad staircase. I wasn't shown the 'upstairs' but looking up I could see beds and a wardrobe. I wondered how these same houses might have housed their occupants in medieval times. Could it be that livestock had occupied part of the ground floor, keeping their owners sleeping above them nice and warm?

~

The seasons were changing and it was beginning to warm up. Quite often now, we would have lunch on the beach, keeping an eye on Danny determined to wade into the water, shoes and all. We celebrated our sixth wedding anniversary, tallying up two in Sydney, one in Durban, one in Brazil, one in Germany and toasting to the next one – more than likely back in Sydney.

I was the first to get restless. April was nearly gone, the season was in full swing and we needed to sell the boat. Money was tight; the rebuilding had cost a lot and I complained to the logbook that Graeme was enjoying himself too much and would carve an eagle on top of the mast next. But the big day did arrive.

30th April 1970
'Puck' and I are still on dry land, but in less than an hour we should be back in the briny. I'm all nervous about whether she will make water, whether the engine will run satisfactorily etc. We are by no means finished – much varnish and paint, plus a few pretties, but apart from that she is OK.

And so, with sweets and drinks offered all around and loud cheers from the shipyard workers – Graeme's friends and helpers – *Puck* slid back into the water. She looked very pretty, a thin red strip at the waterline, the hull newly painted in glossy white, and the Greek flag flying at her crosstrees. The engine started, she didn't make water and soon we were in Mandraki harbour, back in the same spot from which she had been towed three months earlier. Bit by bit we moved back aboard, and I got busy turning the rough unfinished inside into a home: cleaning, painting, fitting carpet, and stitching up curtains, cushions and lastly a new cockpit cover with zip-on sides.

And then I conjured up a minor miracle. I had advertised *Puck* in German boating magazines and Harold, a German man, bought her sight unseen: her journey from Germany to Greece had made her exceedingly sellable. A dozen or so phone calls later and it was arranged that Harold would take possession of the boat right at the harbour-front of Rhodes. He and his girlfriend would travel to Greece in a car that could be lived in (a van of sorts) which we would then take over, the money squared up after their arrival.

Harold and his girlfriend arrived and early in June, four-and-a-half months after the fire, we handed over a beautiful, clean, newly painted and perfectly finished *Puck* with a handshake. The money was sorted out in the cafe across the street and after switching our respective belongings, we moved into the back of an old Ford Transit delivery van. Our friend Nils got out his welding equipment and constructed a seat for Danny that fitted neatly between driver and passenger seats, and we were ready for our overland journey back to Germany.

The journey ends

Saying goodbye was a bittersweet process. Happy to drag it out, we spent a week with Nils and Katrina as guests on their boat. They had invited us, felt we deserved a break, and we met up in Lindos, a little way down the coast. And there we stayed, doing little more than swim, talk, listen to music, eat, drink and sleep in ongoing rounds. Katrina wouldn't even let me help with the dishes.

Unwound and recharged, we eventually hugged our friends for a final goodbye, got into our orange Ford Transit and pushed on. It took another week to call in on the many people who had helped us and spend pleasant hours sitting in the sun, talking and drinking coffee, always pressed to stay longer. Late in the afternoon we'd return to a fabulous spot we had discovered: Epta Piges, (seven springs), an out-of-the-way picturesque valley where we could drive the car over flat rock and pebbles right down to a little stream – a perfect camping spot. We'd cook supper on a small campfire, and soon it would be dark. Danny, walking by then and well and truly tired out, would be the first to turn in. Sleeping until the sun rose, he wouldn't even murmur when later at night we'd move him along the mattress to make room for us.

Our last call was to thank Alexandros, Evangelia and their daughter Georgia, our kind and generous landlords in the

Old Town. We parked outside the town gate and walked the now familiar narrow lanes to our little hideout. My heart already was heavy with many goodbyes, but nothing could have prepared me for this last one. Evangelia cried openly, blessed us one by one, and finally she took the gold chain and gold-set shell pendant off her neck and fastened it around mine. My first feeling was to refuse the gift, *surely we were richer than her*, but perhaps I was wrong there. She was wealthier by far, and I very much hope that if there is a heaven and I get to the pearly gates one day that Evangelia will be there to put in a good word for me. I will have no difficulty recognising her serene presence and her beautiful eyes, and she will recognise me because I'll be wearing her gold chain and pendant: my treasured protection in troubled times to this day.

Before taking the overnight car ferry from Rhodes to Athens we briefly called in on the new owner of *Puck*, to see that all was well. Harold and his girlfriend had settled in well, *Puck* ran like a charm, but sitting in the cabin and smelling the leftover reek from their joints made me uneasy. *Not the best people to hang out with.* Nils had told us that the police had been around asking questions; apparently a boat fender full of 'stuff' had been fished out of the harbour. *None of our business* but noticing our discomfort Harold laughingly reassured us that his stash was well hidden, inside his false leg – which was probably true; Harold was an amputee.

'Would you like a smoke?' he asked.

'No thank you... we've got to go.' The vision of him pushing up his trousers, taking off his leg and rolling us a joint was too much for me.

The journey ends

'Don't go to Turkey,' I said as we left. 'I believe their jails are terrible.'

We would think of Harold's jolly leg again, later, at the Greek border crossing, driving the van that he had brought down for us. Suspicion was obvious. We were asked to step inside the customs house and the car was searched inch by inch – hubcaps off, underneath, everything and everywhere. Luckily nothing was found in the car; his hollow leg must have sufficed. To be fair, we may have aroused suspicion entirely on our own merit. By then we had been living in the back of a van, furnished only with a mattress, for some time and were not a picture of respectability. A bearded man looking cranky over the 'stupid delay' and a tanned woman in a crumpled shirt and cut-off jeans with a half-naked child on her hip fitted the bill of the travelling hippies of the day. We could hardly tell them that we were not.

❦

After the leisurely speed of boat travel, covering the distance back to Germany took no time at all. Getting to Rhodes had taken eight months; coming back took barely two weeks. And that included stopping in Belgrade to stay with John and Margaret, the friends we made at the Australian Embassy on our outward journey. It was our luck to arrive on a party day, some big family event with lots of guests invited. We counted five Aussie couples, plus Graeme and me – 'little Sydney' in Belgrade. Danny found a little playmate in Margaret's daughter, and when invited to stay on for a few days we did, guiltlessly. Expatriate and travelling Australians are not nearly as reserved as they are at home, I noticed.

Danny had again embraced the new travelling mode without a hitch, easy-going even in the security blanket department. All he needed was a towel to go to sleep with and that was easy to come by. Our little Aussie had learned to sleep anywhere, preferably with a diesel engine running. His Belgrade playmate, Margaret's daughter, had a more difficult time. She needed one particular doll to feel secure and I remember the little girl sitting fretfully in front of the clothes dryer watching her doll going round and round with the other clothes. 'Dolly's got to be washed sometimes,' said practical Margaret, 'and the dryer's the quickest.'

~

We dared not stop as we drove over the mountain pass across the Hohe Tauern Alpine range. The old Transit van had been labouring up and up for so long that stopping, even if only to admire the spectacular view, seemed risky. She might not start again in the cold rarefied air and once over the hump, we quickly let her run downhill into Austria, a country of lush pastures and grazing cattle. We stopped in some of the big and famous resort towns, but our mood and our clothes made a poor match with the sophistication of places like Salzburg, and we were soon back on the road.

After Munich we left the Autobahn to dawdle through our beloved Main River region. We had read a great deal *after* we had passed through on *Puck* and felt like catching up on treasures we had missed. I especially wanted to see the famous Heilig-Blut-Altar (Holy Blood Altar) in the St Jakobus Church in Rothenburg. Driving through the crooked one-way streets of Rothenburg we got hopelessly lost but eventually found the church, and a parking spot.

My eagerness to see the altar – carved by Tilman Riemenschneider around 1500 CE to honour a drop of Christ's blood brought back by the crusaders, had been warranted, and sitting quietly in the front pew brought the pace of past weeks to a complete standstill; even Danny became silent. The age and beauty of the many-layered wooden altar, flanked either side by tall stained-glass windows, left me awed at the vision of this remarkable man. Riemenschneider had broken with the tradition of portraying saints as pure and beatific and had carved their faces craggy and serious-looking, showing them as ordinary, real-life people walking this earth like friends.

Looking at the altar made me remember Evangelia, seeing her walk home after Easter Mass, slowly, carefully shielding a burning candle lit at the altar. She needed to get the little flame home safely to smoke the sign of the cross under the newly whitewashed lintel of her house. Her face was like the carved faces on Riemenschneider's altar, serious, lined, real and beautiful. I smiled; yes, she was a saint in her way. *Perhaps being happy and accepting of one's lot makes us saintly ...* and that's how far I got with my reverie before Danny got wriggly and impatient – *must look at that idea one day ...*

～

And then came the last stop, carefully timed so that we could pick up my mother from her workplace at 5 p.m. We wanted to surprise her, and sitting quietly in the car we watched her cross the forecourt towards the gate, looking elegant in her suit and high heels. She glanced at our van parked outside the gate but didn't see us, didn't know the car. Giving a friendly nod to the man at the gate, she was about to walk off in the opposite direction towards the bus stop when I jumped out of the car and shouted 'Mutti, Mutti!' She stopped, turned and next thing we hugged and laughed. 'Kinder, ihr seid hier,' she cried. Yes, Mum, we are here.

We stayed with Mutti for another couple of months, sorting out our gear and making travel arrangements back to Sydney. Graeme confided in the log that he was reluctant to call Australia home,

> because it may not seem that way: We have been on the move for well over four years now and it would be short-sighted to presume that we could settle down ... Anyway, who said anything about settling down – our next goal is to make money quickly to put the next plan into action. A job at Christmas Island, New Guinea, in the "out back" or even Africa may be called for.

And then it was time to leave. Graeme wrote up the last pages in our log in my mother's apartment in Dortmund:

> Our next goal is the obvious one – to make money as quickly as possible so that we can realise the next dreams ... Time too to do all the things we have been forced to shelve due to our travels ... a good stereo ... delve into photography and art, maybe study further in engineering.
>
> Danny of course must be steered along and do some steering of his own – a sister for him too is on the agenda. Plans for the 'next boat', the 'dreamboat', are already drawn, discussed, improved, discarded, and done again in many variations. It is too early to state now, but we are planning to build a 38-foot sloop ... However this is a bridge we must cross when we come to it. Before then there are at least two years of hard work and settled life.

We arrived back in Sydney in September 1970, almost exactly ten years since I had first spotted the Australian coast off

Fremantle from the deck of the migrant ship. I remembered my disappointment, how I had judged the endless strip of land as too flat, deemed the low red-roofed houses incongruous and out of place, the spaces too vast and empty. Australia still felt a little strange, but ten years of travel had made her proportions acceptable, the thought of living there a possibility, perhaps even desirable.

Within days, Graeme found a job working for a former colleague who had set up his own engineering company. A partnership was in the offing and Graeme soon slipped into his former way of life, his last entry into our logbook a mere echo from another world. Australia was his home and he felt at home.

My position was more complex. Within a month of our arrival I was pregnant, not with a sister but with a brother for Danny, as it turned out. Graeme, my close travelling mate, became a largely absent husband working ungodly hours to 'catch up' as he put it, while I became an at-home mum adrift in 1970s Australian suburbia. Sailing out of Sydney Heads again would have been easier for me, but I knew enough about life by then to know that sailing off into the sunset only happens in the movies.

Writing this book, looking back at my travels of so long ago, I have been amazed at how easily the events and experiences have arisen from my memory, fresh, alive and precise down to the smallest detail. The daring and excitement of my travels have clearly left their mark, made more memorable still because it happened in the tumultuous 1960s, a time of ferment and conventions being broken. Young people were beginning to assert themselves and I was more than willing to be part of it.

When I think of the 18-year-old Jutta, restless, immature, brimful with longing – for what, she did not know – I cannot help but marvel at her courage, her drive, her intuitive knowing in finding the ideal antidote for her cramped post-war existence. Sailing the seas was perfect for her. She needed space, wide-open seas, far horizons and the freedom of steering a beautiful boat to beautiful places. She needed distance from her tightly knit family and the liberty of being accountable only to her mate and her ship. She needed the kind of otherworldly, under the stars solitude that invites reflection and opens the heart to love and healing.

And looking in on the 28-year-old returned adventurer, once again I marvel. Stay-at-home Jutta is doing fine, is managing her shore life, her increasing responsibilities, her obvious need to stay put, well enough. She knows herself a little better, is more in tune with her emotional inner world and doesn't mind being alone a lot of the time. She is finding joy in motherhood, has a new sewing machine and is planning to set up a darkroom for her photography. And when times do get tough, as they do, she weathers them as she did those frustratingly calm seas and the storms sent from hell. Her travels have made her strong and resilient and taught her to trust, in herself, in others and in life itself. I feel like hugging her, cheering her on: *good on you, kid.*

Jutta Townes remained in Australia, raising her boys and working in a number of different occupations before finally settling into a career as a psychotherapist. She did not sail deep water again, but kept her vow to live near the sea. Prolific letter writing kept her in touch with her German family and honed her skills as a storyteller. She now lives in Tasmania.

www.ingramcontent.com/pod-product-compliance
Lightning Source LLC
Chambersburg PA
CBHW031228290426
44109CB00012B/208